Medieval Prostitution

FAMILY,
SEXUALITY AND SOCIAL RELATIONS
IN PAST TIMES

GENERAL EDITORS:
Peter Laslett, Michael Anderson and Keith Wrightson

Western Sexuality: Practice and Precept in Past and Present Times
Edited by Philippe Ariès and André Béjin
Translated by Anthony Forster

The Explanation of Ideology: Family Structures and Social Systems
Emmanuel Todd
Translated by David Garrioch

The Causes of Progress: Culture, Authority and Change
Emmanuel Todd
Translated by Richard Boulind

The English Noble Household, 1250–1600
Kate Mertes

An Ordered Society: Gender and Class in Early Modern England
Susan Dwyer Amussen

Porneia: On Desire and the Body in Antiquity
Aline Rousselle
Translated by Felicia Pheasant

Medieval Prostitution
Jacques Rossiaud
Translated by Lydia G. Cochrane

FORTHCOMING

Wet Nursing: A History from Antiquity to the Present
Valerie Fildes

Illegitimacy and Society in Eighteenth-Century Scotland
Rosalind Mitchison and Leah Leneman

Highley 1550–1880: The Story of a Community
Gwyneth Nair

Mobility and Marriage: The Family and Kinship in Early Modern London
Vivien Brodsky

The Country House Society
Jessica Gerard

The Family and the English Revolution
Christopher Durston

Medieval Prostitution

Jacques Rossiaud

Translated by
Lydia G. Cochrane

Basil Blackwell

English translation first published 1988 by
Basil Blackwell Ltd
108 Cowley Road, Oxford, OX4 1JF, UK

Basil Blackwell Inc.
432 Park Avenue South, Suite 1503
New York, NY 10016, USA

British Library Cataloguing in Publication Data

Rossiaud, Jacques
  Medieval prostitution. — (Family, sexuality and
social relations in past times).
  1. Europe. Women. Prostitution, c.a. 1300 – c.a. 1600
  I. Title   II. La Prostituzione nel medioevo, *English*   III. Series
  306.7′42′094

  ISBN 0–631–15141–9

Library of Congress Cataloging in Publication Data

Rossiaud, Jacques
  [Prostituzione nel Medioevo, English]
  Medieval prostitution/Jacques Rossiaud; translated by
Lydia G. Cochrane.
    p. cm. – (Family, sexuality, and social relations in past times)
  Translation of: La prostituzione nel Medioevo.
  Includes index.
  1. Prostitution–Europe–History.   2. Prostitution–France–
History.   3. Prostitution, Juvenile–Europe–History.
  4. Prostitution, Juvenile–France–History.   I. Title. II. Series.
  HQ115.R6713 1988   306,7′4′094–dc19   87–37503
  ISBN 0–631–15141–9

Typeset in 10 on 12 pt Garamond
by Opus, Oxford
Printed in the USA

Endpapers: *Roman de la Violette*, 15th century, Bibliothèque Nationale, Paris,
Ms.F2. 24378 f.31. (Photographie Giraudon)

Contents

Foreword

The history of prostitution has been of marginal interest to medievalists.[1] What studies there are, written by physicians or jurists trying their hand at history, are dated, local and largely anecdotal, and for the most part they are little more than curiosities of scholarly literature.[2] More recently, while historians have certainly not ignored prostitution, their description of it has followed an historiographic concept and a current of thought that attributes its prevalence to the calamities that struck Europe in the later Middle Ages and the moral disorder they brought. It has been

---

[1] This study first appeared as 'Prostitution, jeunesse et société dans les villes du Sud-Est au XVe siècle', *Annales ESC* (1976), pp. 289–325.

Studies of this sort include: G. Bayle, 'Note pour servir à l'histoire de la prostitution dans les provinces méridionales de la France', *Mémoires de l'Académie du Vaucluse*, vol. 5 (1886); J. Chalande, 'La Maison publique municipale aux XVe et XVIe siècles à Toulouse', *La France médicale*, 1912; J.-C. Delannoy, *Pécheresses repenties, notes pour servir à l'histoire de la prostitution à Amiens du XIVe au XIXe siècle* (Amiens, 1943); J. Garnier, *Les étuves dijonnaises* (Dijon, 1867); J. Lacassagne and A. Picornot, 'Vieilles étuves de Lyon et d'ailleurs', *Albums du Crocodile* (Lyons, 1943); P. Pansier, *L'Oeuvre des Repenties à Avignon du XIIIe au XVIIIe siècle* (Paris, 1910).

Nearly all the histories of prostitution treat the subject from its earliest mentions in the ancient world to the current day. Chief among them, *pro memoria*, are: P. Dufour (pseud. for P. Lacroix), *Histoire de la prostitution chez tous les peuples du monde, depuis l'antiquité le plus reculée jusqu'à nos jours* (Brussels, 1851–4), here cited in the edition in 8 vols of 1861; L. Le Pileur, *La prostitution du XIIIe au XVIIe siècle* (Paris, 1908). There is a bibliography in J.-J. Servais and J.-P. Laurend, *Histoire et dossier de la prostitution* (Paris, 1965).

[2] This tendency was initiated by Léon Ménard, who, in his *Histoire civile, ecclésiastique et littéraire de la ville de Nismes* (Paris, 1754), bk 12, p. 23, attributes to the 'scandalous indulgence' of that city's council the existence of public prostitution in fifteenth-century Nîmes. The notion can also be found in nineteenth-century historians, and it still appears in some studies today.

tempting to associate the whore with the soldier, fornication with moral laxity, the municipal brothel with the court of miracles.[3]

An attempt to understand the broad scope of prostitution and its social significance, however, requires its definition in terms of demographic and matrimonial structures, of normal and deviant sexual practices, and of the cultural values and mental attitudes widely shared by the social groups that tolerated it or prosecuted it. This is an ambitious task, but it is the only approach that will permit an exploration of the vast and nebulous zone separating the two levels on which historians of sexuality have concentrated thus far: ideology and morality, and demographic trends.

It is that global analysis that I intend to sketch here, drawing my examples from a network of towns and cities of south-east France that stretched from Burgundy to Provence. My research in the people of the Rhône valley has quite naturally encouraged my interest in this, since the prostitutes' quarter nestled on the riverfront areas of all Rhône cities. Between 1440 and 1490, this geographic area was not gravely affected by war; its cities were recovering or prosperous, so this period was one of relative economic and social stability.[4]

The situation in Dijon, which is described in some detail in Chapters 1 to 4, serves as a backdrop for Chapters 5 to 10. They have been written as a complement to Part I, in order to grasp how a moral system of the sort came to be put into place and how it disappeared.

On the many occasions on which I have spoken of these issues, one

[3] I particularly want to thank professor Georges Duby, who enabled me to present this study in his seminars in Aix-en-Provence and at the Collège de France in November 1974 and February 1975. My gratitude goes also to all who were kind enough to offer suggestions, both in Aix and in Paris, among them G. Bois, A. Burguière, Noël Coulet, Robert Fossier, Christiane Klapisch-Zuber, Evelyne Patlagean, J. M. Pezez, Françoise Piponnier, Karl Werner, and Pierre Toubert, not to mention Natalie Zemon Davis, M. Morineau, and Jean-Louis Flandrin, with whom I have often discussed these problems.

Although I cannot possibly give detailed treatment to all aspects of this vast subject, I have nevertheless chosen to present it in its entirety, at the cost of severely limiting my arguments, paring down the notes, and eliminating nearly all supporting citations to judicial archives. I have treated problems relating to urban youth in 'Fraternités de jeunesse et niveaux de culture dans les villes du Sud-Est à la fin du Moyen Age', *Cahiers d'Histoire*, 21 nos 1–2 (1976), pp. 67–102.

[4] On an earlier occasion I attempted to place the system of prostitution in Dijon within the context of the socio-economic history of the fifteenth century in 'Prostitution, sexualité, société dans les villes françaises au XVe siècle', *Communications* 35, 'Sexualités occidentales' (Paris, 1982), pp. 68–83.

Since the publication of that article, two studies have directed my thought, and I shall cite them frequently. They are R. C. Trexler, 'La prostitution florentine au XVe siècle: partronages et clientèles', *Annales ESC* 6 (1981), pp. 983–1015; E. Pavan, 'Police des moeurs, société et politique à Venise à la fin du Moyen âge', *Revue historique* vol. 264, no. 536 (1980), pp. 241–88. See also Philippe Ariès and André Béjin, *Western Sexuality* (Basil Blackwell).

question always crops up: What was the Church doing? My attempt to answer that question has involved several decisions:

1 The way fifteenth-century Burgundians viewed the world had roots plunging deep into the remote past. This means that I needed to take the thirteenth century, the age of the great theologians, as a point of departure, thus adopting a fairly long chronological span.

2 In my attempt to sketch the history of prostitution over three centuries, I hope to proceed fully aware of a pitfall: Cato remarked to a youth he encountered in a brothel: 'Young man, I congratulate you for frequenting this place; I would not do so if you stayed here.' This is implicit advice for historians: we would do well not to linger in the bordello, but rather to observe all that takes place around it.

3 I have tried to write with an unfettered mind. The area on which I shall concentrate is the south-east of France, but I have not hesitated to draw on examples from northern France, Florence, or Venice when they seemed appropriate.

4 I shall begin with appearances, with signs. The analyses that follow will, I hope, allow me to flesh out their full meaning.

Part I

Prostitution, Youth and Society

1

Urban Prostitution

The towns were not the only place in which venal amours could thrive. Fleeting allusions in urban documentation give us glimpses of a flourishing rural prostitution. Even leaving aside the flood-tides of poverty that increased the numbers of available women on all the high roads of the land, vagabond whores, with or without their 'ruffian' protectors, went from village to village to swell the ranks of the handful of 'women common to all' already there. They adapted their itinerary to the calender of fairs and markets, pilgrimages, or the busiest seasons for agricultural labour. In remote barns, hired farm hands and tenant farmers who shared living quarters would share a whore as well, for several days or several weeks. The German merchants who travelled in convoy to the fairs at Lyons did the same, and riverboatmen on weeks-long trips hired women on shore for rest and relaxation at stops along their way.[1]

[1] R. Vaultier, *Le folklore pendant la guerre de Cent Ans* (Paris, 1965), pp. 121, 281, gives examples of vagabond prostitutes. In Dijon the judicial archives (Archives Départementales, hencefore abbreviated AD, Côte-d'Or, justice criminelle, B 11 360/16 (1498) and B 11 360/33 (1542) contain the interrogations of prostitutes who went into the countryside for the grain and the grape harvests. In Dauphiné certain agreements between local lords and village community assemblies stipulate that the villagers cannot receive prostitutes passing through for more than one night (see P. Dufour, pseud. P. Lacroix, *Histoire de la prostitution chez tous les peuple du monde, depuis l'antiquité le plus reculée jusqu' à nos jours*, Brussels, 1861 edn, vol. 4, p. 151). For whores kept by tenant farmers, see L. Duhamel (ed.), 'Chronique d'un notaire d'Orange', *Annuaire du Vaucluse*, 1881, p. 41: 'The plague began through a whore that the farmhands of Malhet kept in their barn' (1545). See also AD Bouches-du-Rhône, B 2043, fol. 5 (1471) for a similar situation. For the merchants, see Archives Municipales, henceforth abbreviated AM, Lyon, FF inventory Chappe, XIII, 62/67, a suit involving the bathhouse of La Pêcherie (1478). According to witnesses, the German merchants on their way to the fairs were in the habit of going to the bathhouses with whores who had accompanied them on the road. For the riverboatmen, see AD Bouches-du-Rhône, Notaires de Tarascon, 407 E 64, fol. 322v (July 1452), where there is

Nevertheless, it was in the towns and cities that prostitution really flourished, took on complex forms, and became institutionalized. Most of the urban centres of south-east France had a municipal brothel, a *prostibulum publicum*, constructed and maintained by princely or municipal authorities. Dijon, Beaune, Mâcon, Villefranche, Bourg-en-Bresse, Lyons, Bourg-lez-Valence, Valence, Romans, Viviers, Bagnols, Pont-Saint-Esprit, Orange, Avignon, Beaucaire, Tarascon, Arles, Nîmes, Alès, Uzès, Cavaillon, Pernes, Bedarrides and Sisteron all had their *maison lupanarde*, their *bon hostel*, their *bonne carrière* ('good street'), their *Château-Gaillard* (bawdy castle). It might also be called the *maison de la ville*, the *maison commune*, or the *maison des fillettes;* in popular parlance it was usually simply referred to as *le bordel*, the brothel. This list includes only the towns and cities whose archives have been conserved, which explains seemingly surprising omissions. We can state unequivocally, then, that there was no 'good city' that did not have its 'good house'.[2]

More often than not, the urban brothel was built with public funds (that is, with tax revenues) and was leased to a manager (an *abbesse* or a *tenancier*), who in theory held a monopoly of prostitution in the town or city. This manager was responsible for recruiting the 'girls', sometimes with the approval of an official of the judicial system, and for making sure that the women respected certain rules. Managers often provided board and lodging, and they guaranteed order within the small female community. If need be – for example, if the 'abbess' should die or leave during the term of her lease – the city fathers did not hesitate to take over the running of the house themselves.[3]

The size and layout of the brothel varied with the importance of the

---

note of a fight between archers garrisoned in that city and the deckhands employed by a Lyons hauler who were sporting with a woman on their barge. The rectors of the Charité in Lyons complain on several occasions of riverboatmen who carried women from Savoy on their boats (Archives Charité E 4, fol. 101v, 1534; E 5, fol. 304v, 1543).

[2] Repeated proofs of the existence of a *bon hostel* can be found in the minutes of city councils and in the cities' account books. If there is no mention of a municipal brothel in communal records, this does not necessarily mean that one did not exist, for if the city did not own or run the brothel the authorities did not worry about it, except in unusual circumstances, since they had no legal responsibility for it. Beaucaire provides perhaps the best example of this. The city council minutes mention the 'house' only twice, but the records of Beaucaire notaries contain a number of lease contracts for farming it out, recognitions of debts, or wills of the 'public women' who worked there. The same is true of Valence and Lyons.

[3] The term *abbesse*, in this 'sense', can be found as early as William of Malmesbury (*Gesta regum anglorum*, Patr. Lat. Col. 1384–1385), speaking of the *lupanar* founded by Gauthier de Bruges, Bishop of Poitiers. The comparison proved extremely popular. I should note that the title of 'abbess' was used particularly often in the regions in which young men's organizations were called 'abbeys'. The 'abbess' was either a prostitute herself or a former

city. In Tarascon the Château-Gaillard was a modest construction with a courtyard, a garden, two entrances, a kitchen, one common room, and four bedchambers. After an enlargement undertaken in 1447, Dijon owned an imposing dwelling, a main building with two wings flanked by an internal gallery and looking onto a garden. This particular *maison des fillettes* included lodgings for a caretaker, a large common room, and twenty generous-sized bedchambers, each with its own stone fireplace. In Lyons, Beaucaire, Arles and Orange, a whole neighbourhood was reserved for prostitution; in Avignon it extended over several streets with a small, tree-lined square, bordered by rooms at its centre.[4]

The brothel was not customarily a 'closed house' and the women were not usually 'cloistered' there. Public prostitutes, whether they lived in the 'disreputable' streets or lodged elsewhere in the city, were free to solicit in taverns and other public places, but they were under obligation to take their clients back to the 'good house', where a certain amount of merrymaking took place before they moved on to the chamber. The managers found the kitchen nearly as profitable as the bedroom.[5]

Aside from the municipally-sponsored public brothel, every town or city had several other houses of tolerance in the public baths. Everywhere that their operation can be clearly ascertained, the *étuves* served both the honest purpose of bathing and the more 'dishonest' one of prostitution. This continued to be true in spite of innumerable regulations against receiving prostitutes in the bathhouses or specifying hours and days

prostitute, and might even be married. Around the turn of the sixteenth century a male leaseholder (*tenancier*) often took the place of the 'abbess'. An official of the law courts (in Arles and Tarascon it was the *lieutenant du viguier;* in Beaucaire the *châtelain;* in Dijon, the *prévot,* in Lyons, the *roi des ribauds*) admitted or rejected the prostitutes. The 'abbess', who was also an informant for the authorities, was charged with making the 'girls' respect the rules of the trade (we shall see later what that means in terms of mores), with seeing to it that the brothel did not become a gaming house in which blasphemy could be heard, and with making sure that clients stayed no more than one night so the house would not become a den of beggars and drifters. In Tarascon in May 1467, two city officials took over management of the house on the death of the 'abbess' until a substitute could be found (AM Tarascon, BB 9, fol. 276). In Dijon under similar circumstances, two city council members received the 'oath of the girls' (AM Dijon, K 84, 1517).

[4] For Tarascon, see AM Tarascon, BB 16, fol. 16 (1449) and BB 13, fol. 92 (1527). The archives of Dijon contain a good number of mentions of sums spent for the reconstruction or upkeep of what was the best-known brothel in the kingdom in the Middle Ages (AM Dijon K 83 and I 142). Avignon's 'hot' district is described in P. Pansier, *Dictionnaire des anciennes rues d'Avignon* (Avignon, 1930), p. 206. In Beaucaire, the municipal brothel was two or three houses at the centre of a street inhabited by prostitutes. In Orange a house was constructed, rather late, in the 'good street' (AM Orange, BB 10, fol. 91v, 1511) as it was in Arles (AM Arles, BB 6, fol. 171, 1497).

[5] There are many documented instances of prostitutes residing outside the house in Arles, Tarascon and Dijon (AM Dijon, B 151, fol. 64, 1426; B 168, fol. 151, 1508; B 169, fol. 93v, 1517; AD Côte-d'Or B 11 360/17, 1501).

reserved exclusively for men or for women. All the bathhouses employed a good number of young chambermaids, and although the stews were equipped with steam rooms and tubs, there were also a good many bedchambers and an impressive number of beds. G. Bayle, who has published the inventory of an Avignon bathhouse, found beds listed everywhere, but no mention of bathing aparatus anywhere. There were six such establishments in Avignon, seven in Lyons, and seven in Dijon around 1470. The most famous of the Lyons baths, the Etuves Tresmonnoye, were right in the *quartier du Palais*, a minute's walk from the seat of royal justice. In the merchants' parish of St Nizier the Etuves de la Pêcherie were said to be of immemorial age and sizeable enough to serve dozens of men at once. The same was true of the baths of St Philibert, Langres and the Vertbois in Dijon, and of the Servellière and the Pont Trocat in Avignon.[6]

Who were the proprietors of these baths? If not the municipal authorities, extremely prominent persons who were fully aware of the range of their tenants' activities. The Villeneuve and the Barronat families in Lyons, for example, the Faletans, the Bishop of Langres, the Abbot of Saint Etienne in Dijon, or the Buzzaffi in Avignon were only too glad to have the tidy rental fees that an abundant and varied clientele brought to these houses.[7] The stews were well known as permanent centres of prostitution, but they were also houses of assignation and places of procuration. In common parlance in Lyons in the decade after 1470, the

[6] On regulations concerning the segregation of men and women, see AM Dijon, B 148, fol. 15 (1410), where certain bathhouses were reserved for men, others for women. In ibid., fol. 112 (1412), two days of the week are for men only and two for women. Except for the days or hours reserved for one sex, however, it seems that all bathhouses received both sexes. For Dijon, see Garnier, *Les étuves dijonnaises*, under the baths of the Vertbois, Langres, le Palais, St Michel, St Seine, La Rochelle, St Philibert. In Besançon the baths were so evidently places of prostitution that their managers paid a tax based on the number of prostitutes lodging in them (see Lacassagne and Picornot, 'Vieilles étuves'). In Lyons, the Tresmonnoye baths contained twenty or so rooms; those of La Pêcherie perhaps more. There were also the bathhouses of Sabliz (near one of the public brothels), of Bourgneuf, of La Chèvre (near the bridge over the Rhône), of the Augustins, and of Combremont. These establishments were not the exclusive privilege of the big cities: Cavaillon had its public baths as well.

[7] In 1388 the baths of La Pêcherie belonged to one G. Marchis, a wealthy merchant, and in 1446 to the illustrious Barronnat family. At the end of the century the establishment was paying a good rent to the archbishop. The Tresmonnoye baths were the property of Aynard de Villeneuve. In Dijon, the baths of St Michel belonged to the abbey of St Etienne; those of Langres to the bishop; those of the rue des Chanoines to the Faletan family. In Avignon, the Buzzaffi rented rooms for prostitution. Francis de Genas, a confidant of Louis XI who held the office of Général of Languedoc, kept an annual record of earnings from his bawdy house in Valence (AD Drôme, Notaires de Valence, E 2541, fol. 240, 1466, and E 2490, fol. 4v, 1453).

expression *aller s'estuver* had a quite precise meaning that everyone understood.

A third level of prostitution, on the artisanal scale this time, was made up of small, privately-run *bordelages* kept by a procuress in her house and offering two or three chambermaids or women who could be sent for. These procuresses received clients in their homes, might simply act as an intermediary, or, on occasion, used the services of women known to be 'easy'. Women in this last category, the fourth and last level of the structure of city prostitution, freelanced. They went from one inn to another; some were concubines and others 'common to many'; they solicited in the taverns, or in the market squares if they had sufficient official or private protection, for soliciting was dangerous and the competition keen. Finally, on major feast days, at fairs, and when major work projects brought people together, outsiders came to swell the ranks of the local prostitutes, profiting from the temporary influx of day labourers, carters and merchants.[8]

There is an entire vocabulary that clearly differentiates the various levels of amorous commerce, and which incidentally gives proof of the permanence of the phenomenon. Laws and regulations, public proclamations and court records distinguish the prostitutes of the municipal *prostibulum* from women who plied their trade in the baths or in private rooms. In like fashion, *filles communes publiques* (common public prostitutes) were opposed to *filles secrètes* (clandestine prostitutes); *cantonnières* (streetwalkers) were differentiated from both *clostrières*

---

[8] In Lyons in 1478, prostitutes are said to have crowded into the city for the fairs, leaving when they were over (AM Lyon, FF Chappe XIII, 62). In Dijon, a place was set aside for women's hiring fairs for labour in the vineyards, and some took advantage of the opportunity to solicit (AD Côte-d'Or B 11 360/7, p. 914, 1459; ibid., p. 968, 1468; B 11 360/8, pp. 2–20, 1462, etc.).

When an influx of poor women arrived in Valence in August 1502, there were complaints of this 'multitude of disreputable women', but it was soon learned that they had fled Crest, Romans, and other towns because of food shortages (AM Valence, BB 3, fols 36v, 69, 115). Much the same thing occurred in Bourg-lez-Valence in 1504 during one of the century's worst droughts (AM Bourg-lez-Valence CC 31, fol. 825v) and in Montélimar in 1511 (AM Montélimar BB 25, fol. 20). It goes without saying that periods of disaster were unfavourable for mercenary amours: the petitions of prostitutes or bordello managers to have the farm contract lowered always follow times of acute shortage or widespread death, when clients deserted the brothels (AM Dijon, K 83, 1476, 1484, 1495, and 1502 and K 84, 1519, 1520). Conversely, Villefranche-sur-Saône enlarged its brothel in 1454 (*Registres consulaires de la ville de Villefranche*, ed. A. Besançon and E. Longin, (Villefranche, 1905), vol. 1, p. 309). Dijon followed suit in 1446–47 (AM Dijon, B 157, fol. 126), nearly doubling the number of bathhouses there between 1410 (four) and 1470 (seven). New bathhouses opened in Lyons in 1471 and 1473. In other words, the construction of a brothel or the opening of a new bathhouse are good indications of a demographic and commercial upswing.

('cloistered' prostitutes) and the clandestine variety, who were in turn distinguished from the *légières* ('easy' women) and the *vagabondes*.[9]

The authorities did their best to enforce certain sanitary regulations: the municipal brothel and the baths were closed during epidemics, just as commercial gatherings and dancing throughout the city were prohibited. Other regulations were religious and attempted to ensure observation of times of abstinence (essentially, Holy Week and Christmas). Still other regulations were imposed for moral reasons (to keep scandalous spectacles away from the immediate vicinity of a church or out of patrician streets) or vestimentary reasons (so that respectable women could be distinguished from the less respectable, and the sumptuous attire of the latter not tempt poor and pure young girls to a life of sin). Finally, some laws were passed for fiscal reasons (to keep the 'private sector' from threatening the monopoly of the municipal government).[10]

City councils made only somewhat lukewarm attempts to control

---

[9] The Avignon statutes speak of public prostitutes and 'secret' ones, *destrales* (procuresses) (Statutes of 1441, in *Annales d'Avignon et du Comtat Vénaissin*) and *ruffiana publica vel privata* (public or private bawds) (J. Girard and P. Pansier, *La cour temporelle d'Avignon aux XIVe et XVe siècles*, Paris, 1909, p. 128). In Lyons the proclamations of the ecclesiastical court of the *Officialité* distinguish between prostitutes working in the brothels, in the bathhouses, and in chambers (AD Rhône, 1 G 184, fol. 29v, 1468). In Dijon, prostitutes working in private rooms were called *claustrières* (AM Dijon, B 151, fol. 64v, 1426) and on occasion 'easy women, women in love, and trollops' (*filles légières, amoureuses, ou garces*), terms which applied both to the occasional prostitute or to women whose conduct left something to be desired.

[10] On health regulations: In Beaucaire, the city fathers were upset when they realized that the patients at the hospital of St Lazare were in the habit of frequenting the nearby brothel, which they arranged to have moved (AM Beaucaire, BB 2, fol. 29v, 1492). In Avignon, 'public women' were obliged to buy any piece of meat they had touched in the market, but the municipal prostitutes of Nîmes offered the city magistrates yearly a cake made with their own hands, for distribution to the poor.

On prohibited periods: It is significant that some of the lease agreements for the municipal brothels were delivered at the beginning of Lent. This shows a long-standing respect of the Lenten prohibition of sex relations. In this way, after the old *'fermier'* left, the new leaseholder had time to get settled and ready to reopen the house after Easter. In most cities the house remained open Saturdays and Sundays, when business was brisk. The manager had to be careful that no dalliance went on during the hours of divine service, however.

On geographical constraints: These were usually attempts to contain public prostitution within its traditional streets or to make prostitutes keep their distance from a church, either at the request of the inhabitants of an 'honest' street or of the clergy. Examples can be found in Lyons in 1470 (AD Rhône, 1 G 184, fol. 29v); Tarascon (ibid., BB 11, fol. 39); Arles (AM Arles, BB 2, fol. 59v; BB 6, fol. 166), and so forth.

On vestimentary restrictions: Ordinances requiring prostitutes to wear some sort of visible sign can be found everywhere and were renewed frequently (in 1441 and 1458 in Avignon, 1468 and 1475 in Lyons, and so forth). I should note that except for this sign (usually a cord called an *aiguillette* worn on the sleeve), vestimentary restrictions fell into

prostitution, however. It was an exceptional occurrence when the construction of a *prostibulum publicum* was undertaken in order to bring morality to city life, as was the case in Bourg-en-Bresse in 1439, where the municipality wanted to put an end to the scandals being committed daily in the market square. More commonly, the councils voted to give prostitution official recognition 'for common utility' or 'in the interest of public good'. Once the house was built, the city's magistrates and notables seldom managed to contain fornication within the municipal ghetto, nor could they ensure respect of prohibitions, no matter how repeatedly they passed laws. Until the early sixteenth century, attempts at repression were few, short-lived, and ineffective. Prostitutes both public and clandestine, infiltrated the entire city, appearing in the most fashionable parishes as well as in the less savoury *faubourgs* outside the walls.[11]

Emmanuel Le Roy Ladurie quotes Félix Platter, a student from Basel, on an adage once current in Comtat and Provence: 'On the bridge at Avignon you are always certain to encounter two monks, two asses, and two whores.' Avignon in 1550 merely kept alive a state of affairs common to all cities of south-east France fifty or a hundred years earlier. A public proclamation of the ecclesiastical court of the *Officialité* in Lyons shows

the context of more general sumptuary laws applied to all social categories (and never wholly respected).

On fiscal concerns: In Tarascon in 1451, a certain J. Denis is sentenced by the *viguier* to pay a fine of 12 s. cor for having 'kept a fallen women without the court's permission'. Thus the court granted (or refused) the right to introduce newcomers into the 'trade' (AD Bouches-du-Rhône, Viguerie de Tarascon, B 2041/3). In Tarascon in 1473 the city fathers protest because the *sous-viguier* was entertaining public prostitutes for lunch and for supper, 'which is to the detriment of the abbot and to the profits of the brothel' (AM Tarascon, BB 10, fol. 134v).

[11] On municipal governments' lack of zeal: In Dijon in 1426, when the city fathers discovered, thanks to a Lenten sermon, that the brothel was near the school and the schoolboys 'went wild' (*afolissent*) there, they decide to have it moved. This was a pious wish, but the bordello stayed where it was, as did the schoolboys (AM Dijon, B 151, fol. 64v). In Tarascon, the request of the inhabitants of neighbouring houses to close an entrance to the brothel that gave onto the street was denied, since 'it does not do any great harm' (AM Tarascon, BB 11, fols 162 and 181v, 1486).

The Romans bordello was declared *pro servicio reipublicae eiusdem villae* (see U. Chevalier, *Oeuvres historiques*, vol. 1, *Annales de Romans*, Valence, 1897, p. 69, for 1487). Resistance to attempts at reform could come from high places: in Dijon in 1447, the procureur for the bishop of Langres to all intents and purposes became public defender for the *filles secrètes* (AM Dijon, B 157, fol. 161v). In 1486, the police officers who had imprisoned 'dissolute and common women' (priests' concubines) were excommunicated by the bishop and obliged to beg his pardon. The bishop had even declared *coram publico* that 'the mayor had taken his carnal pleasure with some of these women' (AM Dijon, B 166, fol. 35, 1486). In more general terms, certain of Dijon's *échevins* profited from prostitution indirectly, and tolerated houses had the benefit of protection in high places.

that it was no longer an easy matter to distinguish common prostitutes from 'women of estate', and the municipal prostitutes in Tarascon and Dijon complained periodically of too stiff competition and demanded laws against 'debauchery'![12]

Are these exaggerations? That is, are they events felt to be so scandalous that they were deliberately played up? Small towns such as Viviers, Pernes or Bedarrides all kept a town brothel. Tarascon around 1435 counted no more than 500–600 households, but it had a dozen 'public common prostitutes'; in Lyons before 1480 there were at least seventy to eighty prostitutes; and Dijon had more than 100 prostitutes for a population of less than 10,000. Moreover, these figures include only the official public prostitutes, since clandestine and casual prostitution elude estimation. Everywhere in France one can infer levels of public prostitution equal to or higher than those of the late nineteenth or the early twentieth century, when prostitution in France was strictly regulated.[13]

Was prostitution necessarily connected with ports, the crossroads of major routes, or larger centres of commerce, the Church, or the law courts? If this were true, prostitution, if not external to the urban community, would at least have existed at its fringes; it would have been one commercial activity among others directed primarily at outsiders. Or was it perhaps produced spontaneously by the community to satisfy their own needs? In order to answer this question, we need first to analyse the sexual behaviour of city-dwellers and townspeople.

[12] E. Le Roy Ladurie, *The Peasants of Languedoc*, trans. and intro. J. Day, G. Huppert, consulting ed. (Urbana, Illinois, 1974), p. 112; AD Rhône, 1 G 84 (1468); AM Dijon, K 83 (1492, 1498), K 84 (1511), I 142 (1505), and so forth.

[13] In Tarascon the list of prostitutes is taken from notarial archives, so it is necessarily incomplete. In Lyons there were twenty *filles publiques* and *filles communes secrètes* in the two public houses, thirty in the two principal bathhouses, and at least as many in the rest of the public bathhouses. In Dijon we can find from twenty to thirty women in the brothel, and probably there were as many in the bathhouses, whereas a census of eighteen private bordellos in 1486 lists sixty or so, for a city of 2614 households in 1470. These figures agree with what we know of other cities: Amiens had at least fifty public prostitutes in 1453 (see Delannoy, *Pécheresses repenties*). Rheims in 1442 (see P. Desportes, 'La population de Reims au XVe siècle', *Le Moyen Age*, 1966, pp. 463–509) lists twelve 'courtesans' in the parish of St Pierre alone, which would seem to imply five times that number for the city as a whole. To serve as a comparison, a Dijon census for 1872 shows 144 public prostitutes, but the city at the time had a population of over forty thousand. Thus it had at least three times more prostitutes, proportionally, in the fifteenth century.

2

Sexual Order and the Subversion of Youth

Criminal records and the reports of the courts' preliminary investigations and the trials instituted by the city's procureurs-syndics help us to sketch the general outlines of urban sexual economy in Dijon. One image stands out in the vast, truculent and sordid chronicle of the ordinary people in this series of legal documents: it is that of sexual violence.[1]

Sexual Violence

These inquiries, together with civil sentences and the decisions rendered by the mayor in the city council, give us information on 125 cases of rape

[1] On justice in Dijon, see C. Bertucat, *La juridiction municipale de Dijon, son étendue* (Dijon, 1911). The viscount-major and the *échevins* had total legal jurisdiction over the city and its outskirts, and cases that earlier were supposed to be the responsibility of the ducal courts (kidnapping, repeated theft, arson, murder) had been left to the competence of the mayor, who exercised his rights fully in the fifteenth century.

The departmental archives of Côte-d'Or include a good number of criminal investigations and trials: forty large bundles, each composed of hundreds of separate documents, single sheets or thick notebooks, remain from the procureurs-syndics' daily tasks through 1550. These proceedings (series B 11 360) constitute the main source for the demographic and social analyses contained in this study. The two series B 11 336 and B 11 337, which are incomplete, are a mixture of briefs of pardons for civil and criminal cases, including mention of some sentences. Many of the fines for civil offences can be found in series M of the municipal archives of Dijon. Finally, criminal sentences are often transcribed into the minutes of the deliberations of the city council, but in general without accompanying considerations. Aside from J. Garnier, who drew on these criminal records for his study on the bathhouses in Dijon and the Coquillards, the documents have also been used by A. Voisin for a study, 'La nuit à Dijon au XVe siècle', *Annales de Bourgogne*, 1937, pp. 265–79, which presents two or three nocturnal incidents anecdotally.

between 1436 and 1486. This figure does not include rapes committed on prostitutes taken, perhaps against their will, into places of prostitution, nor does it represent anything like the true total for such assaults. We know from victimization studies conducted by socio-criminologists that in societies in which the forces of law and order are stronger than they were in fifteenth-century France and in which taboos have weakened or disappeared, the 'dark figure' for rape, both in middle-sized cities and in larger metropolitan centres, is of the order of seventy-five to eighty.[2] This means that judicial archives reflect only from one-fifth to one-quarter of sexual crimes. Here our series is discontinuous: the documents are stored in bundles, not in register books, and we have hardly any information on eighteen of the fifty years. Furthermore, either out of shame, fear of reprisals, or because the families sought a monetary settlement with the attackers and had no interest in going to court, most of the victims did not press charges (and of course there is no record of proceedings when there is no 'plaintiff').[3] We can thus reasonably estimate that an absolute minimum of twenty 'public' rapes were committed annually in Dijon.

Eighty per cent of these, however, were gang rapes committed by groups of from two to fifteen individuals. After making their preparations, they would force the woman's door at night. They made no attempt to disguise themselves, and interjecting brutal remarks with lewd invitations, threats and insults, they either raped their prey on the spot, often in the presence of one or more terrorized witnesses, or else they dragged her through the streets into the house of an accomplice and had their pleasure of her all night long. Four times out of five, out of fear, the neighbours did not intervene.[4]

[2] On the 'dark figure' (*numerus obscurus*), the ratio of crimes actually committed to those appearing in the statistics, studies carried out in England, the United States, Germany and France on rural areas and large cities all lead to relatively concordant conclusions. They are summarized in R. Hood and R. Sparks, *Key Issues in Criminology* (New York, 1970).

[3] Reprisals were frequent and even struck women placed under the strict safeguard of the city or of the duke (examples in AM Dijon, B 11 360/5, p. 538, 1453 and B 11 360/7, p. 830, 1458). Their families had good reasons, both public and private, to seek an amicable agreement that would avoid a court case that might easily turn against the victim or the plaintiffs and provoke an unfavourable 'social reaction'. Examples of settlements with damages of 18 *gros* accorded the victim, a servant girl, can be found in ibid., B 11 360/9, 1464 and 1465. The procureur-syndic himself encouraged the parties to reach a settlement when the aggressors were the sons of townspeople and when the girl raped was not a virgin or did not belong to a 'good' family (ibid., B 11 360/12, 1475).

[4] At least, this is how the aggression usually took place, but variants existed. The attack could be committed in the street and the victim dragged to the moat outside the city walls. The city watch provided an opportunity or a pretext for some 'gallants' who, if they were members, deserted their posts or, if not , got the watch to open doors for them. Almost all these rapes involved extreme brutality (a pregnant woman dragged through the snow, etc.), but the aggressors never deliberately tried to wound their victim badly or kill her.

Were the perpetrators of these acts outlaws or outsiders? The admirably conscientious reports of the city procureur-syndic, Jean Rabustel, tell us of 400 men involved as protagonists or accomplices in a total of ninety fully documented cases. Only thirty outsiders take part in these assaults. Most of the others – townspeople or their sons or servants – are identified. They come from all levels of society, but the overwhelming majority of them are artisans and day labourers, not pimps or protectors. Only one-tenth of the attacks can be put down to thugs operating under the leadership of a chief. But 85 per cent of the assailants are *jeunes fils* (sons of burghers) and unmarried journeymen, one-half of them between the ages of eighteen and twenty-four. Assaults are not strictly connected with holidays, nor with heavy summertime drinking, nor with times of intensive agricultural labour, but are spread throughout the year.[5]

It would be inaccurate to conclude, however, that all young women in Dijon lived in terror after nightfall. Many women and girls had no reason to fear rape. Attacks occurred perhaps once or twice a month, maintaining an atmosphere of insecurity only among certain groups in the female population. Dijon was a middle-sized city, and public security was no less there than in other towns. Brief episodes of civic turmoil – the Ecorcherie, the Coquillards, and the royal occupation – were not reflected in a higher incidence of rape. The city was relatively prosperous: ducal officials, men of law and churchmen lent support to commerce and the crafts, and this was the period of the full expansion of Burgundian

---

[5] The aggressors came from all professions: vintners, weavers, fullers, butchers, barbers, goldsmiths; even young clerics have a place among them. We have identities for 398 participants in such crimes between 1436 and 1486 (out of a total of 430 to 450). Of these, 18 were without question married, 99 were probably bachelors (marriage-aged sons of established families), 166 others, journeymen or serving men, were certainly bachelors. The matrimonial status of 115 others is uncertain. Out of a total of 125 rapes (1436–86), 98 were collective, with 65 out of 82 rapes collective between 1492 and 1542. In the 73 fifteenth-century preliminary investigations for which we have records, the group was composed of an average of six persons. Only 20 per cent of the rapes were committed by ten men or more.

The age of the attackers is known, for the fifteenth century, in only nine cases (20 to 29 years of age, with an average age of 25). In the first half of the sixteenth century, however, when the overall average age at marriage remained stable between 1450 and 1500, we know the age of 72 attackers, who were from 16 to 36 years of age, with an average of 24 years, 10 months.

The distribution by months of the 207 rapes committed between 1436 and 1542 (for a monthly average of slightly more than 17) shows a slight decline in March (14 cases), May (11 cases), September (12 cases), and October (14 cases). These last two months are not surprising, as it was a difficult period and the time of the grape harvest. Does the lower level in May have a cultural significance? Youth festivities and public dances were numerous at that time of year, which would seem to confirm the moralists, Gerson in particular, who claimed that collective festivities 'socialized' and tempered the violence of mores.

power. Furthermore, Dijon was not a princely capital: professional soldiers and bands of young pages were not involved and had little to do with setting the tone of social relations.

Although the *échevins* of the city council kept careful minutes of their deliberations (conserved in their entirety), they give not the least hint of such disturbances. The viscount-mayor certainly reported to his city council on the sentences meted out for crimes and kidnappings, but the *échevins* never discussed or denounced these aggressive gangs. Only once or twice in fifty years is there mention of 'nocturnal disorders', but such events are immediately put down to vagabonds and foreigners, not to the city's own rowdies who appear in Rabustel's charges.[6] The apparent complacency of the city council's deliberations should not mislead us, however, especially since the magistrates did not have jurisdiction over such cases and seldom discussed matters outside their competence. Brief allusions in similar documents in Lyons, Valence and Tarascon to the 'insolences' committed *campana pulsata* (after the evening curfew) and the rare mentions of scandals or of armed 'gallants' probably refer to acts similar to those described.[7] We can conclude, then, that sexual violence was an everyday dimension of city life. There was probably less of it, proportionally speaking, in smaller towns, but it was an even more serious problem in the largest cities. One cannot help but think of the Languedoc chroniclers whose ghosts Emmanuel Le Roy Ladurie evokes and who, haunted by obsessive fear of urban insurrections, prophesied that the poor would carry off and possess the wives of the rich and hold them in common. Georges Duby and Jacques Le Goff had good reason to analyse the importance of women in both social conflicts and age-group rivalries.[8] The first place to seek the cause of this sort of behaviour is in demographic and matrimonial structures.

[6] AM Dijon, B 161, fols 50 (1458) and 138 (1454). Rabustel was procureur for thirty-six years (1436–72). He was rigorously conscientious and he showed humanity in applying the rules of a justice that was intransigent towards the poor.

[7] Jacques Du Clercq describes the climate of violence in Arras in his *Chronique* (see J. A. Buchon, *Choix de chroniques et mémoires sur l'histoire de France*, Paris, 1838, pp. 1–318). Jean Déniau has noted similar situations in Lyons (*La Commune de Lyon et la guerre bourguignonne, 1417–1435*, Lyons, 1934, p. 159). There are mentions of nocturnal 'scandals' in Valence (AM Valence, BB 3, fol. 89v, 1503), in Tarascon (AM Tarascon, BB 12, fol. 355, 1516), Beaucaire (AM Beaucaire, BB 5, fol. 102, 1525). In general, the scarcity of these references should not surprise us, since the city fathers showed little interest in crimes that only exceptionally struck women of their circles.

[8] See E. Le Roy Ladurie, *The Peasants of Languedoc* trans. and intro. J. Day, consulting ed. G. Huppert (Urbana, Illinois, 1974), p. 197; J. Le Goff, *La civilisation de l'Occident médiéval* (Paris, 1964), p. 376; G. Duby, 'Au XIIe siècle, les "jeunes" dans la société aristocratique', *Annales ESC*, 1964, pp. 835–46 (available in English translation, 'Northwest France: The "Young" in Twelfth-Century Aristocratic Society', in M. Ferro (ed.), *Social Historians in Contemporary France: Essays from Annales*, Harper Torchbooks, New York and London, 1972, pp. 87–99).

Matrimonial Order

When a serious offence had been committed and a complaint registered, the procureur and his clerks went without delay to the scene of the crime and interrogated the victim's neighbours. Thus we have available an impressive series of depositions taken (unlike those in civil investigations) from the humbler levels of society. We see men and women, adolescents and the elderly, the married and the unmarried who, under oath, report their 'quality' and their age to the courts. After 1500, we also have a number of interrogations of the suspects themselves, for the most part 'youths', which give us information on dates of marriage, among other things, thus permitting an estimate of age at marriage and of the gap between spouses. The witnesses' perception of calendar time, which was approximate at best, is quite comparable to that of the citizens of Rheims in the 1422 census: nearly identical for men and women, it is relatively accurate for the age groups of first marriages.[9] The documentation at hand is too sketchy to permit precise conclusions concerning age at marriage, but we can discern some long-term trends.

Age at Marriage

These sources provide information between 1500 and 1550 on only 84 individuals, 52 men and 32 women, all from the lower end of the social scale. The average age at first marriage is 24.5 years for men and 21.9 years for women.[10] Although the sampling is perhaps ridiculously small, these data are confirmed by two other series that are based on larger samplings. The average age difference between husbands under thirty years of age and their wives (150 couples) is less than three years; on the other hand, we can see an abrupt decline in the number of marriageable girls between

---

[9] Applying the method used in P. Desportes, 'La population de Reims au XVe siècle', *Le Moyen Age*, 1966, p. 496, to married couples to compare male and female perception of age, 50 per cent of both men and women choose figures rounded to the tens; 40 per cent of men and 37.5 per cent of women choose even numbers, and 10 per cent and 12.5 per cent, respectively, odd numbers. These results do not change perceptibly during the first half of the sixteenth century. As in Rheims, we can see that the persons involved forget their exact age as they grow older. In general, we cannot speak of a tendency for women to understate their age. All we can see is a sort of clumping, grouping ages around milestone years; thus the same individual would tend, through time, both to overstate and then understate his age, though only by one or two years. In statistical analysis this cancels out.

[10] Out of fifty-two married men, only four married under twenty years of age, and four after thirty. Very few girls were married before the ages of sixteen or seventeen in the fifteenth century, and seventeen or eighteen in the sixteenth.

the ages of sixteen and twenty-five: at age twenty-two, 75 per cent of women are married.[11]

We have no direct standard of comparison for the fifteenth century, but it is legitimate to compare the average age of husbands between twenty and thirty years of age (the age decade during which the overwhelming majority of men married) and wives between fifteen and twenty-five years of age (for whom the same remark applies). Out of 350 cases documented between 1500 and 1550, the average age for men is 26.8 years and for women 22.5. These figures, admittedly, have no absolute value. Nevertheless, if we subject two identical series of couples (300 cases), between 1440 and 1550, to the same calculations we can see that the average age for married men is stable at 26.8 years, but the average age for women drops to 21.5. This corroborates the average age difference between husbands and wives among 'young couples' (four years rather than three, although the second series is not identical, since it includes husbands of under thirty years of age and their wives of all ages).

Speaking prudently, and because the respondents themselves give their ages only within a year or so (time perception remains unchanged in these social strata between 1450 and 1550), we can fairly safely conclude that the average age at marriage remained stable for men during the century of demographic growth between 1450 and 1550, at twenty-four to twenty-five years of age. It was thus moderately high (and may be slightly underestimated, since I have omitted men over thirty from my calculations). In the same period, average age at marriage increased from twenty/twenty-one years to twenty one/twenty-two years for women. Why should the age at marriage remain stable among males at a time of economic and demographic change? Let us try to explain.

Matrimonial 'Custom'

The age gap between spouses can be reckoned directly and precisely from the data given in these investigations. Between 1440 and 1490 we have a sampling of 241 couples who declare their age on the same day (furthermore, this figure corresponds approximately to the number of

---

[11] When women give testimony we can be fairly sure of distinguishing wives from marriageable girls: the former are always given as 'X, wife of Y' and the latter as 'X, daughter of Y'. Looking at the latter group alone and dividing them into two-year age levels (to correct for faulty age perception), we get, out of 216 women between eighteen and twenty-five years of age (witnesses under that age are relatively few), 87 girls eighteen or nineteen years old, 82 twenty or twenty-one, 24 aged twenty-two or twenty-three, and 24 aged twenty-four to twenty-five. The break in the series is thus situated between twenty-one and twenty-two years of age. (In this age group, as in Rheims, the attraction of the round number 20 is not clearly stronger than 25.)

couples in a parish in Rheims in 1422). Three structual elements clearly emerge:

(1) Age inversion is rare. In 14.5 per cent of couples the husband is younger than his wife (which is within one per cent of the situation in Rheims in 1422), but only in 11.7 per cent of the cases is the difference significant (greater than two years). Such an inversion is exceptional both at first marriages and with couples in which the husband is elderly. Naturally, it is among couples in their thirties that it is most frequent. I would thus be willing to suggest that marriage with an 'old woman' (a widow, for the most part) is characteristic of a late marriage for the man. The infrequency of this inversion probably signifies that in Dijon in the fifteenth century, as in other cities of France under the *ancien régime*, in general young men rejected the social promotion by marriage with an 'old woman'.[12]

(2) In 85.5 per cent of these couples, the husband is older than his wife, the average age gap being 7.9 years. But if husbands under thirty years of age are on the average 4.2 years older than their wives (the largest difference is eight years), couples in their thirties show an average age gap of six years (the greatest difference being sixteen years), and husbands in their forties and fifties are almost eleven years older than their tender young wives (the largest gap is thirty-four years). There is nothing remarkable in this, since what we see here are the effects of second or third marriages, which always accentuate differences in age. This situation remained largely unchanged during the first half of the sixteenth century, with only a slight tendency toward the equalization of ages among young couples.[13]

These age gaps are perhaps comparable to those in Rheims, but they are less than those in Tuscany.[14] Nevertheless, in spite of slight variations,

[12] Among 'young couples' (husbands under thirty years of age), the proportion of age inversions is 14.5 per cent; among those with husbands in their thirties, 20 per cent; for husbands in their forties and fifties it falls to 10 per cent. This means that a man whose first marriage came relatively late (around thirty years of age), taking an 'old woman' as his bride, married a younger woman when his first wife died. I should add that in Lyons in the eighteenth century, in spite of a relatively high proportion of age inversions, couples who fell outside matrimonial custom were still treated to a charivari (M. Garden, *Lyon et les Lyonnais au XVIIIe siècle*, Paris, 1970).

[13] During the first half of the sixteenth century (in a sampling of 204 couples), 'inverted' marriages represent only 15 per cent of the total, a barely perceptible rise in comparison to the fifteenth century. On the other hand, 31 per cent of husbands under thirty years of age have a wife older than they. The only notable change in matrimonial customs thus concerns first marriages.

[14] Desportes, 'La population de Reims', p. 501, gives an approximate average of ten years, which implies that differences in age were even more striking in Rheims than in Dijon. For Florence, see D. Herlihy, 'Vieillir à Florence au Quattrocento', *Annales ESC*, 1969, p. 1341.

identical marriage structures can be discerned in Florence as in Rheims and Dijon: relatively late marriage for men, very few inverted age relationships, and marked age differences, the husband typically being older. Other cities probably followed the same pattern; matrimonial order in the fifteenth century presented mature husbands and younger wives. Hence in the business negotiations that marriage represented, although the terms of the exchange were multiple and included ethnic origin, profession, social status and wealth, we can assume that the 'freshness' of the woman was an asset sought by a man of established position, even in the minor trades.[15]

(3) A closer view of the realities of the marriage market shows that 30 per cent of men from thirty to thirty-nine years of age had a wife who was from eight to sixteen years their junior (from ten to sixteen years in 20 per cent of the cases), and 15 per cent of the forty- and fifty-year-old husbands had a wife who was from twenty to thirty-four years younger than they. This means that these men chose their companion from an age group in which they competed with younger men. I am not so naive as to deduce from this that there was a shortage of wives for young men; still, we should note that nearly one-third of the marriageable girls and 'remarriageable' women under thirty years of age were claimed by men who were 'established', if not elderly. This syphoning off of young wives was considerable enough to be clearly felt by the young in sixteenth-century cities, as it had been in the fifteenth century.[16] Without entering into the familial or affective consequences that they brought to couples, such age gaps seem to me to have caused both a certain amount of social tension between penniless and wifeless young men and more fortunate men who had both; and, even more, a rivalry between marriageable young men and married men or widowers of over thirty years of age. This rivalry may have contributed to age-based solidarities and collective behaviour patterns unique to young men.

[15] There was no difference between the customs of the rich and those of the poor in such matters. There are several reasons for this: the attraction of a young wife, first, but also worries concerning security, both for the husband whose old age is thus 'assured' and for the young woman who perhaps opts for a man of mature years – when she can choose – not because he can offer her a better 'situation' than a younger man, but for increased peace of mind, since he is further from the 'follies' of youth. There may be a still deeper reason for this behaviour: men and women did not perceive the stages of life in the same fashion. Eustache Deschamps notes in his *Miroir de Mariage* that old age begins for women at the age of thirty, but for men at fifty (cited in J. Huizinga, *The Waning of the Middle Ages*, Anchor Books, Garden City, New York, 1954, p. 33).

[16] Village and city were not noticeably different where the behaviour of groups of young people was concerned. Women circulated in city society a good deal more freely than in the village. Still, young men in the city could hardly be unaware of it when their elders 'syphoned off' young women. One young woman out of four was put out of reach of the men who, by their age, might legitimately have claimed her.

Age Groups, Collective Rites and Mediating Institutions

When we apply concepts such as age groups, collective rites, and mediating institutions to traditional societies, we may very easily fail to get a satisfactory answer. Some historians go so far as to apply to the fifteenth or the sixteenth century a too removed 'ethnographic model' or a 'sociological model' that leads to anachronisms. Paul Veyne, following Philippe Ariès, even goes so far as to write that village youths participating in charivaris were playing out a rite that had become simply customary.[17]

I believe, to the contrary, that urban societies of the waning Middle Ages, like those of the Renaissance, tended to maintain and above all to develop the importance of age groups. The arguments that Ariès uses to refute this idea do not persuade me: apprenticeship, far from integrating the child into the adult world, frequently had the effect of keeping him out of it, at least temporarily. Both Bronislaw Geremek and Natalie Zemon Davis have noted certain traits of this tendency. Apprenticeship could certainly transmit a *savour-faire*, but not a *savoir-vivre*. S. N. Eisenstadt has emphasized the fundamental role of immigration in youth solidarity, as the rootless sons of newcomers were encouraged to band together with others of their ilk, and my own ongoing research shows that the populations of Rhône valley cities were largely composed of recent immigrants. Finally, the conditions of family life encouraged adolescents to seek the company of their peers. Many of them lacked the presence in the home of a father capable of providing an adult role model, since the head of family was entering old age just as they were reaching their twenties. Above all, the conditions of communal life in the city encouraged the young to search out a suitable role model outside of the home.[18]

It may well be true, as David Herlihy has suggested, that in more evolved cultural areas and in wealthy milieux in which the woman held an enviable position, maternal education profoundly influenced the sensitivities and the social attitudes of the young. In most French cities, however, which lay far distant from Florence, a male-oriented morality

[17] P. Ariès, *L'enfant et la vie familiale sous l'Ancien Régime* (2nd edn, Paris, 1973), p. vii; P. Ariès, *La France et les français* (Paris, 1972), p. 872. See also P. Veyne, *Writing History: Essay on Epistemology*, trans. M. Moore-Rinvolucri (Middletown, Connecticut, 1984), pp. 196–7.

[18] B. Geremek, *Le salariat dans l'artisanat parisien aux XIIIe–XVe siècles* (Paris, 1968), pp. 32–5. N. Z. Davis, 'City Women and Religious Change in XVIth century France', in D. G. McGuigan (ed.), *A Sampler of Women's Studies* (Ann Arbor, 1973), republished as chap. 3 of N. Z. Davis, *Society and Culture in Early Modern France* (Stanford, 1975); S. N. Eisenstadt, *From Generation to Generation: Age Groups and Social Structure* (Glencoe, 1956).

encouraged 'the boys', unless they were born into patrician families, to form aggressive bands that disturbed order.[19]

These gangs of young males that troubled the Dijon night have some quite distinguishing characteristics. First, they were all more or less of the same age. In eleven of the fifteen groups that form the basis of this analysis, more than one-half of the participants are of the same age cohort, and the presence among them of one or two older bachelors – experienced hands – does nothing to negate this homogeneity. Two-thirds of the groups have a strong socio-professional orientation: they are made up of journeymen and craftsmen's sons from the same or closely related trades, or of young men of the same social status. In similar proportions, these were also streetcorner gangs, comprising only from three to five individuals who knew each other well. Finally, and this is an essential trait, in more than 80 per cent of cases, the young men had never before faced charges of group delinquency. In other words, the *juvenes* of these walled cities, victims of boredom, roamed the city in the evening, quite spontaneously on the lookout for adventure or for a good brawl, taunting the night watch, chasing girls, and organizing a rape.[20]

Is it fair to call these assaults gang rape? This is a 'crossroads of ambiguities', the socio-criminologists tell us, and with good reason. Any explanation of it must include the particular gang's motivations, the imprudence of a specific girl, vengeance, private or collective, the seizing of an offered opportunity, and the demands of clan rivalries.[21] In this society in which images of violence were a daily experience and the sexual impulses of adults met with few constraints, the aggression of the night gangs quite naturally translated into sexual violence. It seems to me that there are two principal reasons for this:

[19] Herlihy, 'Vieillir à Florence', p. 1345.

[20] On the structure of groups:

a) Age homogeneity: the 15 utilizable groups date from the first half of the sixteenth century, but there was no change in age at marriage between 1450 and 1550. I define a group as homogeneous when more than half the individuals who comprise it are within five years of age.

b) Socio-professional structure: 34 fifteenth-century groups show strong homogeneity (25 groups of sons of workingmen in the same profession or sons of men of the same social status); eight groups show average homogeneity (clerics, sons of merchants, plus a majority of artisans' sons); one group show weak or no homogeneity (domestic servants, soldiers, artisans, valets, etc.). During the first half of the sixteenth century, this same distribution is true, respectively, of 23, 8 and 2 groups.

c) Numerical values: in the fifteenth century, 54 of 98 gangs had from three to five members.

[21] *Image du viol collectif et reconstruction d'objet, Déviance et contrôle social*, no. 15 (Paris: SEPC, 1974), compiled by a team of researchers from the Chancellerie and the University of Bordeaux, presents an analysis of rape from the socio-criminologist's point of view, a consideration of the significance of rape in contemporary societies and a summary of current work on adolescent gangs.

(1) To acquire the privilege of masculinity. Masculinity is a social role, an acquired behaviour. One recurrent image, the cock and the hen, accurately reflects the relative place of man and woman in the fifteenth-century French city. By her very nature, the hen needed to be mastered and dominated. Add to that an extremely Manichaean vision of young women, who could only be pure or public. This is what lent legitimacy to the actions of these young cocks: their attacks were always accompanied by degrading insults, humiliation of the victim, and blows. Well before they passed on to the act itself, the aggressors exculpated themselves, and from the outset the woman they chose was treated as guilty and viewed as a mere object and as obliged to submit.[22]

Every year in Dijon a hundred or so individuals were implicated in rapes. If we exclude the outsiders, the repeat offenders and the adult instigators, there remains a minimum of fifty to sixty young men aged between eighteen to twenty-four years. This means that half the city youths had participated at least once in this sort of attack. It is, in my opinion, quite possible that this type of aggression constituted a rite of passage to manhood and of admission to neighbourhood gangs.[23]

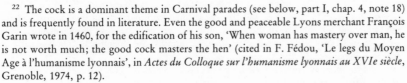

[22] The cock is a dominant theme in Carnival parades (see below, part I, chap. 4, note 18) and is frequently found in literature. Even the good and peaceable Lyons merchant François Garin wrote in 1460, for the edification of his son, 'When woman has mastery over man, he is not worth much; the good cock masters the hen' (cited in F. Fédou, 'Le legs du Moyen Age à l'humanisme lyonnais', in *Actes du Colloque sur l'humanisme lyonnais au XVIe siècle*, Grenoble, 1974, p. 12).

[23] I am basing my estimate on the number of young men between eighteen and twenty-four years of age in Rheims, a city comparable in Dijon. In Dijon in 1422 this age group comprised 750, out of a city population of 10,000. In seven years in Dijon there were at least 700 men cited in such cases. Exclusion of the categories mentioned leaves from 350 to 400 unmarried men among them.

How, though, could illegal group behaviour of this sort exist? Why was the judicial system unable to establish the criminality of such actions?

(1) The surveillance of moral conduct in urban areas was the responsibility of municipal authorities. When the behaviour of a woman was felt to be particularly scandalous (flagrant adultery or intolerable concubinage), the *échevins* of the city, accompanied by the night-watch, had a legal right to surprise the guilty parties, oblige them to open their bedroom doors and impose a fine on them. (Examples of such visits are in AM Dijon, B 157, fol. 161v, 1447; AD Côte-d'Or, B 11 360/8, p. 22, 1461; AM Dijon, series M, *Amendes de nuit*.) Sometimes the authorities publicly conducted women to the brothel if they failed to heed warnings or had insufficient protection (AD Côte-d'Or, B 11 336/63, fol. 98; AM Dijon, B 161, fol. 110v). The charivaris and ass-back cavalcades were carried on 'legally' and probably without physical violence, but they were marked by extraordinary moral violence. This 'policing of mores' was at the time delegated by the judicial system to the youth brotherhoods and, on occasion, to groups of young men who requested authorization from the mayor to surprise a particular concubinary couple (usually a priest and his mistress) to chastise them or drive away the woman (AD Côte-d'Or, B 11 360/2, item 150, 1450). Visits of the sort often ended up in genuine violence. Above all, the bands of young men amused

(2) Although the participants made full use of this opportunity to satisfy their sexual desires (the women were raped repeatedly), for many of them – poor journeymen, domestic servants and penniless sons of established families – collective rape expressed much deeper impulses or frustrations: it was a denial of social order. When they raped her, they marked the young widow or the marriageable girl by destroying her social standing. They attacked the serving girl rumoured to be 'kept' by her master, the servant-mistress of a better-off journeyman, the priest's concubine, or the wife who had been 'left' temporarily and who, they take care to add, should by rights 'provide' pleasure to the companions'.[24]

---

themselves – this time without official permission – by surprising lovers and making them pay a gage, spying on priests' concubines and 'knocking at the door' of 'engaged' couples. It was thus an easy matter to 'legitimize' any plot aimed at a woman who aroused desire. We can conclude that gang rape had a place at the borderline between culture and subculture.

(2) All violent acts without delegation of authority were punished, but unless it was committed against a respectable Dijon wife or a child, rape did not incur strict penalties, and such sanctions were hardly disuasive. When the guilty parties were identified (not always the case), they were imprisoned. If the victim withdrew her complaint (which often happened, for the reasons mentioned), the assailants were freed immediately. If she did not, they usually were freed on bail and later were fined in proportion to their means and the reputation and social status of the victim. If they were poor, they were punished by 'long emprisonment' (for weeks more often than for months), by flogging and, occasionally, if they were outsiders, by banishment.

Furthermore, competing jurisdictions and appeal to a higher court helped undermine the efforts of the mayor and the public prosecutor. In fact, urban judicial authorities aimed at using as many judiciary privileges as possible on behalf of the townspeople, at the risk of seeing a criminal case mitigated into a misdemeanour punishable only by a fine, but in the interest of keeping the accused and his goods out of the hands of ducal justice. A number of delinquents were pardoned by the duke, while others demanded judgement by the bishop of Langres, and clerical privileges seem to have been extended, somewhat oddly, to hosemakers, butchers, and torch manufacturers. It was customary, what is more, to free all prisoners on the occasion of the formal entry into the city of a member of the royal house, who would then pardon all but the debtors. This occurred seven times between 1450 and 1475.

As the social reaction to rape was only rarely favourable to the victim, a young Dijon citizen could permit himself the rape of a woman without being considered criminal or held to be 'bad' (*meschant*). There is documentation of artisans' sons who participated in several rapes, armed attacks and innumerable brawls before the mayor made up his mind to banish them temporarily. As for notables' sons, the cruel sports of their youth had little effect on their careers, and they could end their lives with their honour intact.

[24] The depositions of both victims and assailants offer glimpses of resentment towards the affluent. The 'companions' knew full well that young and pretty serving girls were often 'kept' by the master and his sons. There were many chambermaids made pregnant by their employer, given sums of money and married off. A butcher's assistant, one G. Robelin, declares to a young serving girl that 'her master was keeping her' and that he 'would make his pleasure of her too' (AD Côte-d'Or B 11 360/4, item 364, 1449). A weaver's son tells one Jaquette, twenty-two years of age and a serving maid of an attorney, 'I have a right to have a

City notables and heads of large households had a stake in quelling this turbulence. They offered their sons, their domestics and their working-men liberal opportunities for municipally-sponsored fornication (and they took advantage of it themselves). They may perhaps also have compromised with unmarried men by accepting some of the ways they expressed their solidarity and not objecting to the rowdy public behaviour of their 'joyous brotherhoods'.

Mediating Functions

Now that we have a firmer understanding of the complementary nature of matrimonial order and the subversion of the young, we need to return to the question of the place and the significance of 'youth abbeys' in urban society.

It is well known that young men's organizations could be found under a wide variety of names in both towns and villages. Natalie Zemon Davis has given us an excellent analysis of them, emphasizing the role that they played in rural communities in the socialization of the young, the control of their impulses, and the defence of the community and its traditions.[25] Nevertheless, when she bases her conclusion on the example of Lyons (in reality an exceptional metropolis), she is led to make too great a distinction between rural youth abbeys and their urban counterparts and to oppose the *maugouverts* – the organizations of 'misrule' – of the sixteenth century to the *bachelleries* – unmarried men's societies – of the previous centuries. Davis claims that the conditions particular to the larger cities of the Renaissance, new elements in the apprenticeship system and the diffusion of a new culture restricted the social range of recruitment of these brotherhoods, which now welcomed both married and unmarried men and became associations dedicated to good neigh-

---

go at you just like the others' (AD Côte-d'Or, B 11 360/31, 1533). Two journeyman masons call out in the street to the niece of the viscount-mayor (she was sixteen and her conduct was beyond reproach), 'We are going to f--- you; we can f--- you just as well as the others' (ibid., B 11 360/18, 1505). Bitterness is also directed at workingmen with enough income to keep a servant: one Mongin, an unmarried carpenter, had a serving girl who six 'companions' attempted to rape (ibid., B 11 360/5, p. 619, 1454). Men say of a pregnant woman who was a widow and the servant of a priest, 'We will have our share just like the priests' (ibid., B 11 360/7, p. 817, 1458). A woman left alone when her husband went to work outside Dijon for several days was told that 'she was obliged to give pleasure to the companions, even to they themselves, and that they would pay' (ibid., B 11 360/11, 1471). Widows were solicited in the same manner (ibid., B 11 360/13, 1479).

[25] N. Z. Davis, 'The Reasons of Misrule: Youth Groups and Charivaris in Sixteenth-Century France', *Past and Present*, 50 (1971), pp. 41–75. My own conclusions on the youth brotherhoods can be found in J. Rossiaud, 'Fraternités de jeunesse et niveaux de culture dans les ville du Sud Est à la fin du Moyen âge', *Cahiers d'histoire*, 1–2 (1976), pp. 67–102.

bourly relations, adding to their supervision of matrimonial mores social, political and religious criticism. Without going into all the problems raised by Davis's arguments, I shall limit my remarks to the continuity that I see in the structure and the objectives of these groups in the urban milieu from the end of the fourteenth to the mid-sixteenth century.

(1) In all the cities of south-east France the abbeys of *jovens* or the joyous brotherhoods were institutions recognized by and integrated into the city's body politic. The abbot, his treasurer and his priors were often elected in the presence of city council members; the association's internal quarrels were arbitrated by the city council, which also controlled its finances, granted or refused permission for its public activities and set the limits of its jurisdiction. This was true from Dijon to Arles, in the sixteenth century as it was in the fifteenth. The few traces of conflict between the abbeys and the urban authorities should not mislead us: almost never was an abbey formed spontaneously; they were instigated or controlled by the urban collectivity.[26]

(2) Youths exercised a jurisdiction over the unmarried and the married alike. This fundamental notion remained true throughout the sixteenth century. We should note, however, that the abbey's 'rights' were negligible in the first marriage of a young couple (amounting to a few pennies or a share in the wedding party). They were relatively high when the union was seen as a threat to the young or when matrimonial customs were transgressed. In that case, the organization could levy fines that went into the group's coffers and were used, in part, to organize banquets. The groups' jurisdiction amounted to coercion only when the couple refused to submit to such customs. Then a charivari or a forced ride on ass-back, with no physical violence, but which ended up in a drinking bout, helped youths put up with a situation that in their hearts they found intolerable.[27]

When they performed these activities, however, the 'kings', 'prince abbots' and their henchmen compromised with matrimonial order by

[26] How could it possibly be otherwise in cities, where any gathering was suspect? On one occasion, men who had organized a ninepins contest without permission from the judiciary were prosecuted (AM Dijon, B 157, fol. 99v, October 1445).

[27] Jean Gerson defends the Feast of Fools, since 'it permits the people to run wild, as one gives air to new wine to avoid having the barrel explode' (cited in C. Gaignebet and M. C. Florentin, *Le Carnaval: Essais de mythologie populaire*, Paris, 1974, p. 44). Many of the notables were conscious of the 'therapeutic' virtues of festivities, and my observations on the distribution of rapes in the calendar year seems to confirm the accuracy of their views. By definition, however, participation in a charivari could not have constituted a 'rite of passage' for a young man, as stated in C. Gauvard and A. Gokalp, 'Le charivari en France au Moyen Age', *Annales ESC* (1974), p. 704, since people of all ages joined young men in these disturbances, which did not serve as a trial for the participants.

coming to terms with the situation.[28] As for the new bridegrooms, they had good reason to accept the abbey's rights: by compromising with the young they wiped out their 'error' and protected themselves against possible violence. Furthermore, husbands controlled these youthful demonstrations: their representatives sat on the city council that held authority over the 'abbeys', and some of them were members of youth brotherhoods themselves.

(3) Youth solidarity did not extend to both sexes: the troops ranged behind their leader dancing a noisy saraband around the dwelling of the 'guilty couple' or following mockingly after the ass did not work for the protection of the woman as they did the man. Although men were on occasion the victims of these rites, responsibility for the scandal denounced by the young was almost always laid to the woman. She was seen as dominating, unfaithful, perfidious when she snared a man younger than herself, and imbecilic (which was her nature) when she accepted marriage with a greybeard or, if she did so willingly, guilty of treachery toward eligible younger men. Youth groups punished the husband who beat his wife, to be sure, but only in the month of May, and only if he was particularly quarrelsome or was an outsider to the community. It was these same young men, who had gained the esteem of their peers by well-publicized fornication, who in May directed public scorn at young girls whose virtue they chose to suspect (and girls had no solidarity structure to back them up), reserving the right to target them for collective violence at a later date.

Contemporary vocabulary is profoundly indicative: every young male living in the town above the poverty level owed it to himself to join the great band of the *gars* ('the boys') who gave chase to *la garce* (one of many terms for a whore). That was how one became known as an *homme joyeux* (a real man, 'one of the boys') whereas a *fille joyeuse* meant a prostitute. The *abbé* of a youth group held a position of influence and prestige (their 'queens', the *reinagières*, played an insignificant and purely accompanying role), whereas the term *abbesse* referred to the manager of a bawdy house.[29] In my view, then, until the beginning of the sixteenth century and possibly a good deal later, the youth abbeys (with the exception of the so-called *abbayes bourgeoises*) were institutions for

---

[28] In Beaucaire, the abbot of the youth association was assisted by four 'priors' (two each for married and unmarried men) (AM Beaucaire, BB 4, fol. 63v, 1515). This meant that only a small fraction of married men (probably the younger ones) were represented. This was true at the end of the fourteenth and the beginning of the fifteenth century (see R. Vaultier, *Le folklore pendant la guerre de Cent Ans d'après les lettres de rémission du Trésor des chartes*, Paris, 1965, pp. xvii, xviii, 55).

[29] The same could be said of *bons companions*, which had positive connotations, and *bonnes dames*, another term for prostitutes.

conserving and passing on the most traditional sort of misogyny. They contributed to keeping women subservient, at least in the middle and lower levels of society.

The 'companions' who roamed the city at night in search of prey – those *ephèbes noirs* (black adolescents) of the medieval city[30] – underwent their apprenticeship in adulthood among their peers and under cover of night. Anonymously and through violence, they embodied a true counter-force controlling marriage. When these same young men and their wealthier peers forced their victims to parade on ass-back through the city, or when they taunted couples at their second marriages, they were not merely carrying on rites whose meaning they no longer understood, nor were they simply actors in a collective psychodrama in which the roles and the situations had remained fixed from time immemorial. The kings, abbots and Mad Mothers who led them – in broad daylight – only rarely and in mitigated form expressed the frustrations of youth. The abbey was simply the opposition to 'his lordship the State of Marriage'. Above all, it was somewhat like the municipal brothels, an institution for harmony between age groups and social groups, and between newcomers and native townspeople and citydwellers. It integrated; it socialized; it amused. However, in the last analysis, both in their more aggressive behaviour and in the organized mockery of the *chahut*, young people also proved themselves faithful followers of an order of which they expected to be a part one day.[31]

Literature, legend and popular mythology have retained only the more benevolent aspects of these youth solidarities. The champions of a popular culture largely defined by laughter and what is called the Gallic tradition would do well to look twice,[32] for these groups of grotesque maskers who resemble the comic characters of farces and *sotties* lead us to forget the victims, most of whom were 'abandoned' to a life of vagabondage or prostitution.

[30] The events described in P. Vidal-Naquet, 'Le Philoctète de Sophocle et l'éphébie', *Annales ESC*, 1971, pp. 623–38 come to mind. (This article is available in English as 'The Black Hunter and the Origin of the Athenian Ephebeia', in M. Ferro (ed.), *Social Historians in Contemporary France: Essays from Annales*, Harper Torchbooks, New York and London, 1972, pp. 212–9.)

[31] Natalie Zemon Davis has quite rightly seen that the village *bachellerie* transmitted a set of traditions. As for Paul Veyne (*Writing History*, pp. 196–7), he is partly right: young people behaved like the faithful, yes, but they were faithful not to a rite but to a moral code. Aggression was almost always committed in the name of 'matrimonial morality' and the charivaris and *chevauchées* punished 'bad' fiancées or guilty wives. However, none of the 'joyous companions' dreamed that he could remain young forever, and all knew they would later be on the receiving end of such customs.

[32] This 'cultural' image surfaces in M. Bakhtin, *Rabelais and his World*, trans. H. Iswolsky (Cambridge, Massachusetts, 1968) and somewhat less clearly in Gaignebet and Florentin, *Le Carnaval*.

3

Victims, Procuresses and Prostitutes

The Consequences of Rape

There were a large number of available women in the city: widows, wives temporarily separated from their husband, unmarried young girls. They alone took on the full burden of the feminine condition. They were also the preferred targets of all male unruliness. The victims of collective rape, whose ages ranged from fifteen to thirty-three years, were girls and women of marriageable or remarriageable age. Child rape was rare. Perhaps many such rapes were never admitted, but I would conjecture that the rape of a child under fourteen or fifteen years of age was perceived by all as an extremely serious social crime. The interrogation of one victim of the sort bears witness to this: the investigators seek out the least details of an occurrence that seems to them (as to the witnesses) monstrous.[1] This is also true of procuration when the girl offered was twelve to fourteen years of age: when this happened justice was for once prompt and rigorous. For this reason, marriage for girls of less than fifteen years of age should be considered the exception in an urban environment and contrary to custom and social consensus. Furthermore, this society distinguished clearly between childhood and adolescence, not only for girls, but also for boys, who, for identical misdemeanours received sentences that varied in severity according to their age.

Sixty per cent of the plaintiffs in rape cases are unmarried. Half of the rest are normally married women, their husbands being absent for a few days or a few weeks. It is clear, then, that both the girls and their aggressors were part of the community. The marginalised had no place in

---

[1] For example, AD Côte-d'Or, B 11 360–3, p. 242 (1444); B 11 360–12 (1473); B 11 360–18 (1504).

these sports. Socially, however, these women belong to the least affluent levels: they are servant girls, the daughters or wives of day labourers, or of waged textile workers. Only seven of them are the wives of master craftsmen, and only one comes from a more comfortable background.[2] This is hardly surprising, since it was an easier matter to commit rape on humble folk. The sentences or fines were lighter, swift vengeance was seldom to be feared, and social reprobation was tempered, for a sense of community was less strong among day labourers, who were, for the most part, newly established in the city, and came from different regions of the country. Furthermore, the notables held that the 'honesty' of a woman was relative to her 'estate', and the wife of a worker could not aspire to the 'honesty' of a burgher's wife. Finally, the aggressors preferred to attack isolated women, weak women, women who (except for the serving girls and chambermaids) were old maids or had remained widows too long and thus were suspect or scorned in a society in which the dominant morality was matrimonial. In this age, a woman's destiny was dependent on her *fama publica*, which amounted to snippets of gossip and rumour.[3] The most highly prized victims were the 'good ladies of priests', who were led a merry dance, engaged girls (sometimes on the eve of their marriage), women separated from their husband (even with his agreement and that of their families), and any girl accused of 'dishonest' conduct – often calumniously since many young immigrants had to earn their bread by going from one large city house to another for a week or several days

---

[2] For the fifteenth century, the average known age of forty victims is: servant girls, 17; unmarried young girls, 20; women alone, widows or separated, 25. In only one exceptional case was the woman 47 years old. For the first half of the sixteenth century, 47 examples, the average age is 22½ years.

Social status: Out of 101 cases, 18 servant girls, 24 young girls, 14 widows, 13 wives temporarily 'left', 3 separated wives, 8 wives living with their husband, 9 outsiders passing through, 6 women of unknown status. Twelve of the victims had shown proof of truly 'immoral' conduct before the rape.

Family ties: Out of 95 utilizable cases, 50 had either a husband, an uncle, relatives, or brothers in the city; the others were in service far from home. Out of 64 cases there are 18 servant women, 31 daughters or wives of workingmen in the fullers' and weavers' trades or in the vineyards, 7 wives or daughters of master craftsmen, 3 of sergeants or messengers, 4 of archers or garrisoned soldiers, 1 merchant's widow.

[3] One woman's judgement of another is revealing: 'The said Jacote is a woman who was never married and [is] of little governance' (AD Côte-d'Or, B 11 360/16, 1494). Another confession shows to what point a moral code could be widely diffused and internalized: a seamster's wife was attacked in the street by three 'companions' who would have raped her if she and her servant had not put up a stiff resistance: 'Even though she was a good woman *as far as possible in her estate*' (emphasis added) (AD Côte-d'Or, B 11 360/20, 1509). Being 'of little estate' was naturally connected in notables' minds with 'unruly conduct' (ibid., B 11 360/2, p. 153, 1432).

at a time, arousing the suspicion, merited or unmerited, of young men on the lookout for any fair game.[4]

The consequences of rape were the same, in the long run, as those of dubious or dishonourable conduct. The victim, who lost her good name in almost all cases, encountered real difficulty in regaining her place in society, and even in her own family. If she was unmarried, her price on the marriage market sank; if she was married, she could be abandoned by her husband. Even when her neighbours had testified on her behalf, they invariably saw her as sullied by what she had undergone.[5] She herself felt shamed, guilty, and the object of scandal. The rapists achieved their ends in this: in her own eyes and those of her associates, the status of a raped woman was brought singularly closer to that of a common prostitute. Rendered vulnerable, psychologically and physically, she had little hope of regaining her honour as long as she remained in the city.[6]

[4] Examples of a woman separated from her husband with his consent (ibid., BB 11 360–5, p. 627, 1454), of another who had fled her conjugal roof (ibid., BB 11 360/8, p. 35, 1461), of wives who frequented or received other couples too often, even if they were in the company of their husbands (ibid., B 11 360/3, 1442). One carpenter's wife was raped 'because she is bawdy and laughs a lot' and called to people in the street by their name (ibid., B 11 360/3, p. 317, 1447). There are also women who venture out in the evening (perhaps accompanied by a relative), for it was not 'the hour for women to go about the city' (ibid., B 11 360/14, 1485; B 11 360/5, 1453; B 11 360/5, p. 607; B 11 360/9, 1464). Another case summarizes the vulnerability of young immigrants and explains the majority of the rapes: Jeanne, fifteen years of age, tells her meagre history. She had left her masters, roast meat purveyors, in whose house she had been raped by a domestic. She took lodgings with a woman and worked as a day labourer in the fields or in the city and was happy with her lot, for she lived better than when she had been a servant. But she occasionally went for several days without work, 'and since it was known that she came and went and was idle, she was immediately hunted by the young men of the city, who pursued her so that she began to give them pleasure of her body' (ibid., B 11 360/16, 1492).

[5] This is why families were reluctant to enter a complaint. To cite two cases: in July 1425 a valet indecently assaulted a ten-year-old girl named Regnaulde. He did not actually rape her, but his act was sufficiently scandalous to merit him a sentence of being publicly flogged on market day. The victim's parents requested and obtained remission of the sentence, 'so that the said Regnaulde not be dishonoured' (AM Dijon, B 151, fol. 54v). In 1455 a young woman was put into prostitution by her mother-in-law, who was banished but not flogged for it, for the judges expressed their fear 'that in this case the son would abandon his wife' (ibid., B 11 360/6, item 676).

[6] There are many examples of this. A pregnant woman was raped by Picard archers. When the city opened an investigation, she refused to admit the rape. Only after the child was born did she withdraw her first deposition, made 'out of shame' (ibid., B 11 360/12, 1473). Another women accepts a settlement 'fearing to be defamed by legal procedings' (ibid., B 11 360/19, 1464). Catherine, twenty-six years of age, knew that the ducal archers had for several days been carrying on wildly and that they wanted to carry her off to the brothel. She went there on her own, 'to avoid having them lead me there shamefully . . , and so the neighbours will not be scandalized' (ibid., B 11 360/6, p. 772, 1457). There were also reactions from the neighbours. In December 1483, Jeannette, a servant who for two years

Thus violence was often a prelude to forced prostitution or procuration, and tensions within marriage increased prostitution.

Procuration and Pimping

The model for profiting from the prostitution of women came from on high. In each city, officers of the municipal or princely authorities were charged with enforcing the regulations concerning prostitution and with the registration of prostitutes, on acceptance and payment of a tax, or else of their rejection. These men were known from Arles to Dijon for trafficking in female flesh. The *sous-viguier* of Tarascon, a nobleman named Ferrand de Castille, was little more than a pimp; J. de Marnay, the provost of Dijon, turns up now and then with his henchmen, using force against women he intended taking off to the municipal brothel or to the bathhouses run by his procuress friends.[7] Procuration – *maquerellage* – was a specifically female activity: out of 83 cases of 'private bordellos' that I have located in Dijon, 75 were kept by women. Literature has all too often presented the figure of the aged and superstitious crone acting as go-between and has indulged in a detailed description of her withered body, twin in ugliness to her depraved soul, which the author then goes on to denounce.[8] We do indeed find a few 'ancient' widows among the Dijon madams, but 41 of the 67 women about whom we have information were married and carried on this profitable commerce to round out the family budget with the agreement of their husbands –

---

had served her locksmith masters well, was raped by a band of toughs, and 'out of fear, no one dares receive the said Jeannette, even her former masters' (ibid., B 11 360/14). In 1527, the mother of a victim wanted to take her away from Dijon, for, as she declares, 'never would she have honour in this city' (ibid., B 11 360/29). The same year, a servant woman was attacked and insulted by three rowdies and was chased out of her lodgings when she complained of it to her landlady, who said that 'since she had been charged with these nasty things, she would not have her any longer, unless she could know for certain if [the girl] was a decent woman or a wicked whore' (ibid., B 11 360/29).

Thomas Aquinas had outlined the consequences of sexual seduction, and in the process he expressed many contemporary ideas on female sexuality: if the seducer does not marry the seduced woman as reparation for his act, she will find it more difficult to marry. She may be led to give herself over to debauchery, from which only her intact modesty had kept her thus far.

[7] For complaints on Ferrand's conduct in Tarascon in 1444, see AM Tarascon, BB 7, fol. 183v; for 1470, see ibid., BB 10, fol. 63; for 1473, ibid., fol. 134v, and so on. In Beaucaire, the *sous-viguier* was 'illiterate, leads a dissolute life, frequents bandits and pimps' (AM Beaucaire, BB 2, fol. 112v, 1495). In Avignon, Lyons and Dijon, sergeants managed bathhouses and rented rooms for prostitution.

[8] See J. Bailbé, 'Le thème de la vieille femme dans la poésie satirique du XVIe et du début du XVIIe siècle', *Bibliothèque d'Humanisme et Renaissance, Travaux et documents*, vol. 26 (1964), pp. 98–119. The same image can be found in Villon and in the *sotties*.

artisans, carters, innkeepers.[9] Furthermore, there was an extraordinary range within the profession. Some procuresses limited their activities to arranging assignations, others supplied the young women, some openly kept a bordello in their house, and an elite among them worked for an upper-class clientele, providing for Monsieur le Gouverneur de Bourgogne, Monseigneur le Bailli, or the Deacon of Blois lovely young things of varying degrees of innocence and quick to succomb to the charms and promises of these 'good talkers'. We can imagine these procuresses as valued confidants and persuasive women skilled in establishing relationships with other women. They recruited rape victims (when the perpetrators did not keep them for their own purposes too long); they solicited women 'constrained by marriage', kept on too short a leash, or beaten; they took in 'abandoned' poor girls and even went searching for recruits at the gates of the hospitals.[10]

Bathhouse managers stood at the peak of this hierarchy. There was Jeanne Saignant, called around 1460 'the finest *maquerelle* in Dijon', who reigned for twenty years over the bathhouse of St Philibert. She had good backing: a fun-loving husband, a brother who was a priest, a protector who stood in good grace in the ducal court, and several lovers. She enjoyed going to see 'the charming activities taking place in the chambers', and she boasted to young men and priests, even in public, of the 'tasty flesh' (*chairs de haute graisse*) that she had to offer in her stews, promising all a fresh supply daily. Furthermore, she was 'enchanting', and good enough company to have maintained the friendship of two 'women of estate' who came to her house for their assignations. She was also intelligent enough to feign indignation when she had led a new servant girl into prostitution. Her girls stayed with her because they owed her money, and for twenty years she laughed at the city *échevins* – when they were not among her clients.[11]

The *ruffians* – pimps and 'protectors' – pale in comparison with the procuresses. (The exception were the colourful and vagabond *bélitres*, who were more accurately beggars, but who pimped for a *ribaude* when the occasion arose, while she also lived as much by begging and petty theft (*sur le bonhomme*) as by her body.) Most of the prostitutes, both clandestine and public, had their 'friend' or their 'fiancé', but even though such men might syphon off a part of her earnings, they do not seem to have been organized into bands, nor did they live by procuration alone.

[9] Out of 75 *maquerelles*, 8 have insufficient data to tell, 41 are married, 14 are concubines or are engaged, and 12 are widows.

[10] Examples in AD Côte-d'Or, B 11 360/5, p. 584, B 11 360/8, B 11 360/14, and so forth.

[11] On Jeanne Saignet, long protected by J. Coustain, first Valet de Chambre of Duke Philippe le Bon, see J. Garnier, *Les étuves dijonnaises* (Dijon, 1867) and AD Côte-d'Or B 11 360/8, item 986.

They were for the most part hosemakers, seamsters, cobblers, barbers or clerks – all professions that lent themselves to this traffic since a great number of people came in and out of their workshops. There were also small groups of fullers, butcher's assistants or archers who protected and exploited the prostitutes of the faubourg or of the public brothel. Such men were not part of the criminal underworld (the case of François Villon would be out of place here), and it seems to me quite revealing that the slang of the Coquillards, who at one time made their headquarters in the Dijon brothel and extorted the prostitutes, had no terms for prostitution and procuration. Such activities were so clearly public that there was no need for the protective screen of a secret language or an underground society.[12]

Prostitutes, 'Clandestine' and Public

Contrary to a number of popular beliefs, the world of prostitutes was not peopled by vagabonds and foreigners. Penitent prostitutes in Avignon at the end of the fourteenth century came from the Rhône valley; two-thirds of the women in Dijon were born in the city or its immediate surroundings, and most of them had lived in the city for more than a year. Only 15 per cent of them were only passing through or were following chance companions. Daughters of artisans or workingmen, wives of masters or servants, only one out of five came from the more affluent milieux. For most, separation from their family or the loss of their father or mother had made them vulnerable at a young age. For almost all, prostitution had begun around seventeen years of age, but one-third of them had been obliged to sell themselves before they were fifteen. Half had been constrained into prostitution by force (27 per cent of these were victims of public rapes), and nearly a quarter had been prostituted by their family or pushed into prostitution by an intolerable family environment. Only 15 per cent or prostitutes seem to have offered their bodies on their own initiative and without constraint.[13]

Only exceptionally did a woman fall directly into public prostitution.

[12] Complaints against the conduct of these 'ruffian' protectors can of course be found in the deliberations of the city council, but they are not distinguished from vagabonds, foreigners and idlers (for example, in AM Valence, CC, 31 June 1483; AM Arles, BB 2, fol. 93v, 1435; AM Tarascon, BB 12, fol. 226v, 1507). On the Coquille, see J. Garnier, *Les compagnons de la Coquille* (Dijon, 1842).

[13] Global data on public and clandestine prostitutes in Dijon between 1440 and 1540: It goes without saying that we are dependent on the image that the prostitutes give of themselves or on the information furnished by the law courts. Biographical sketches contained in the interrogations and the depositions of Dijon citizens are the source for the following conclusions.

One example is a certain Catherine, married for two years to a Beaucaire riverboatman. 'Out of madness', she went off with a lover, also a riverman and a pimp, and she soon found herself shut up in the municipal brothel in Avignon. There was also a noble widow in the Île-de-France who, separated from her suite on pilgrimage, was kidnapped by a chance companion, and spent several days in the Grande Maison in Dijon.[14] The average age for prostitutes is a clear indication of the normal career of a woman in the 'trade'. Average age for the *filles secrètes* who worked in the private brothels was seventeen years, for chambermaids in the bathhouses, twenty, and for the women of the *prostibulum*, nearly twenty-eight. Almost all had, in fact, begun their careers with occasional prostitution, combining day work with 'abandonment' to one or several men whom they served as temporary concubines or forced servant girls. Soon bought or recruited by the procuresses, they became chambermaids in the public bathhouses, satisfying a demanding manager and a numerous clientele. Soon or later they ended in the Grande Maison, either because they were no longer earning their keep in the bathhouse, or

---

(1) Geographical origin: Out of 146 cases, 38 women are from Dijon, 45 from the Burgundian plains, 63 from more remote regions. In 123 utilizable cases, 21 women come from big cities, 33 from villages, and the immense majority from middle-sized cities or towns.

(2) Stability: Out of 130 cases, 69 women had permanent residence in Dijon, 42 were moderately stable (chambermaids or domestics in service for more than six months), 19 were vagabonds or women passing through.

(3) Matrimonial status: Out of 136 cases, 60 per cent were unmarried, 32 per cent married, 8 per cent widows. To the contrary, only 20 per cent of the prostitutes of the public brothel admit to having been married.

(4) Family situation: Out of 96 cases, the father is alive in two-thirds of cases, the mother in nearly one-half. Less than one-third of prostitutes are orphans with neither father nor mother.

(5) Social status: Out of 61 cases, less than a quarter are daughters of merchants or wealthy fathers. The others are equally divided between peasants' and artisans' daughters. When they are married, however, 2 out of 3 are the wives of journeymen in the minor trades or of labourers.

(6) Reasons for entering prostitution: Out of 77 cases, 12 were prostituted by a mother-in-law, a godfather, her mother, an uncle or aunt; 8 were driven to prostitution as the result of family conflict, 8 were forced into it by sheer poverty, 17 by forced procuration, 21 after a rape. Only 11 admit they came to their profession by choice.

(7) Age at first prostitution: Out of 48 cases, an average of 17 years of age.

[14] See P. Pansier and J. Girard, *La cour temporelle d'Avignon aux XIVe et XVe siècles* (Paris, 1909), p. 196, and AD Côte d'Or, B 11 360/12, 1475.

because they had been taken to the municipal house by their pimps, by the city authorities, or by the women who worked there.[15]

It was in the 'public place', the city brothel, that the greatest proportion of foreign prostitutes could be found. Many came from the north-west, sorely tried by various crises and by war, where life was hard for women. Flanders, Artois, Picardy, Hainaut and Barrois provided women for the bordellos of all the cities of the Rhône valley. Typically, they started from Arras, Liège, Amiens or Tournai, then worked in three or four cities sometimes moving on independently, sometimes in the company of others, resembling a female 'Tour de France' as in the later *compagnonnage*. Popular language was right: the 'abbess' of the brothel was the 'mother of the girls'.[16]

When they were admitted into the city brothel, prostitutes had to swear an oath to the authorities, pay their weekly rent to the madam, give a few pennies to the night watch for protection, and contribute to heating costs. Furnished with a *nom de guerre* – Margot la Courtoise, La Petite Normande, Marion la Liégeoise, etc. – bejewelled and finely dressed, they then 'earned their fortune' outside churches, in the marketplaces, or in the taverns. They sang in the streets in the evening to attract customers, whom they brought back to the Grande Maison. They were supposed to turn away married men and under-age youths and not to share a customer with another girl, although they could have several men at once, on the condition that the men were not related. Fees were one *blanc* the *esbattement*, a sum equivalent to what a woman could earn in half a day's

[15] The averages have been established from a sampling of 39 public prostitutes, 10 prostitutes from the bathhouses, and 19 prostitutes from private brothels. In the sixteenth century a clear decline in average age for public prostitutes can be seen (37 cases, average age twenty-four years, ten months). Several examples confirm these averages. Jeanne la Rousse left her parents' home at the age of sixteen. She went first to live with some priests, then in a rented room by herself, then moved to the city brothel of Troyes (ibid., B 11 360/26). Among sentences handed down by the mayor of Dijon, we find Simone Plateau, who was first a concubine, then a prostitute in a private brothel, then a prostitute in the municipal Grande Maison.

[16] This tendency can be seen in Villefranche-sur-Saône, Avignon, Beaucaire and Tarascon. In Dijon, out of 66 prostitutes in the brothel, 53 come from distant regions, including 26 from the country areas or the cities of north-west France. A good description of this 'wandering' is given in the confession of Jeanne d'Arras (AD Côte-d'Or, BB 11 360/18) who, in four years, went from Arras to Amiens, then to Lille, Douai, Thérouanne, Mex, Pont-à-Mousson, Neufchâtel and Nancy. She was twenty-two years of age when she settled in Dijon in 1504. Examples of 'compagnonnages': five common whores left the bordello of Verdun to work in the harvests in Burgundy before they went to a city (ibid., B 11 360/33, 1542). In Dijon in 1433, a common whore is sentenced for having said to a woman that, since she was of their 'trade', she should give them 'wine', the equivalent of the 'welcome' imposed in Dijon on outside prostitutes who came to work in their city (ibid., B 11 336/45, fol. 219). The expression *mère des filles* is used by a man from Lille (ibid., B 11 360/19, 1508).

work in the vineyards. They could expect from three to six times that when they agreed to spend the night with a 'young son'.[17]

Although on occasion prostitutes were beaten or kidnapped by a group of individuals intent on making use of them gratis, they benefited from special safeguards and were efficiently protected. The 'sign' that they wore was not only a mark of infamy, but also a guarantee against possible violence. They had men friends who were not pimps, and could be seen chatting with them in the evening in their chambers or in the common hall.[18] Before 1490, we seldom see a prostitute charged with criminal offences, and they avoided theft and procuration. A saint's image or their rosary in their hand, they heard mass at the church of the 'Jacobins' (Dominicans) or of the Cordeliers (Franciscans), they went on religious retreats at Easter and Christmas to ward off sin (sometimes it was the city who obliged them to do so, providing for their upkeep) and should they happen to blaspheme or drink, they gave generous alms and could turn to their confessors. At times they speak of themselves as victims, cry over their past, and indulge in moralizing; at other times they hold themselves no more sinful than many others. In the last analysis, they do not seem to have been unduly worried about their eternal salvation.[19]

A prostitute may have arrived fairly late in her career in the public brothel – never before twenty years of age in the fifteenth century – but

---

[17] Prostitutes paid rent and they paid off the nightwatch (AM Dijon, I 142, 1434). They were exempt from the tallage (ibid.), which was also the case in Besançon (see J. Lacassagne and A. Picornot, 'Vieilles étuves de Lyon et d'ailleurs', *Albums du Crocodile*, Lyons, 1943). They ate their meals either at the Grande Maison or the tavern (ibid., K 83; AD Côte-d'Or, 8 II 360/7, item 964). They sang or chanted in the streets in the evening (R. Vaultier, *Le folklore pendant la guerre de Cent Ans*, Paris, 1965, p. 218, and A. Eysette, *Histoire administrative de Beaucaire depuis le XIIIe siècle*, Beaucaire, 1884–9, vol. 2, p. 284). Félix Platter describes their rich clothes and their wiles for luring young men to the brothel.

Prostitutes usually received a customer for a half-hour. This is the length of time always cited by a prostitute or a madam to assure the authorities that the 'contract' had been fulfilled, or to get a customer to relinquish a bedroom (AD Côte-d'Or, B 11 360/4, 1450; B 11 360/8, 1462; AM Lyon, FF Chappe XIII, 62/67. Sometimes there were candles to measure the time, and in Italy prostitutes were called 'whores by the candle'.

It goes without saying that it is hazardous to attempt a global estimate of fees, but one *blanc* seems to have been the current price in the fifteenth century for the most expeditive service (AD Côte-d'Or, B 11 360/2, p. 115, 1433; B 11 360/5, 1454; B 11 360/10, 1467). In June 1462 a woman could be hired for two *blancs* to do a day's work in the vineyards. Young 'clandestine' prostitutes, fifteen to seventeen years of age, were paid from 2 to 6 *blancs* (ibid., B 11 360/11, 1469; B 11 360/14, 1480). In the bathhouse of St Philibert, members of a group that also dined well left Jeanne Saignant 3 or 4 *gros* for a good evening (ibid., B 11 360/8, p. 986). On occasion the prostitutes also accepted payment in kind – a good dinner (ibid., B 11 360/17, 1500).

[18] There was a fireplace in the rooms, and the 'companions' came there to get warm and talk (ibid., B 11 360/10, 1467, and B 11 360/23, 1515).

[19] Except in a port city like Arles, only exceptionally can one find provocative behaviour

she could not remain there for long. When she turned thirty her seniority would begin to show, and it was then time to make plans for the future.[20] A period of uncertainty followed. Some continued their careers in the 'trade' as abbesses and managers of bathhouses, thus assuring themselves a comfortable old age. Others chose a cloistered retreat in an institution for penitent prostitutes. These foundations were few, however, and each took in only a few women. They imposed age regulations for admission and sometimes standards of beauty (in Avignon a prostitute had to be under twenty-five years of age and pretty to be accepted). Furthermore, these charitable institutions were not always regarded kindly by the authorities, for they encouraged poor girls to take up prostitution in order to solicit aid. Thus such institutions took in only an 'elite' of poverty and penitence.[21]

A certain number of prostitutes who fell into a life of vagabondage must have known abject poverty, daily rounds of begging, rags, the hospital and death. The majority, however, had an excellent chance of finding a new place in society at thirty years of age. They had little to fear from the violence of the young and were still marriageable. In no way the objects of social rejection and often with contacts among the clergy and men of law, ex-prostitutes could easily find a place as a servant or a wife.

---

on the part of prostitutes. One such case was in Valence in May 1501, where the public prostitutes made an improper exhibition of themselves in front of virtuous young women on their way to the public washbasins (AM Valence, BB 3, fol. 21). as for their sentiments concerning their 'trade', one says of another woman who 'put her in the trade' that she will 'curse her all her life' (AD Côte-d'Or, B 11 360/5, p. 533, 1452). Another says that 'she has been put to evil' (ibid., B 11 360/18). A third, thirty years old, cries out to a fresh thirteen-year-old that 'if she knew that she was already *ribaude* she would wring her neck' (ibid., B 11 360/31, 1532). However, a common whore who was called *paillarde* (lecherous) by a young patrician woman answers 'that she is no worse than she' (ibid., B 11 360/18, 1505). Only in one will (out of five made by prostitutes of Beaucaire and Tarascon) have I found any mention of anxiety about infernal torments as punishment for a dissolute life (AD Gard, Notaires de Beaucaire, 2 E 18–31).

[20] In the fifteenth century, out of 43 prostitutes in the Dijon brothel whose age is known, 7 were over thirty, the youngest was twenty-one, and the average age was 27.9 years. In the sixteenth century (up to 1542), out of 41 cases, 3 declare more than thirty years of age, the youngest is sixteen, and the average age is twenty-four years, ten months. This lower age may be due to more efficient repression of clandestine prostitution or perhaps to the first effects of a decline in female labour.

[21] The statutes of one institution for penitent prostitutes in Avignon, as translated at the end of the fifteenth century, are savoury indeed: 'there will be received . . . only young women of the age of twenty-five years who in their youth were lustful, and who by their beauty and formliness could still be prompted by worldly fragility and inclined to worldly voluptuous pleasures and to attract men to the same totally' (see P. Pansier, *L'Oeuvre des Repenties à Avignon du XIIIe au XVIIIe siècle*, Paris, 1910, p. 40). In Lyons the Grand Hôpital could receive only twenty-five penitent prostitutes (AM Lyon, BB 25, fol. 206v, December 1507, repeating older regulations).

For many city-dwellers, public prostitution was a stage in atonement for wayward conduct. Many men felt compassion and sympathy for prostitutes, and charity dictated that neighbourhood benevolent associations and and city authorities help the 'repentants' by providing a dowry to facilitate marriage for them. Marriage was the most frequent end to a career of making a living with her body for women who had roots in the city.[22] This was why they made wills in the city and chose to be buried there. It may well be that prostitutes, far from being marginalised in the city, assumed a real function there.

[22] There are a great many examples of prostitutes whose marriage was facilitated by the city government or the neighbourhood *aumônes* (charitable groups) cited in Pansier, *L'Oeuvre des Repenties* (vol. 3, pp. 18 and 19; vol. 4, p. 19, and so on). One mention specifies that she will be an 'honourable woman'. In Beaucaire a worker marries a prostitute from the brothel and the contract drawn up before a notary gives specific mention of her social status (AD Gard, Notaire de Beaucaire, 2 E 18–82, November 1480). In Dijon, before Easter, a prostitute from the Grande Maison was engaged, and 'we hope to have her married eight days from now, and she will be a good woman' (AM Dijon, 1 142, April 1516). P. Dufour (pseud. P. Lacroix), *Histoire de la prostitution chez tous les peuples du monde depuis l'antiquité le plus reculée jusqu' à nos jours* (8 vols, Brussels, 1861 edn.), vol., 4, p. 38, cites a confirmation of the statutes of the Grande Boucherie de Paris (1381), which forbids apprentice butchers from marrying a woman who had been a public prostitute or was still one. If one of them did take a wife of the sort, he would be unable to use the facilities of the Grande Boucherie, but he could still cut meat at the Petit Pont. This means that the case was far from unusual.

4

Prostitution and Society

Clientele: The Young and the Not So Young

We find it time and again: the young frequented the brothel and the bathhouses; the local young, not just young men passing through. But was this a minority or a mass phenomenon? Were these outcasts or the city's own sons? Were their visits rare or regular? How did they view their conduct, and how were they judged by others?

Perusal of the briefs of the notaries of Tarascon and Beaucaire who did business in the municipal brothel reveals the existence of a stable local clientele. Trial witnesses are local residents of all trades. We know that in Lyons between 1471 and 1478 men of all ages from twenty-two to forty years of age and of all conditions – weavers, knifemakers, fishermen, clergy – frequented the bathhouse of La Pêcherie. In Dijon, incidents in the brothel that required the intervention of the procureur show us a large population of workingmen, artisans and merchants, most of them fully identified, from eighteen to forty years of age, three-quarters of whom lived in the city.[1]

During a trial in Lyons in 1478, witnesses for the prosecution state quite openly that they frequented that establishment in order to *s'estuver*

[1] AM Lyon, FF Chappe, XIII, 62/67 (1478). For the clientele of the brothel in Dijon between 1442 and 1492 we have 107 persons, 87 of whom are identified by profession (28 different professions). Foreigners and outsiders, including domestic servants, soldiers and the poor, form only slightly more than one-quarter of this population (in the first half of the sixteenth century, 19 out of 63 clients). Socially, 47 are artisans or workingmen, 11 merchants or engaged in the more enviable professions, 9 clerics or clerks in the judicial system, 10 domestic servants, 5 soldiers, 5 poor. Thus the municipal brothel was not a den of destitute or vagabond men, nor was it a haven for an affluent clientele, who represent less than 30 per cent of customers.

(bathe, with connotations of another sort, as we have seen) or *s'ébattre* (literally, to sport or frolic). In Dijon in 1461, in an identical context, a notary's clerk twenty-two years of age, Didier Maire, declares that 'for two years now . . . he has been several times to sport [in Jeanne Saignant's bathhouse] as the fellows do day and night'. Others state 'that they have taken their pleasure there'. In 1457, however, the procureur himself notes that 'two young men had gone to sport in that house [the municipal brothel], as unmarried young servant-journeyman are wont to do'. He adds elsewhere '. . . as young men go to sport . . .'. Other evidence from a later date but just as indicative of the norm confirms this 'custom' of journeymen and young men of burgher families.[2]

Notables and men of law were not in the least scornful of these young fornicators. The only persons who aroused suspicion or concern were those who frequented the brothels several nights in a row or spent on a grand scale. The others were, for the authorities, *bon jeunes fils*, 'good young sons, regulating themselves and living agreeably'.[3] As for the customers themselves, they felt no guilt. Quite to the contrary: when two serving men of the abbot of Clairvaux testify concerning a brawl that they had witnessed, they declare that 'Nature had moved them to go sport', and a school clerk confides, 'Monday last between two and three hours after noon, nature moved me to go sporting in the *maison des filles*'.[4] Thus, 'nature moves them', 'nature impels them', they go to the brothel 'to take their pleasure'. One 'companion' lying with a prostitute responds to an insistent knocking at the door, 'We are married for the night'.[5]

All these statements clearly prove that no one went to the brothel furtively. The texts are numerous, clear and unequivocal: for young men, whoring was a way of life, and it is likely that this practice was not imposed by 'Nature' alone but also by their age group and their elders, married men and notables. Indeed, the *bon jeunes filz* and the peaceable 'companions' owed it to themselves to go 'sporting'. This might constitute one of the rites practised by adolescent groups, whether they were organized into abbeys or not. It was a proof of social and physiological normality. Indeed, those who, for one reason or another, did not frequent the brothel from time to time could be suspect in the eyes of their companions (were they keeping a servant mistress? did they

---

[2] AM Lyon, FF Chappe, XIII, 62/67; AD Côte-d'Or, B 11 360/8, pp. 37 and 986, investigations of charges against Jeanne Saignant of 1461 and 1464, and ibid., B 11 360/6, item 772 (1457); B 11 360/19 (1508), and so forth.

[3] This moral judgement was expressed by the procureur-syndic himself and is written on the margin of an investigation concerning a young man, witness to a brawl in the Grande Maison (AD Côte-d'Or, B 11 260/15, 1490).

[4] Ibid., B 11 360/6, item 772 (April 1457), and B 11 360/15 (1490).

[5] Ibid., B 11 360/6, item 772.

have their own *ribaude*?) or of older men (were they committing grave offences against social morality? were they seducing decent girls or wives?).

In this way, almost all married men, even if they respected their marriage vows, had used the services of the public prostitutes during the five to ten years of their 'youth'. Husbandly behaviour could on occasion be influenced by this. In 1457, a prominent Dijon notable, the honourable Etienne Chambellan, a man of some forty years of age and *receveur* (tax collector) for the Duke of Burgundy, was told of a band of archers who attempted to throw a clerk out of the brothel window whom they had taken for a priest. 'This was not right,' he comments, 'the house was common to all and all manner of people could go there and be there safely, under the safeguard of the city and of the duke.' Does that mean that the toleration of the habits of 'youth' was extended to others?

Access to places of public prostitution was in theory closed to married men and clerics, with the rules enforced more strictly for married men at night than by day. The abbess had to swear when she took on her lease not to admit married men. If she did infringe this rule, there was a complaint, and the matter came to the attention of the authorities, she was liable for a fine just like the man who had committed the adultery.[6] But the regulation was never respected. First, it did not apply to outsiders. For the townsfolk, the affair was more delicate. On the understanding that prohibitions were not too blatantly transgressed, a man could reach an understanding with the abbess or with the agents of the authority charged with supervising prostitution (but who also made their living out of it). A great degree of tolerance seems to have reigned in Dijon. We know, in fact, that the watch did not usually search the brothel and open the bedroom doors: the sergeants relied on the prostitutes' word.[7] How many married men frequented their local municipal brothel is hard to tell, but we can get some idea from the following: 'Matthieu Beauprestre, mason, and J. Desgranges, also a mason, although they are married men and *have their wives in this city*, [emphasis added] are in the habit of going publicly, day or night, to the brothel, committing mortal sins [blasphemy] and scorning God, the Holy Church and the State of

---

[6] In Tarascon the abbess was sentenced to pay 48 s. cor., and one E. Gras, a married man, to pay 75 s. cor. (AD Bouches-du-Rhône, B 2043, 1477). We would need to know the circumstances of the affair, however, before concluding that severity was the general rule.

[7] The mayor's office in Dijon accused the provost, Richard Faultrey, of having transgressed custom by visiting the chambers of the municipal brothel and demanding of the girls 'from one, one *gros*, from another, three, under the pretext that they had taken in married men or priests or clerks, which the said provost of the said place has no business knowing about if there is no plaintiff' (AD Côte-d'Or, B 11 360/8, November, 1463).

marriage, and giving a bad example to others.' With what crime were they charged? They had gone to the brothel and had stabbed a customer with a dagger – on 25 May 1466, the feast of Pentecost![8]

All the same, even if married men could strike a bargain by giving a few extra coins to the abbess or the provost, they were never safe from arbitrary application of the law. A better and cheaper solution was to frequent the bathhouses. They were not subject to police visits and the girls were younger; furthermore they were safer, since they all had hiding places and more than one exit. Married men went to the bathhouse of La Pêcherie in Lyons and that of St Philibert in Dijon.[9] Jeanne Saignant preferred to have married men as customers because they paid better. In fact the average age of her clients was higher than those of the public brothel, and they were often 'men of estate' and 'honourables'.[10]

Finally, in all cases of procuration and brawling in the brothel or the bathhouse, members of the clergy are listed as present, named and given as residents of the city. Virulent anti-clericalism, old wives' tales and good yarns passed on in farces aside, clergy still made up 20 per cent of the clientele of the bathhouses and the private bordellos of Dijon. We find secular and regular clergy, aged monks and mendicant friars, canons, priests and dignitaries of the church. Some even were members of the night gangs. Still, the constant denunciation of clergy in this sort of business indicates a reprobation among the common people that implies not only condemnation but a certain concern for the dignity of the clergy. I doubt that priests' frequenting of prostitutes was seen as truly scandalous, at least not by the majority of the faithful. Everyone was scandalized, however, by a priest who kept a concubine, one who used the services of the go-betweens, or one who was especially attractive to

[8] AD Côte-d'Or, B 11 360/10. They were accompanied by other men who were not charged.

[9] The infrequent visits of the watch in the baths had few consequences for the clients. According to his own statement, O. Fremyot, the *échevin* named to the watch, had on several occasions gone into the common hall of the bathhouse of St Philibert in Dijon 'without, however, doing any harm or displeasure to anyone, even though he had found there priests and married men and women at extraordinary hours' (ibid., B 11 360/8, fol. 2, 1463). In 1467, the provost's lieutenant was sued for allowing brutalities in the bathhouse of Marion la Liégeoise (ibid., B 11 360/10, November, 1467).

[10] The average age of bathhouse customers (27 cases) is thirty years, three months; less than twenty-seven years in the public brothel. Out of 104 clients (between 1440 and 1540), there are 24 law clerks and men of the law, 21 clergy, 18 artisans, 17 journeymen, 11 merchants and burghers, 5 high officials, ducal or royal, 5 domestics in noble houses, and 3 men of war. Two-thirds of the clientele thus belonged to affluent milieux, which is the reverse of figures for the public brothel. As for private bordellos, the procureur admits that they 'offer an opportunity to notable personages who would not for anything agree to act ill' (ibid., B 11 360/15, 1486).

young girls and married women.[11] There were three reasons for this. This society allowed fornication for all unmarried men, and secular priests and the monks of the older orders were not held in such reverence that they were thought to be gifted with heroic virtues. Husbands and fathers preferred to see the lusty young clerics of the urban churches frequent the public houses or the houses of toleration rather than see them making overtures to their own wives or daughters. They laughed at priests' fornication, perhaps, but did not condemn them for it.

Conversely, the laxity of certain doctors of the Church concerning problems of sexuality had led many clergy to attach less extreme importance to the old interdicts. This relaxing of sexual morality produced an image of the prostitute that in many ways resembled the way city councils viewed her. There were both city fathers and clerics who thought that the common whore exercised a dual function.

Prostitution and Collective Attitudes

The same notables who reveal their obsessive fear of the sharing of women were conscious of other phantasms expressed obliquely at each social revolt: there were images of a golden age suspended at the deepest level of consciousness among the poor; there was a desire to return to the primitive community. Here, too, the opening of the brothel responded not only to a need for collective security, but gave the 'companions' partial satisfaction to their innermost impulses. The Grande Maison welcomed them, in common, and they exchanged the *filles communes* (girls common to all) under the benevolent protection of the authorities. Its prostitutes were exercising their *ministerium*[12] – their ministry – and their *métier*. The word is used constantly, and hardly by chance: prostitution had a function.

---

[11] The situation seems identical in Lyons. For Dijon I shall cite only the most revelatory events: priests show no hesitation in causing scandal in the brothel (ibid., B 11 360/4, items 359, 1449); the chaplain of Monseigneur le Maréchal goes there (ibid., B 11 360/6, p. 783, 1457), priests participate in night rapes (ibid., B 11 360/5, p. 624, 1454; B 11 360/12, 1475, etc.); in June 1502 the *échevins* say that the abbot of St Etienne had caused several 'insolences' at night, armed, and in disguise (AM Dijon, B 168, fol. 51); the procureur of Monsignor de Langres defends the fornicators under his jurisdiction against the mayor's office (ibid., B 157, fol. 161v, 1447), the vicar-general's clerk is living in concubinage in the Chapter house (ibid., b 11 360/11, 1469), Messire le Promoteur keeps whores in his house (ibid., B 11 360/18, 1506), and so forth. Public opinion was most concerned about clergy who had married women visit them in their houses (ibid., B 11 360/8, 1463; B 11 360/13, 1476, etc.).

[12] The term is used by the prostitutes themselves, by city-dwellers, and by the municipal authorities.

Not only did prostitutes have a social responsibility; they had a moral responsibility as well, since they contributed to the defence of collective order. The arraignments of the procureurs and the lawyers' briefs insist on a point that was never questioned: the *filles communes* helped to defend the honour of women 'of estate' and protect them from unruliness. They also participated in the struggle against adultery in two ways. In theory, they had sworn an oath to denounce any man who broke his marriage vows, and their failure to do so was counted as a lesser evil for the community since it avoided more scandalous turns of event. They also had a responsibility towards the city's young and to outsiders among the journeymen, tempering their aggression and keeping them from more serious crimes.[13] Finally, they were more active than anyone else in hunting down 'clandestine' prostitutes and 'depraved' wives, whom they threatened to carry off to the municipal brothel.[14]

Responsible citizens were fully aware of all this. This is why, in all criminal proceedings against imprudent procuresses or brothel managers, public prostitutes or their abbesses, solicited by the judicial authorities, figure among the witnesses for the prosecution. This is why the brothel could be called 'the city's house', why the proprietors of bathhouses were so often prominent figures whose 'honour' remained intact, and why the

[13] I have no intention of playing the devil's advocate or of cultivating paradoxes, but I will note a series of facts: 1. Given the brutality of prevailing mores and morality, the bordello avoided an even greater insecurity. One example: on Saint Catherine's Eve in 1439, three journeymen 'wanted to find a priest's woman to sport with' (and we know what that signified). Since one of them had already been arrested for such activities, they decided to go to the municipal brothel on the rue des Grands Champs instead. After this they played some rather rowdy tricks without grave consequences, but that was the reason for the interrogation (ibid., B 11, 360/2, item 149, 1439). 2. In the course of a trial involving the bathhouse of La Pêcherie in Lyons the defence took good care to explain that the public baths operated on permission by decree of the kings of France and by custom in the 'good cities of the kingdom', *ad evitandum majus malum*, and, by that token, 'one does not seek to corrupt the good girls and honourable women'. Furthermore, in 1535, when prostitution began to be more severely punished by the authorities and condemned by public opinion, the governers of Besançon specify in an ordinance on brothels and bathhouses that 'in order to forestall [worse] for youth and to avoid greater evil, the houses of dissolute whores are tolerated by the Church' (L. Le Pileur, *La prostitution du XIIIe au XVIIe siècle* (Paris, 1908), p. 109).

The strongest of these justifications for prostitution seems to me to be the idea that it limits the number of female adulterers. Indeed, in terms of social morality, female adultery was one of the gravest possible crimes. This is why I suggest that when a prostitute welcomed a married man, it was indeed a lesser evil for the community.

[14] Examples of public prostitutes' raids on their 'secret' colleagues can be found in AD Côte-d'Or, B 11 360/5, p. 633 (1454); B 11 360/8, p. 986, 1460; B 11 360/9 (1465); B 11 360/15 (1489), etc. Of course, the number of these forays was related to the prosperity of prostitution. They were more frequent in bad years, and increased in the sixteenth century when public reprobation of clandestine prostitution ran higher.

managers of their baths were considered honest men and women. Sober notaries went *in prostibulo*, as they said, to write up briefs, and they accepted payments out of the house revenues. City consuls received the oath of the prostitutes, discussed prices and earnings with them, exempted them from local taxation, tolerated their presence at certain public events, accepted an annual gift *coram populo* from the hands of the abbess, encouraged the manager to recruit 'beautiful and titillating partners for lechery', had the girls participate in urban festivities and in sports competitions for young people, made use of them on the occasion of princely entries, and from time to time insisted they take on public responsibilities.[15]

The cities of south-east France were of course agitated now and then by brief flare-ups of purifying morality: all it took was a lethal epidemic, a catastrophic harvest, or the arrival of a flamboyant preacher to sway people's minds for a time and lead them to penitence. When this occurred, cities seemed to discover for the first time the crimes of the procuresses and the depravity of the bath managers, and concubines and unauthorized prostitutes were ordered to leave the city. These were violent but short-lived purges that chroniclers and journal-keeping burghers noted carefully, since such unforeseen reactions were considered miraculous.[16]

It is perhaps true that all we know of 'clandestine' prostitution comes from the criminal trials to suppress it; we also know that when such trials

[15] The husband of Casotte Cristal, Thomassin, was provost of the workers in the mint in Lyons; Jeanne Saignant's brother was a priest; in Tarascon or Beaucaire, notaries often went to do business in the public brothel, and certain of them even received a stipend from it (AD Bouches-du-Rhône, Notaires Tarascon, Muratoris, 395 E 14, fol. 616, 1436). In Nîmes, every year on the feast day of the Charité, the municipal agency for distributing aid, the prostitutes of the municipal house came in procession to offer a *fougasse* to the consuls, for distribution to the poor. The first consul kissed the abbess and gave her in return wine or a sum of money (AM Nîmes, RR 5 inv. ms.). In Alès, the lease agreements for the brothel specified that the manager must keep there 'beautiful and agreeable young whores' or 'beautiful and titillating partners for lechery' (AM Alais, inv. ms. Bardon, vol. 2, pp. 553 and 683). The city of Pernes organized games and contests with prizes on the occasion of St Bartholomew's Day: between an archery shoot and a children's foot race there was a race for municipal prostitutes (AM Pernes, inv. ms. CC 27). Princely entries were an occasion for *tableaux vivants* in which nude prostitutes appeared allegorically as Truth, the Graces, and so forth. It was unimaginable that young girls of patrician families, or even the daughters of artisans, offer their charms to all eyes in this manner. Civic responsibilities were the same everywhere: in Toulouse as in Besançon or Amiens, prostitutes were expected to pitch in to fight fires (just as they combatted the 'fire' of lechery).

[16] Except for calamitous years in which the vagabond poor, rowdies and whores were expelled pell-mell, and in spite of a timid respect of the Lenten prohibitions, it is above all after a particularly influential religious event that we can see a slight trace of improved mores, and not only in sexual behaviour. Thus in Dijon in 1426, the Lenten preaching of the 'very notable preacher and good moral friar J. Foucault of the order of the Cordeliers'

were initiated, the procuration they were aiming at had been going on for some years and was not about to be stopped.[17] To offer two examples: In 1478 inhabitants of the rue de la Pêcherie in Lyons wanted to put an end to the activity of the manager of the bathhouse, Casotte Cristal. The city supported them, but only half-heartedly. Casotte won her case, and her baths continued to flourish. As for Jeanne Saignant, she had done business for fifteen years when the city resolved to charge her with a number of serious infractions. It took four years before they put an end to her activities, and only then because Jeanne had dared to blackmail two young women from the better families of Dijon. In these cases, both the plaintiffs and the charges against them seem quite odd: it is difficult to take seriously plaintiffs who are business rivals of the defendant and jealous of a flourishing trade, and although the preambles to the indictments denounce 'scandals and dishonesties', the accusers and their procureurs hardly bother to discuss them. Doubtless, they had few illusions about the efficacy of this sort of argument, and they take care to interject complaints of a more disturbing nature. When Casotte Cristal was under attack, she (and most of the girls she employed) was accused of speaking Flemish and of being in regular contact with Burgundy. Thus her establishment was a threat to 'city security'. This came at a time when the conquest of Burgundy seemed uncertain and war threatened to break out in the north of the kingdom. The best argument for her condemnation was an accusation of espionage to the profit of the king's enemies, not trafficking in women. The échevins of Dijon used similar arguments against Jeanne Saignant. They did not so much concern the 'orgies' that she organized as the death threats she had made and the love philtres she was accused of pouring into the drinking vessels of some customers with whom she was smitten. Philtres, enchantments, sorcery: this was surely what brought on the fall of the great procuresses. As for the lesser fry, it

---

moved the city fathers to action. Brother Foucault demanded the removal of public prostitutes from the grasp of the young and of their 'enclosure', but he also wanted the city to forbid blasphemies and foul oaths, chase the merchants out of the cemeteries, abolish markets held on feast days, and so forth (AM Dijon, B 151, fol. 64v, 19 March 1426). The first investigation against Jeanne Saignant (ibid., B 11 360/8, p. 986) was launched soon after the general chapter of the order of the Prêcheurs had met in Dijon.

[17] See, for example, the cases of Marguerite, 'hostess' of la Muraille, a procuress for more than ten years (ibid., N 11 360/5, p. 533); of J. de Bouchaud active for eleven years (ibid., B 11 360/4, B 11 360/9), of Marie du Château, for more than thirteen years (ibid., B 166, fol. 81v, and B 167, fol. 16v), of Pierre Bouju (who committed several rapes) and his wife during a dozen years or so (ibid., B 166, fol. 141). One sentence requires close scrutiny: a procuress was banished for five years in 1488, but it was 'because this time she had profited from her niece, and was besides accustomed to do so in spite of remonstrances' (ibid., B 11 337/4). In Tarascon, La Pintresse (the drunkard), accused of the same offence, was brought before the consulate in 1467 (AM Tarn, BB 9, fol. 283), but we find her at liberty in 1472–3 (AD Bouches-du-Rhône, B 2043, fol. 7v).

took their admission of having carried off married women or seduced young girls into prostitution – crimes against the family – to convict them, since prostitution and procuration were not in themselves enough to trigger social repercussions.

How could it have been otherwise? Popular opinion in this domain drew from two cultural currents, one lay, the other religious, both of which were shot through with contradictions.

Jurists had an overwhelming influence in setting the tone of urban society. A number of city councillors were men of the law who had attended the universities, and it was young law clerks who led the 'joyous societies'. (In Burgundy the only two 'kings of youth' known in the fifteenth century were law clerks, and one of them was at the same time 'king of the *Basoche*', the law clerks' association.) It was they who organized cavalcades and wrote or played in farces and *sotties*. They were the heirs of a goliardic tradition that was all the more alive for their own display of its basic values at all urban festivities.[18] A 'king of love' elected in Dijon in 1440 has left us an astonishing drawing of his carnival procession: dressed as a king cock, he parades amid masked figures and blatantly male animals and he is blowing on a rose he holds in his hand. The allegory is plain, and the presiding spirit in the retorts and bawdy word-plays that surround the drawing further reinforces the significance of the grotesque and exaggeratedly male figures. It is the spirit of the *Roman de la Rose*, the exaltation of Nature, and the search for physical pleasure. Many of the notables had been members of one of these law clerks' circles, thus they were all the more inclined accept this moral message. The influence of these waggish clerks was taken up by the 'companions', who saw in these notary's assistants and law court clerks indispensable allies, a source of yarns and tales to be turned to farce, purveyors of witticisms, and informants on scandals and family negotiations gleaned in the privacy of the bathhouse and the corridors of the law courts.[19] As accomplices to the city's gilded youth and essential members of the bands of 'good companions', the law clerks fulfilled the function of latterday mass media in urban society. There is little wonder that these young hotheads displayed a certain 'goliardism', not only in their extremely free attitudes, but in their vocabulary: 'nature moves them',

[18] L. Petit de Julleville, *Les comédiens en France au Moyen Age* (Paris, 1885), p. 141. My commentary on a drawing of the parade of the 'king of love' in Dijon can be found in J. Rossiaud, 'Fraternités de jeunesse et niveaux de culture dans les villes du Sud-Est à la fin du Moyen Age', *Cahiers d'Histoire* 21, nos. 1–2 (1976).

[19] In 1497, clerks and journeymen played 'The History of King Ahasuerus and Queen Esther', in 1509 they mounted the 'Play of Saint Suzanne's Day' in place St Michel (AM Dijon, B 131). These subjects lent themselves to savoury allusions to oldsters who carry off virgins.

'nature impels them', they go to 'take their pleasure', to 'play' and 'sport' in 'charming activies' with young women obedient to 'Venus'. By this logic and according to the teaching of Jean de Meun, such women were indispensable accomplices and objects of scorn.

Even in this domain, however, Church doctrine was not unequivocal. We know that sexual morality had become somewhat more flexible in the thirteenth century under the influence of the canonists and great theologians: St Thomas Aquinas, P. de La Palud, Johannes de Bromyard had helped mitigate ancient taboos, had argued for the use of contraceptive practices in certain circumstances, and had, albeit timidly, rehabilitated pleasure. In short, they had modified the hierarchy of sins of the flesh at the same time as they attenuated the gravity of these sins, all within the framework of marriage, of course. Both the Dominican and the Franciscan friars had read the doctors: could their teachings avoid having consequences? The end result was a somewhat hazy excuse for certain forms of behaviour outside of marriage.[20]

If, at the end of the Middle Ages, fornication was no longer a sin reserved to the bishop but could be absolved by the parish priest, was it not because the lowest orders of the clergy – those closest to the people – were obliged to allow this outlet for poor men who found marriage unattainable?[21] For pastors, the prostitute was thus both an auxiliary and a witness. She was poor and humiliated, but in a certain sense she took part in the struggle against vice. She was also its victim. She stood witness to the misery of the human condition. When some Dijonnais expressed their anti-clericalism by calling trollops 'jacobines' (after the Dominican nickname of 'Jacobins') and saying that only whores followed the processions of the mendicants, the insult cut both ways. Above all, it was the mendicant friars who were concerned with the salvation of their Mary Magdalenes, considered them future penitents, accepted their contributions, and authorized them to follow their crosses and be buried in their churches.[22]

As for the poor journeymen and the artisans of the city's faubourgs, they occasionally made a show of scorn for prostitutes, but it was much tempered by their social proximity. The morrow was also uncertain for them, and they knew all too well that calamities leave in their wake a trail of victims who must live out their miserable fate. This explains the double

[20] See J.-L. Flandrin, *L'Eglise et le contrôle des naissances* (Paris, 1970), pp. 55–68, and J. T. Noonan, *Contraception: A History of its Treatment by the Catholic Theologians and Canonists* (Cambridge, Massachusetts, 1966).

[21] Fornication was never considered licit by the Church, but it is known that there was debate on the question in the councils of Vienne and Basel.

[22] AD Côte-d'Or, B 11 360/9, 1465. A master carpenter is the author of this statement, but the epithet *jacobine* was in current use.

series of names for prostitutes: some are insulting (*ribaudes, savates* – old slippers – and so on). Others show signs of pity, connivance and sympathy: prostitutes are *bonnes dames, fillettes, belles filles, filles joyeuses*. Prostitutes were not rejected by the social community; society was as ready to add victims to their ranks as it was to embrace them when their penitence had been accomplished. The hell of the *filles* was but a purgatory that lasted only as long as their 'youth'.

* * *

In all fifteenth-century France from Burgundy to Provence, prostitution, official or tolerated by all the powers that be, thus appears as the natural result of demographic structures, of a certain social order and a specific moral code. It exercised a mediating function, and the bordello, like the 'joyous abbey', was considered an institution for harmony between age classes and social groups. All the young and many of the less young went to fornicate freely in the brothels. Prostitution, municipally sponsored or not, tempered the aggressive nature of adolescents, though it failed to eliminate it. All the city's youth, from burghers' sons to kitchen boys, had tracked down 'whores' (*chassé la garce*) and had raped a poor girl at least once during their young years without being rejected by the city. Only when they persisted in aggressive behaviour were they considered criminals. When this happened, social status entered into the picture: the future of young men of the burgher class was not compromised in any way; the *médiocres* could pay up or seek a pardon; the less fortunate were banished. Pimps fared better than gamblers, however, and raping a chambermaid was less dangerous than stealing a penny. Male adolescence was a dangerous and turbulent time, a period of resentments and frustrations, but it was also a time for adventure, night-time mascarades, and free sex. Literature does not dwell on the subject, but the poets who wept for their lost youth enjoyed remembering how mad it had been.

Women, on the other hand, had little to be nostalgic about. they were married young and lived hemmed in by prohibitions. Their role in festivities was a minor one, their civic space and time was much inferior to that of young males, and they had no sisterhood organizations or companies of their peers. If now and then girls gathered on winter evenings to sew and gossip in their *escreignes*, it was under the gaze of their mothers and old women who were taking note of their attitudes and supervising their conversation. There were undeniably some widows who carried on the family business with great competence and some well-born girls who could permit themselves a few liberties in their bearing, but these were minorities of age or wealth. For the rest, under the sway of a father, a master, or a husband, youth was a time of uncertainty and insecurity. It is hardly surprising that at an age at which sons led a free life and claimed the right to direct the mores of others, daughters and wives were offered the edifying tale of Griselda.[23] Liberty was not for them: they were to 'fear God, their husband, and dishonour'.[24] The Church consoled them, whereas the word of the clergy – who could be tolerant accomplices, but also could be severe – left husbands or young men indifferent. They accepted it in varying degrees, adapting it or transforming it. On one point (but it was fundamental) the spirit that animated groups of adolescent males paralleled the morality preached by the churchmen: the exaltation of Nature implicitly paralleled the condemnation of what was counter to nature. It seems to me probable that husbands operated within marriage 'according to nature', just as they did, for the most part, with the prostitutes. Furthermore, the free fornication of young men with professionals very probably had little effect from a demographic point of view.

This liberty of male behaviour did not survive the 'crisis of the Renaissance', and there are clear signs of urban communities' progressive rejection of prostitution between 1520 and 1570. I can only sketch this change in the broadest terms here. The wide spread of prostitution revealed the precariousness of the female condition, to which the first decades of the sixteenth century brought a gradual improvement.[25] Women slowly conquered their part of the city's space, acquired an identity of their own, and became less vulnerable – a process that may well be tied to the slow re-evaluation of the couple that has been described by Natalie Zemon Davis and A. Burguière.[28] Religious polemic

---

[23] Cited in E. Sullerot, *Women on Love: Eight Centuries of Feminine Writing*, trans. H. Lane (Garden City, New York, 1979), pp. 73–4.

[24] These words come from Guillemette, the wife of a vintner (AD Côte-d'Or, B 11 360/11, 1471). As this shows, the social image of the wife was well internalized by the persons concerned. Other examples of female submission to the model can be seen in ibid., B11 360/11 (1469).

[25] We find the first notice of the participation of women – 'honest' women – in nocturnal mascarades (accompanied or not by their husbands) in Dijon in 1515 (ibid., B 11 360/23). In 1508 goodwives of the rue St Pierre lodge a formal complaint with the mayor to protest against the invasion of their street by concubines and procuresses (AM Dijon, 1 142). In Orange – but in 1567 – women offer to manufacture gunpowder for the defence of the city (AM Orange, BB 16, fol. 115). It seems that from the 1530s on (the first example is from 1533) certain women played a positive role in the organization of charivaris. But it was particularly in the way a wife was identified that the model which up until then had been reserved for patricians' daughters began to spread to other levels of the population (X, daughter of Y, wife of Z).

[26] A. Burguière, 'De Malthus à Max Weber, mariage tardif et esprit d'entreprise', *Annales ESC* (1972), p. 1134; Davis, *Society and Culture in Early Modern France: Eight Essays* (Stanford, California, 1975), chap. 3, 'City Women and Religious Change in Sixteenth Century France'.

had greatly contributed to a modification in the relationship between husband and wife. The Church was forced to pay greater attention to women, both married and unmarried. Some currents in the Catholic Reformation displayed a new rigorous attitude that echoed the intransigent austerity of the emissaries of Protestantism. Concubinary priests were denounced, along with pimps and procuresses. In a parallel movement, social reactions to prostitution slowly changed. The outbreak of syphilis was in no way responsible for this: city councils never deliberated on the *mal de Naples*; at the most, they periodically ejected prostitutes affected with it. Futhermore, the epidemic outbreaks of syphilis came thirty years or more before the closing of the brothels, and it is known that contemporaries did not consider sexual relations to be the only cause of contagion. If the public houses came to seem more dangerous, it was not because Dame Pox haunted them, but because brawls and murders increased there when garrisoned soldiers or unemployed workingmen fought with the pimps and beat up the scions of burgher families. For the first time, prostitution and criminal behaviour appeared to dovetail.[27] In time, poverty worsened and the price a woman could command in the work market sank dangerously low.[28] Municipal authorities, backed by the Church and the monarchy, reached the point of taking rigorous measures against what had come to be viewed as a social scourge that generated civic disturbance and brought down divine punishment.[29] The bathhouses were shut or closely supervised, priests' concubines and 'clandestine' prostitutes were periodically banished, and so forth. One after another, the municipal brothels closed, and the edict of Amboise, soon after 1560, put an end to the resistance of the most venerable of them. Prostitution did not die with the municipal brothel, but it became more expensive, more dangerous, and more shameful. In spite of a momentary respite, the age of classicism was on the

[27] In Orange, the bordello was ransacked in 1523 by the pages of Monsignor de Bayard (AM Orange, CC 417, fol. 40); in 1525–6 by soldiers (CC 419, fol. 10); in 1536 (CC 428, fol. 50) and in 1537 by the Lansquenets (CC 429, fol. 12v). In Dijon it was sacked in 1495 (AM Dijon, K 83), and again in 1499 (ibid.), 1514, 1525 (K 84), 1527 (I 142), 1536 (K 85), and 1542 (ibid.).

[28] Le Roy Ladurie, *The Peasants of Languedoc*, trans. and intro., J. Day, G. Huppert, consulting ed. (Urbana Illinois, 1971), p. 111.

[29] An ordinance of the general police in Dijon of the mid-sixteenth century describes the situation in these terms: 'because the greater part of the said male children [of poor families] beg and for not knowing a trade put themselves to theft and bad living . . . and several girls of the above-mentioned sort put themselves to whoring, going to the bordello, and living idly . . .' From about 1520 on, pestilence, famine and civic disturbance were commonly attributed to lasciviousness, blasphemy and the corruption of morals (AM Dijon, I 142).

horizon, and it promised branding and the whip to the prostitute, and scorn and opprobrium to her customers.[30]

Should we attribute the sexual liberty that I have just described to the 'scandalous indulgence' of the city councils, to troubled times, to a taste for intense living before death – in short to a 'moral crisis'? Once again: no. Prostitution was just as fully developed in zones of peace as it was in areas touched by war; it flourished better in expanding metropolitan centres than it did in cities in decline; it was just as tolerated in bastions of the Church as it was in regions poor in catechetics. Its prosperity arose out of an order that long pre-dated the calamities of the fourteenth century and that probably was contained in germ in the Gregorian attempt at reform. It was the double-faced and distorting mirror of monarchist absolutism and the Counter-Reformation that made what had been once an essential dimension of medieval society appear as scandalous decadence.

---

[30] Starting in the 1520s in Dijon, priests' concubines and 'clandestine' prostitutes were banished from the city every four or five years, or else obliged to transfer to the brothel. In Lyons, the Tresmonnoye, Pêcherie, Chèvre and Sabliz bathhouses were demolished or abandoned. In Dijon, all the bathhouses were closed before 1560. In Le Puy, the brothel was moved to the faubourg; in Tarascon and Cavaillon it was transformed into a hospital (1527–8); in Alès it disappeared in 1553, and in Dijon it was closed once and for all in 1563.

Part II

Prostitution and the Evolution of Social Attitudes

5

The Relaxation in Social Mores: the Legalization of the Whore

The world of prostitution in France of the mid-thirteenth century had some distinctive characteristics. The *meretrix* had for some time been a familiar figure in the street or in the tavern: the prostitutes of Provins and Troyes were known throughout the West, and in Paris the *fillettes* haunted the student quarter and plied their trade near the cloister of Notre Dame, and near Les Halles and La Grève. The Church accepted alms from prostitutes, university professors reflected on their condition, and the authors of *fabliaux* portrayed them as indispensable accomplices in the human comedy of urban life, crafty but always ready to lend a hand. Studies are lacking on urban prostitution in the middle of the thirteenth century, but similar conditions seem to have prevailed in western cities from that time to the middle of the fifteenth century. The prostitute was a character omnipresent in literature, in proverbs and sayings, in the *fabliaux*, and in regulations governing their profession. We find traces of them in the taverns and the public bathhouses; 'lovely ladies' converged on the fair of Le Lendit; the 'daughters of joy' kept shop in several places in the city of Troyes: a thirteenth-century poem proclaims that 'there are more brothels everywhere than there are other houses'.[1]

In December 1254, however, St Louis ordered the expulsion of all 'women of evil life' from his kingdom and the confiscation of their belongings and even their clothing. In 1256 he repeated the order to expel women 'free with their bodies and other common harlots', but he adds

---

[1] As Marie-Thérèse Lorcin has written, 'the prostitutes had not the slightest reason to hide. ... Everyone knew them. There was the "whores' street" just as there was the "herbalists' square" or the "goldsmiths' embankment"' (M.-T. Lorcin, *Façons de sentir et de penser: les Fabliaux français*, Paris, 1979, pp. 42ff.).

that it would be desirable to drive them out of respectable streets, to keep them as far away as possible from religious establishments, and, when feasible, to force them to lodge outside the city walls.[2] In 1269, on the eve of his departure for his second crusade, he sent the regents a letter reminding them of the decree of 1254 and urging them to enforce it strictly so that this evil could be extirpated root and branch. These ordinances were also aimed at the suppression of gambling, blasphemy, injustice and usury. They were part, as is known, of a penitential effort of vast scope designed to lead a shriven people before the divine judge. The king's wishes in this matter were in keeping with the Church's desire to subordinate the crusade to Jerusalem to the reform of Christendom, and they were not unconnected to declining population growth and to the first upheavals that shook western society. In Italy the first groups of *penitenti* were already forming.[3]

The king's decrees were not only unrealizable; they also ran counter to intellectual speculation and to the evolution of mores. Many a young person – cleric, bourgeois or noble esquire – who no longer believed in the imminent end of the world and who had every intention of living his youth fully scoffed at King Louis' exaggerated piety and blamed it on his entourage of mendicant friars haunted by Joachimite prophecies.

The ordinances of 1254 and 1269 may well have been inapplicable, but they none the less had some effect. Royal officials, princes and bishops took inspiration from them, and their edicts, aided by the increasing pauperization of prostitutes, branded prostitution with a lasting seal of infamy.[4]

In Avignon, which was perhaps precociously touched by eschatological currents of thought (and was also affected by the struggle against heresy), statutes of the mid-thirteenth century stipulate that Jews and prostitutes must not touch foodstuffs, or they would have to purchase them. The statutes of Salon-de-Provence, enacted in 1293 under the influence of the archbishop of Arles, echo this prohibition, and in all probability other cities followed suit. The twelfth-century texts from that region collected by Pierre Pansier, on the other hand, contain not the slightest trace of an effort to expel prostitutes. It was only beginning with the second half of the thirteenth century that the *meretrix* was declared

---

[2] *Ordonnances des rois de France*, vol. 1, p. 65, art. 34 (1254); ibid., p. 77 (1256); p. 104 (1269). See also *Les propos de Saint Louis*, presented by D. O'Connell, with preface by J. Le Goff (Paris, 1974).

[3] The king severely punished malefactors guilty of public sins and scandal. He threatened terrible tortures to crusaders who blasphemed or frequented prostitutes.

[4] See the extremely cruel measures against prostitutes and procuresses at the end of the thirteenth and the beginning of the fourteenth centuries cited in B. Geremek, *Les marginaux parisiens aux XIVe et XVe siècles*, trans. D. Beauvois (Paris, 1976), p. 240.

impure and was marked for social exclusion, along with Jews and lepers. Like the leper, she polluted what she touched, her hand contact alone was held abominable. She was to be viewed as an untouchable.[5]

If this was the case, honest folk had to be able to recognize a prostitute in order to avoid her, which is why prostitutes were obliged to wear an external and visible sign of their profession. Formerly, municipal governments were content to forbid them the coif or the veil worn by respectable women: in Arles in the later years of the twelfth century, any respectable woman who saw a prostitute wearing a veil could, and in theory was obliged to, rip it off. Now prostitutes were obliged to wear an *aiguillette* – a knotted cord falling from the shoulder and of a colour contrasting with that of their dress. This *aiguillette* soon became a mark of infamy, like the Jews' *rouelle*, a round felt patch worn on clothing, or the lepers' revolving rattle. Prohibiting 'disreputable' women or girls from wearing a coif or a headdress seems to have been widespread in the Middle Ages. In Dijon as late as the middle of the fifteenth century, taking off a woman's headdress was equivalent to accusing her of prostitution or debauchery. Many young men who did just this were attempting to demonstrate their claim on the victim.

Conversely, official prostitutes would remove the headdress of a rival who operated 'in secret', or they would so the same to a man to reveal

---

[5] A. R. de Maulde (ed.), *Coutumes et règlements de la république d'Avignon au treizième siècle* (Paris, 1897), art. CXXXVII, p. 200 (the editor dates these statutes at 1243). L. H. Labande, *Avignon au XIIIe siècle: L'éveque Zoen Tencarari et les Avignonais* (Paris, 1908, reprint edn., Marseilles, 1975), pp. 163–4 situates them in 1246. In all probability they are of a later date, perhaps later than the first ordinance of St Louis or the first time the king passed through the Rhône valley. The statutes of Salon concerning prostitution are transcribed, with many other texts, in P. Pansier, *Les courtisanes et la vie galante à Avignon du XIIIe au XVIIIe siècle*, Bibliothèque Calvet, MS 5691. For commentary on them, see N. Coulet, 'Juif intouchable et interdits alimentaires', in *Exclus et systèmes d'exclusion dans la littérature et la civilization médiévales* (Aix-en-Provence, 1978), pp. 207–21. On the concept of 'untouchableness' see M. Kriegel, 'Un trait de psychologie sociale dans les pays méditerranéens du Bas Moyen âge: le juif comme intouchable', *Annales ESC* (1976), pp. 326–30. See also M. Kriegel, *Les juifs à la fin du Moyen âge dans l'Europe méditerranéenne* (Paris, 1979), esp. pp. 39–59.

Noël Coulet thinks that the Church, reacting to laxity in daily religious practice, now wanted to mark the separation between the Christian and the Jewish communities in order to ensure that *nulla sit communio*. I concur entirely with this opinion, taking into account the new tone of spirituality and the efforts of the king. It is certain that the king's decrees were an attempt to put an end to an increasing 'confusion' in urban geography, social estates and clothing. Burghers rented chambers to prostitutes in 'honest' streets, and many prostitutes were married. Some wore rich outfits that made them indistinguishable from the young women of the bourgeoisie – who, in turn, seem to have benefited from a relative freedom of comportment towards the middle of the century, at least in the larger cities. The statutes of Avignon in 1246(?) specify that married prostitutes were to be expelled from the city, were not to live alongside honest folk, and so forth.

him as one of their clients or someone whose conduct they judged to have been immoral or hypocritical. They also pulled off the hats of men they wanted to entice into their chamber. Their conduct to some extent expresses a challenge to male power.[6]

Like Jews and lepers, the prostitutes, at least in central and northern France, fell under a special jurisdiction. The situation in the south is at present little known, but from the Lyons area to the Artois there was in each urban seigneury a *roi des ribauds* (literally, king of the ribalds) who had authority over the women, and a similar function existed within the households of princes and of the king. The monarch of debauchery was often the executioner as well (as was the case in Amiens in the fourteenth century). He reigned over the rabble, he supervised prostitution and disciplined women of doubtful morals, and he exercised control over lepers.[7]

In this fashion, the *meretrices* were segregated from the community, at least in theory. They plied their trade in expressly designated areas, they were marked with a special sign, and they were subject to the hangman and his men-at-arms. Their isolation was far from perfect, however: they were never considered as impure as Jews or lepers, even in the eyes of the severest censors. Lepers were forbidden access to the prostitutes' quarter under pain of terrible sentences. Lepers were dead, in the civil sense; not so prostitutes.

On occasion, social communities and the authorities considerably tempered these segregative measures. The fact remains, however, that even when they were whittled down or interpreted generously, the royal

[6] This conduct seems to have been common among all the public prostitutes in Florence (see R. C. Trexler, 'La prostitution florentine au XVe siècle: patronages et clientèles', *Annales ESC*, 1981, p. 996). It was also the practice in Avignon, where the statutes of 1441–58 forbade the official prostitutes from *homines rapere per raubam . . . Nec capucia ipsorum amovere seu retinere* (see J. Girard and P. Pansier, *La cour temporelle d'Avignon aux XIVe et XVe siècles*, Paris, 1909, p. 162 and added p. 29. A friend of the student from Basel, Félix Platter, had his *barrette* removed by a courtesan in Avignon in this manner, after which he followed the 'beautiful Champenoise from Troye'.

[7] On the *roi des ribauds*, see P. Dufour (pseud. P. Lacroix), *Histoire de la prostitution chez tous les peuples du monde depuis l'antiquité la plus reculée jusqu'à nos jours* (in 8 vols, Brussels, 1861 edn), vol. 4, pp. 27ff. for Cambrai, Saint Amand, Mâcon, Noyon, Douai and Tournai. For Arras, see R. Muchembled, *Popular Culture and Elite Culture, 1400–1750*, trans. L. Cochrane (Baton Rouge, La., 1985), p. 124. For Lyons see *Le livre du vaillant des habitants de Lyon en 1388*, intro. C. Perrat, published by E. Philipon (Lyons, 1927), p. 172; G. Guigue, *Les registres consulaires de la ville de Lyon* (Lyons, 1926), vol. 2, p. 111 (1414). For Lyons and the king of the ribalds of the Hôtel royal, see M. Rey, *Les finances royales sous Charles VI; les causes du déficit 1388–1413* (Paris, 1965), pp. 22–8; and in particular A. Terroine, 'Le roi des ribauds de l'Hôtel du roi et les prostituées parisiennes', *Revue d'Histoire de droit français et étranger*, 1978, pp. 253–68. The position was attached to the service of the royal larder, the hunt, the footmen and the musicians. This 'king' kept order under the authority of the *maître de l'hôtel*.

ordinances aiming at containing this 'gangrene' and rejecting the women infected by it, along with the urban statutes they inspired, constituted a permanent menace to the prostitutes. But whereas nearly all lepers disappeared, victims of the widespread turmoil of the beginning of the fourteenth century, and the Jews were effectively kept at a distance and lived in fear of the persecution before they were expelled from France, prostitutes saw the relaxation and eventually the disappearance of the constraints to which they had been subjected. We need to review briefly the stages of these important changes.

It was between 1350 and 1450 that the cities institutionalized prostitution, setting up a *prostibulum publicum* when the city did not already have one. The Castelletto in Venice opened its doors in 1360 (not long after the municipal brothel in Lucca) in a group of houses in the parish of San Matteo di Rialto belonging to the patrician Venier and Morosini families. In 1421 the Ca Rampani was added to the complex. Florence took a similar decision in 1403; Siena in 1421.[8]

The chronology seems to have been somewhat different in Provence. In Tarascon the 'house' mentioned in 1374 was enlarged in the 1390s and improved in 1449. In Sisteron the construction planned in 1394 was completed in 1424. The towns of Pernes and Cavaillon followed suit in 1430 and 1437. In Auvergne, in Saint Flour, the consuls rented a house for the city's *filles* in 1402, then bought it in 1443 and rebuilt it extensively. The 'great house' was functioning in Dijon in 1385, and a second one was opened at the beginning of the fifteenth century, to be transformed into a vast and comfortable dwelling in 1447. A number of other examples could be cited. To summarize: in this general movement toward municipal control of prostitution there were two periods of rapid acceleration. The first was in the decades bracketing 1400, the second in the 1440s: the brothel in Villefranche-sur-Saône opened in 1439 and was enlarged in

[8] For Venice see E. Pavan, 'Police des moeurs, société et politique à Venise à la fin du Moyen âge', *Revue Historique*, vol. 262, no. 536 (1980), pp. 241–88. For Florence and the cities of Tuscany, see Trexler, 'La prostitution florentine', pp. 983ff. For the enlargement of the prostitutes' quarter in Amiens, see A.-A. Dubois, *Justice et bourreaux à Amiens dans les XIVe et XVe siècles* (Amiens, 1860); for Dijon, see J. Rossiaud, 'Prostitution, sexualité, société dans les villes françaises au XVe siècle', *Communications* 35, 'Sexualités occidentales' (Paris, 1982); for Pernes, see AM Pernes BB 27 fol. 1; for the house in Saint Flour, rented in 1402 and acquired by the city and repaired at city expense in 1443, see A. Rigaudière, *Saint-Flour. Ville d'Auvergne au bas Moyen âge*, 2 vols (Paris, 1982). For Sisteron, see Lacroix/Dufour, *Histoire de la prostitution*, vol. 4, p. 147; for Montpellier, where prostitutes were solidly established in the city before 1465, see ibid., vol. 4, pp. 175ff. For Toulouse, see J. Chalande, 'La maison publique aux XVe et XVIe siècles à Toulouse', *La France médicale*, 1912. For Tarascon, see M. Hébert, *Tarascon au XIVe siècle: Histoire d'une communauté urbaine provençal* (La Calande, 1979), pp. 54 and 111 (new developments at the end of the fourteenth century); for enlargements of the brothel in 1449, see AM Tarascon BB 8, fol. 16.

1454; the one in Bourg-en-Bresse opened in 1439, the one in Tours in 1448, and the one in Amiens during the same period.[9]

This *prostibulum* (or the block of streets that occasionally took its place) was set up at one of the main crossroads in the town: in Venice it was at the Rialto, in Florence, between the Mercato Vecchio and the Baptistry of San Giovanni; in Notre Dame du Puy, at the place de la Plastrerie (a major marketplace). In Toulouse, the great 'abbey' was at first installed outside the walls and was moved inside the city in 1425, as was the Montpellier brothel several years later.

Were the city authorities attempting to bring morality to urban life by herding these women into a ghetto? It does not seem so: the city brothels and the 'good streets' were by no means difficult to find and public prostitutes 'earned their fortune' in the squares, the streets, the taverns, or near churches. In Venice in 1358, although prostitutes were ordered to remain within the confines of the Rialto district and were forbidden to enter the taverns, they solicited in taverns and later practised their trade there. Soon there were *hostariae* (the term first appears around 1420) in all districts of the city. In 1448 prostitutes boldly promenaded around piazza San Marco, and if the city government – the Signoria – reissued the regulation to stay within the compound area it was only intermittently and without any real intention of enforcing it. In Florence, the attempt to contain prostitutes within the Chiasso de' Buoi was an exceptional event, and, according to the earliest archives of the city's Board of Morals, the *Onestà*, a great many prostitutes were working outside the principal bordellos in 1441 and the authorities made little effort to pursue them.

The same was true in all French cities. As we have seen for Dijon, outside the official public brothels, prostitution in the public bathhouses, the inns and the taverns was common knowledge and was tolerated. Minor 'bedroom' prostitution in private bordellos was tolerated by the neighbourhoods, which played an essential role in this domain. Let me offer four examples of this.

> 1 In 1387 in Paris (where areas reserved for public prostitution were scattered throughout the city), the burghers in the neighbourhood protested when the curé of St Merri persuaded the Provost to move to expel the harlots from the rue Baille-Hoe, arguing that their business would suffer. The burghers appealed to the *Parlement*, won their case, and the ladies were reinstated.
> 2 In Montélimar in 1423 – a calamitous year – the consuls of the

[9] For Tours, see B. Chevalier, *Les bonnes villes de France du XIVe au XVIe siècle* (Paris, c 1982), p. 223. For Villefranche-sur-Saône, A. Besançon and E. Longin (eds), *Registres consulaires de Villefranche* (Villefranche, 1905), vol. 1, pp. 110v and 309. For Bourg-en-Bresse see Rossiaud, 'Prostitution'.

city expelled from their lodgings the 'women of evil life' who lived and practised their trade outside the the official brothel. The women took refuge in the principal inns of the city, where, until 1438, the innkeepers were happy to lodge them. At that date the plague was threatening the city, and their expulsion from the inns was suggested. The proprietors agreed, but on the condition that the bathhouses, the taverns, and other such places be included in the decree. When the epidemic had passed, the innkeepers calmly went back to their former practice, and in 1447 they obtained from the dauphin – the future Louis XI – the right to receive as they saw fit *claustrières* and *cantonnières* (prostitutes who operated in the private bordellos and streetwalkers).

3 In Alès in 1454 the *viguier* decreed by proclamation, 'Let no woman dare to keep a brothel, public or private, except in the accustomed places, and let no inhabitant dare to give lodging to a concubine, married or unmarried.' There was an immediate hue and cry from the citizenry, and the proclamation was rescinded.

4 In Avignon, as a last example, the officers of the temporal court had the right to enter the houses of the townspeople under the pretext of recognizance of fornication, adultery or concubinage. When 'abuses' arose from this practice, the matter was brought to the attention of Pope Paul II, who decreed, in a bull dated 13 December 1465, that searches of the sort could be carried out only on presentation of a formal and written request signed by friends, relatives or neighbours of the suspected delinquents.[10]

Thus there was official recognition in Alès and in Avignon that the neighbourhood held authority where mores were concerned, and all serious control over such tolerated or unofficial bordellos was, of necessity, abandoned. This was why in the middle of the century – in Metz, Strasbourg, Paris, Dijon, Lyons, Cavaillon or Arles, just as in Venice or in Florence – prostitutes were installed even in 'respectable' or 'honourable' streets and in houses or rooms rented by burghers. Thus prominent men lived well on the profits from the public bathhouses. Preachers of the 1500s did not fail to criticize these customs and these ill-gotten gains.

This was the case in Dijon. When in 1423 the city prohibited

[10] See the map of organized prostitution in J. Favier, *Paris au XVe siècle, 1380–1500, Nouvelle histoire de Paris* (Paris, 1974), p. 81. All the *quartiers* of Paris are represented. The affair of the rue Baille-Hoe is reported in Lacroix/Dufour, *Histoire de la prostitution* and in Geremek, *Les marginaux*, p. 263. For Alès, see AD Gard, Bardon, MS *Alès*, vol. 1, p. 119. For Montélimar, see Pansier, *Les courtisanes*, p. 69, citing from Coston, *Histoire de Montélimar*, vol. 1, p. 510. For Avignon, see Pansier, *Les courtisanes*, added p. 19 and p. 354, citing from AM Avignon, box 11, item 20.

municipally-authorized prostitutes from using violence against the clandestine prostitutes or trying to drag their unofficial rivals to the city brothel, setting a fine of 100 *sous* for this act, one cannot really speak of a municipally-sponsored ghetto.

Exceptions had always existed, as shown by *Les lettres royales, accordées par Charles V et Charles VI aux Lombards*. Lombards could not be accused of rape of women of 'evil life' found in their dwellings, nor could they be troubled by charges of simple fornication. The Lombards established in Languedoc thus solicited authorization to keep prostitutes or concubines reserved to the pleasure of the master and his friends or his clients (1366).

In Avignon, article 78 of the statutes of 1441 prohibited gaming in the taverns, brothels, houses of 'disreputable' women or inns. Exception was made for houses 'in which knights and gentlemen agree to stay and to game'. This article was simply borrowed from the 1246 statutes. In the fifteenth century as in the thirteenth, the meeting places frequented by patricians (and which served purposes other than dicing) were not touched by the repressive measures.[11]

In like fashion, time constraints nearly disappeared. In the fourteenth century, places of prostitution had to close at nightfall in Paris, Beaucaire and Venice. As early as the 1390s, however, the hours of the Castelletto in Venice were prolonged to the third bell, nones, or 9.30 p.m. In Dijon and Tarascon in the mid-fifteenth century, the women and their clients could make use of the 'great house' in the evening, and many a workingman spent the night there. The *prostibulum* effectively fulfilled its function: in

---

[11] For Dijon, see AD Côte-d'Or, B 11, pp. 336–7. For the Lombards, see Lacroix/ Dufour, *Histoire de la prostitution*, vol. 4, p. 153, and for Avignon, Bibliothèque Calvet, MS 3180, fols 22–3. As for the situation in the mid-fifteenth century, in Cavaillon before 1477 'public women' were scattered throughout the city. In Dijon, dozens of private bordellos existed between 1460 and 1480. In Strasbourg, there were nearly sixty establishments of prostitution (fifty-seven, to be exact). In Lyons almost every neighbourhood soon had public baths and 'rooms for women'. In Metz, the courtesans were settled in 'respectable' streets (see *La Chronique de Philippe de Vigneulles*, 4 vols, ed. C. Bruneau, Metz, 1927–33, vol. 3, p. 299). In Paris there was the widespread prostitution on which the Bourgeois commented as early as 1436–38.

This proliferation lent legitimacy to the sermons of the preachers of the end of the century: 'The city today, like Sodom and Gomorrah, builds a brothel on every square; at the head of every street flies the banner of prostitution' (M. Menot, *Sermones quadragesimales*, Paris 1525, fol. 23). According to Olivier Maillard, 'in every neighbourhood prostitution is spreading out' (*serm. quadr.* no. 21, fol. 127v). 'In the time of St Louis the houses were built outside the city; today it is full of them' (ibid., fol. 67); 'there are here prostitutes who keep brothels and who keep them their life long' (*Sermones de adventu quadragesimales dominicales*, Lyons, 1503, sermon 38, fol. 75v; 'you burghers who rent out your houses *ad tenendum lupanar*' (O. Maillard, *serm. quadr.*, fol. 67), and so forth. See below, chapter 8, note 1, for fuller discussion of these references.

the cities of the Rhône valley the municipal bawdy house was open at all hours.[12]

Above all, it was open on the Lord's day. Dijon was in no way exceptional in this, as this was true in Alès, and seems to have been true everywhere before the 1480s, since Michel Menot and Olivier Maillard refer in their sermons to the workingmen's custom of going in a group to the brothel on Sundays. The only restriction and the only truly sacred moment was during solemn high mass, when both gaming and Nature's games were to cease.[13]

Even more significant is the oblivion into which the traditional periods of abstinence had fallen – Ember days, the vigils of major feast days and Lent. In the fourteenth century, municipalities leased the 'great house' at the beginning of Lent, which shows that the old prohibition was probably respected. When the old 'farmer' left, the new one had time to get established and to recruit girls before reopening after the Easter holidays. In Arles, Dijon, Uzès and Albi, prostitutes took no time off except for Holy Week, when the city's consuls granted them and the manager an indemnity for loss of earnings. In Venice, the Castelletto was idle just as seldom, closing only for Christmas Eve, Christmas Day, Holy Week and the feasts of the Resurrection, and the four feasts of the Virgin and their respective vigils. On Ascension Day and the feast of St Mark – times of rejoicing and large crowds – the city council took care to have the house in operation.[14]

---

[12] For Paris, see Geremek, *Les marginaux*, p. 242: the streets designated for the prostitutes served as their gathering place during the day. In the ordinances and the regulations of the fourteenth century they were obliged (and the obligation may already have been theoretical) to leave the houses at twilight. For Beaucaire, see the ordinance of 1373, which states 'Let no prostitute go about the city once curfew has sounded' (A. Eyssette, *Histoire administrative de Beaucaire depuis le XIIIe siècle* (Beaucaire, 1884–8), vol. 2, p. 234 and added p. 28. For Venice, see Pavan, 'Police des moeurs'. These prohibitions were probably the ones least respected. In Avignon they seem not to have been effective in the thirteenth century. The statutes of 1246 state: 'we decree that no one after the sounding of curfew may make noise or confusion in the taverns, the brothels, prostitutes' houses, or the inns'. This article prohibits noise and disturbances, but not fornication. For Dijon, see above. In Tarascon, repairs were made to the bordello 'in order for women and others to be able to remain there both day and night' (AM Tarascon BB 8 fol. 16, 1449).

[13] In Avignon, the proclamations of the civil court specified that the prostitutes must not open shop *diebus sabativis*. This was in 1441–58 but, as I have pointed out, these articles simply reiterate others from the thirteenth century. In Alès at the beginning of the sixteenth century the 'abbot' of the brothel was forbidden to permit any sort of game of chance during divine service, under pain of a month in prison on bread and water (AC Gard, Bardon, *Alès*, vol. 1, p. 173). Olivier Maillard denounces the workingmen's habit of leading their companions to the bordello on Sundays (*Sermones de adventu*, no. 4, fol. 36).

[14] In Uzès in the fourteenth century the prostitutes left the city at Easter-time. The same was true in Albi (Lacroix/Dufour, *Histoire de la prostitution*, vol. 4).

Three remarks need to be made, obvious as they are:

1 Regulation by the municipality reflects common practice: not only did it determine the rhythm of activities in the authorized brothel, but also in the public bathhouses and in the private brothels that followed the practices of the municipal *prostibulum*.
2 Such regulation clearly defined the few times sexual activities were severely prohibited: the period of the Passion of Our Lord and the hours of solemn high mass. When we think of the hundreds of days of abstinence listed in the penitentials of the early Middle Ages (and analysed recently by Jean-Louis Flandrin), we realize that their omission constitutes one of the most striking illustrations of the secularization of the period.[15]
3 Public prostitutes were, in fact, the category of the city's labour force with the least restrictions on its working week.

Prostitutes may have worked more hours, but they did not, for all that, earn any greater reputation for impurity. The prohibition on touching foodstuffs still figured in the statutes of Avignon in 1441 but for the most part these statutes reiterate the earlier ones of the thirteenth century and at this point they seem out of touch with reality. For some time in nearby Languedoc cities (In Nîmes, in particular) the girls from the municipal brothel kneaded with their own hands the *fougasse* cakes that they offered to the consuls for distribution to the poor. The kiss that the First Consul accorded the 'abbess' during this ceremony *coram populo* clearly shows that the city's prostitutes were no longer considered untouchable.[16]

Consequently, the use of the *aiguillette* as a mark of society's reprobation was gradually transformed or abandoned. Had it ever been imposed universally? We know that in many cases Jews were able, individually or collectively, to avoid wearing the *rouelle*. No distinctive mark seems to have been inflicted on Florentine or Venetian prostitutes in the fifteenth century, and in France such marks became highly discreet, had changed meaning, or had fallen into disuse. As early as 1389, King Charles VI had accorded the women of the 'great abbey' in Toulouse the right to replace their distinctive *chaperon*, a hood decorated with plaited cords, with a thin contrasting edging on one sleeve. In Avignon in 1413 a

[15] See J.-L. Flandrin, *Un temps pour embrasser: aux origines de la morale sexuelle occidentale (VIe–XIe siècle)* (Paris, 1983).
[16] Statutes of Avignon 1441, in *Annales d'Avignon et du Comtat Vénaissin*, 1914–16, p. 178 (article 116). For the customary gift made to the 'abbess' in Nîmes in 1412, see AM Nîmes, inventory RR 5 (1480): *quando portaverunt panem caritatis per ipsas factum juxta morem*. See also Du Cange, *Glossarium*, s.v. 'osculum'; L. Ménard, *Histoire des antiquités de la ville de Nismes et de ses environs. Nouvelle édition* (Nîmes, 1826), bk 8, vol. 97, 'don à l'abbatissa' in 1399.

sumptuary ordinance of the Papal Legate reserved to the *viguier* and the judges the right to grant dispensations (which the constabulary was already selling to the prostitutes).[17]

At this point, city governments limited themselves to promulgating or reinforcing older sumptuary regulations that prohibited the wearing of rare furs or precious ornaments by prostitutes. These proscriptions must be seen in context, however: they were so sweeping that their impact was slight, and the frequency with which they were repeated reveals their ineffectiveness. In Amiens, Paris, Dijon, Lyons or Metz, *ribaudes* could dress as they pleased; in the 'good streets' of Avignon they could even wear elaborate girdles, wimples, furs and silks.

Prostitutes were no longer subjected to an ignominious jurisdiction. The office of the *roi des ribauds* was abolished in Lille as early as 1364; it disappeared in Lyons soon after 1400; in 1441 in Arras it was called 'shameful and of great infamy'; in 1449 the last king of the ribalds of the royal household, who had occupied the post for twenty years, was not replaced. The nearly total disappearance of these 'kings' – a function that had given rise to striking contradictions – had one aspect of even greater importance: it signified that from that moment on, public prostitutes fell under the jurisdiction of the ordinary courts (as had long been the case in the south of France), and thus their cases were handled by the same police officers and the same judges as for the rest of the citizenry. Discipline was no longer enforced among them by a hangman 'king' and his henchmen, but by a woman who may or may not have been of their trade – an 'abbess', a 'queen' or a 'rectoress' – whereas the more general supervision of morals passed either to the criminal courts or, more often, to the confraternal institutions or the territorial abbeys.[18]

The disappearance of the king of the ribalds some time before the middle of the fifteenth century confirmed a reality: the end of social exclusion. It seems that in many places the rape of a woman of 'evil life'

[17] For Toulouse, see Chalande, *La maison publique*, p. 65; Lacroix/Dufour *Histoire de la prostitution*, vol. 4, p. 175. For Avignon, see Pansier, *Les courtisanes*, p. 55.

[18] For the disappearance of the king of the ribalds, see above, note 7. The authors who have written about this position have not fully grasped the importance of its disappearance. I refer in particular to Robert Muchembled (*Popular Culture*, p. 124), who interprets the refusal of one city-dweller to whom the position was offered as a condemnation of prostitution. In reality, just the opposite was true, as the situation of prostitution in Arras up to 1493 clearly shows. The last mention of the king of the ribalds in Lyons dates from 1414. When the position persists in scattered localities between 1400 and 1450, the responsibilities that accompanied it seem to have been less extensive than before. 'Abbesses' existed in brothels in the south of France as early as the end of the fourteenth century. In Geneva, public prostitutes had a 'queen' from 1413 on. In 1459, the bishop J. Louis recalled that they had to choose a queen, 'the better to regulate their life' (see H. Naef, *Les origines de la Réforme à Genève*, Geneva, 1936, pp. 219ff.).

was treated like the rape of any woman of the lower echelons of society and was subject to the same sentences.[19]

Generally speaking, police regulations and initiatives on the part of princely or municipal authorities to restrict the freedom of action of prostitutes, which had been frequent from 1400 to 1440, became less frequent after that date and often disappeared entirely. Symbols of exclusion were forgotten, and signs of integration now carried the day. Although repressive measures were numerous at the end of the fourteenth century, they illustrate both the development of the phenomenon and the ineffectiveness and incoherence of the struggle to combat it. Examples can easily be found in monographs on the various cities. All such laws disappeared between 1434 and 1440 and from 1470 to 1480. They reappeared everywhere during the only difficult years which that generation experienced, between 1458 and 1460, when repression was not aimed at prostitution alone.[20]

The young Charles VI had already shown an interest in the fate of prostitutes in Toulouse, and their requests concerning vestimentary regulations had been fully debated in the council before they were in part granted. It is true that the royal Hôtel, like all princely households, kept a

[19] The opinion that from a juridical point of view the rape of a prostitute was not a crime derives from Joost de Damhouder (*Practica rerum criminalium*, Lyons 1558; and *La Practicque et enchiridion des causes criminelles*, Brussels, 1571). The latter work states, 'but to rape or force easy women who have exposed themselves in public places or in the bordello there is no punishment, for they must be abandoned to everyone.' This author was writing in a period of moral reaction, however, and Bronislaw Geremek (*Les marginaux*, p. 267, n. 79) cites him as cited in J. Foyer, *Exposé du droit pénal normand au XIIIe siècle* (Paris, 1931), p. 36. It is possible that at that time a rape of an 'easy' woman was not severely punished. In the fourteenth and the fifteenth centuries, it was not public prostitutes who were exposed to acts of violence of this sort, but the 'secret' prostitutes and women who failed to respect conjugal discipline. Those who advocated rigour – the preachers in particular – occasionally recommended such actions as a punishment.

Everything shows, to the contrary, that the official prostitutes had effective defences: the privileges accorded in 1389 by the seigneur de Chandieu to the burghers of Eyrieu, near Valence, stipulate that anyone who raped a dissolute woman or a woman of the brothel would pay a fine of 100 *sous*. These privileges were confirmed by Charles VI (*Ordonnances des rois de France*, vol. 7, p. 316). In Avignon it was against the law to drag off a public prostitute by force or insult her (see Girard and Pansier, *La cour temporelle*, p. 171). In Tarascon the fines inflicted for insults or for blows were the same whether the victim (or the guilty party) was a prostitute or the wife of a labourer or an artisan (see AD Bouches du Rhône B 2043, fols 2, 7, 7v, and others (1471–3)). In Dijon there was no noticeable difference between the sentences handed down for the rape of a 'public woman,' an 'easy' woman, or a woman 'of little estate'. In Metz the murder in 1469 of a 'common prostitute' was punished by death, even though the guilty party was a goldsmith and a citizen of the city (see *Chronique de Philippe de Vigneulles*, vol. 2, p. 400).

[20] In Frankfurt, Strasbourg and Mayence the Inquisition pursued beghard friars and beguine nuns as well (see J. C. Schmitt, *La mort d'une hérésie: L'Eglise et les clercs face aux béguines et aux béghards du Rhin supérieur du XIVe au XVe siècle*, Paris and New York,

group of common prostitutes, but they lived in the shadows in the basement rooms, along with odd-job men and men-at-arms. The *roi des ribauds* ruled over them and recruited newcomers as needed. These court whores served the royal guests, but they had no access to the great halls and took no part in the ceremonial life of the court. It was in all probability during the reign of Charles VII that the 'girls who followed the court' emerged out of the shadows, and their rectoress was granted the honour, in May of each year, of offering the King of France the 'bouquet of renewal', surrounded by her staff of girls and in the presence of the assembled court. By the beginning of the sixteenth century this custom was considered to be age-old. The monarchy was no longer ashamed of its 'ladies of joy'.[21]

The change in mores within the court of France did not escape the attention of critics: the austere Bourgeois of Paris noted that the King kept three or four 'common law' concubines and, with unprecedented scandal, had appeared in public with the first among them, Agnès Sorel. Philippe le Bon, Duke of Burgundy, acted in like manner and, somewhat

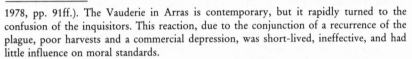

1978, pp. 91ff.). The Vauderie in Arras is contemporary, but it rapidly turned to the confusion of the inquisitors. This reaction, due to the conjunction of a recurrence of the plague, poor harvests and a commercial depression, was short-lived, ineffective, and had little influence on moral standards.

All I can do here is to indicate a tendency, a movement of the periphery toward the centre, for it is a vain exercise to pose the problem in terms of integration or marginality. As Roger Chartier and Jean-Claude Schmitt have rightly remarked in their dictionary, *La Nouvelle Histoire* (Paris and Retz, 1978), s.v. 'marginaux', it is the dominant morality that defines marginality. Marginality according to the statutes and marginality of condition do not necessarily coincide. Only a minority in society carries within itself all the values of integration: one can head a household, have a fixed residence, and still be 'of low estate'. Around 1400, retail butchers were marginal in relation to the *grande bourgeoisie* of Paris, but the weavers by no means scorned them. Should they have done so, the butchers would not have cared less.

[21] The texts that speak of this ceremony have been collected in Du Cange, *Glossarium*, s.v. 'meretricalis vestis' from royal letters of 1535, 1538 and 1539, with mention of the 'gift from the lady of the daughters of joy following the court of the king'. In 1535, Olive Sainte received from Francis I a gift of 90 *livres* 'to help her and the above-mentioned women to live and meet the expenses that it is incumbent on them to make to follow the court as usual'. From this we can deduce that a distinction was made between the 'ordinary' ladies of easy virtue, who belonged to the household of the king's Hôtel, and the 'extraordinary' ones who were recruited on the occasion of festivities. The renewal day bouquet or the bouquet offered on St Valentine's Day are attested by several ordinances between 1539 and 1546. It was in exchange for this bouquet that the king offered money to the *filles*.

It is evident that this group of ordinary prostitutes existed well before the beginning of the sixteenth century. When he experienced some health problems, Charles VIII gave the order to send all the 'ladies of joy' away from the court (see Y. Labande-Mailfert, *Charles VIII et son milieu: 1470–1498: La jeunesse au pouvoir*, Paris, 1975, p. 471). The responsibilities of the king of the ribalds before 1449 is one proof of this. I think that the Valentine's Day ceremony and the May ceremony must have appeared in the middle of the fifteenth century, later, the temperance of Duke Charles seemed to the chroniclers, accustomed to princely liberties, extraordinary and disquieting.[22]

The Bourgeois certainly did not approve of the new moral code. He thought that the King's conduct set an unfortunate example, and he quite lucidly established the connection between the expansion of prostitution in Paris and changes in the mores of the court. 'The court is a sign of the morals of the people', as it was commonly said. It is tempting to conclude that the monarch had no intention of creating a scandal, and that his attitude was not out of step with social practice.[23]

The king was not the only one to receive a gift from a prostitute 'queen'. Let us look briefly at the ceremony, already mentioned, that took place in Nîmes, and probably in many other cities of Provence and Languedoc. On Ascension Day the citizenry gathered in the principal square to honour the *Charité majeur*, the city agency for the distribution of alms. The prostitutes participated in the ceremony as a group, and they did not stand with the various paupers' groups. They were not beneficiaries of public charity; they practised charity, as did the other urban trade associations. Thus they participated in a ritual of integration. We can find the logical complement of this ceremony in Pernes (and the same event is attested in Arles at the beginning of the sixteenth century), where the 'public women' took part in the games on the feast day of the city's patron saint, running races after the young people and before the children. Their little community had full membership in the larger urban family.[24]

---

for it is then (see below) that one can observe the most marked changes in the moral climate of the court. Furthermore, starting with the 1470s, the princes ritually offered a sum of money to the prostitutes who followed their court or were close to it. Thus King René gave money three times a year to the prostitutes of Marseilles, Aix and Tarascon – at Epiphany, at the beginning of Lent, and in May. They most probably offered him flowers (see G. Arnaud d'Agnel, *Les comptes du roi René*, 3 vols, Paris, 1908–10, vol. 3, pp. 45, 48, 50, 197, 216, and so forth).

[22] 'He kept three or four common prostitutes as his mistresses. He always protected loose women, of whom through his laxity Paris had far too many, and got himself a very bad reputation with everyone because it was almost impossible for the law to correct the prostitutes in Paris, since he always protected them and their bawds' (*Journal d'un bourgeois de Paris, 1405–1449*, ed. A. Tuetey, Paris, 1881, pp. 382–3, cited from *A Parisian Journal 1405–1449*, trans. J. Shirley, Oxford, 1968, p. 363). The good canon also imputes the laxity of Parisian authorities to Ambroise de Loré, baron de Juilly and Provost of the city between 1436 and 1445. He goes rather far when he attributes to 'the people' his own hostility, which is political in origin and came largely from his 'Burgundian' past. When the Duke of Burgundy awaited an English embassy at Valenciennes, he had the public baths of the city prepared 'with everything required for the calling of Venus' (J. Huizinga, *The Waning of the Middle Ages*, Anchor Books, Garden City, New York, 1954, p. 109).

[23] Cited in Lacroix/Dufour, *Histoire de la prostitution*, vol. 5, p. 179.

[24] In Pernes the games celebrated twice a year (24 January and St Bartholomew's Day) included a men's foot race, wrestling matches, and competitions in jumping, crossbow

In the fifteenth-century city, the family was a common image in public monuments and in places of worship, and neighbourhood festivities were organized much like family festive gatherings. Civic imagination relied heavily on images of the family, since the family was where shared experience and solidarity were the strongest; it was the visible sign of roots and of success; it was at one and the same time an unshakeable model and a constantly threatened reality. What do we find, however? When in the 1480s Olivier Maillard (and many others with him) began to fight for the reform of morals, they denounced the habit of having the city prostitutes participate in weddings and banquets in 'good society'. Were they exaggerating the facts? Not in the least. The custom seems to have been widespread. We learn from Philippe de Vigneulles of a decree in Metz in 1493 'that the said women and girls be found in no festivities and at no dances, weddings or festivities held near the city, and that no one lead them dancing, on [pain of a fine of] the sum of ten *sous*'. The chronicler, a notable who was quick to defer to the governing families of the city, would not have missed the opportunity to castigate the custom if the wine merchants of the faubourgs had been involved, but here it was city festivities and burghers' customs that were targeted. Furthermore, the municipal government of Arras took a similar decision in the same year, prohibiting the 'daughters of joy' from going 'to houses, public places, congregations and assemblies at feasts and solemnities'.[25]

During these family gatherings prostitutes ate, drank, danced and talked with the men, their mothers and their wives just like the assembled kin. They were not simply invited along to exercise their profession. Whatever resulted from the merrymaking took place within the family and festive space.

Marie-Thérèse Lorcin has drawn conclusions based on an analysis of 150 *fabliaux* composed in the north of France during the thirteenth century that merit summarizing briefly.[26] Prostitutes resident in the city could be on good terms with 'respectable' people, and they joined in all the rites of living in society. Their children lacked neither godfathers nor godmothers. The clients of the brothels were normal men who had not yet settled down in marriage. The prostitute could be 'reformed' only by

---

shooting and archery, after which there was a foot race for the 'public women', followed by one for children (AM Pernes, inv. ms. CC 27 (1458). For Arles, see AM Arles CC 318, fols 91, 11v; CC 564, and so forth (1557). In Boulogne on St Martin's Day the city fathers sent four barrels of wine to the public prostitutes (Lacroix/Dufour, *Histoire de la prostitution*).

[25] Olivier Maillard: *[quod] meretrices non vocarent ad bonas societates et ad nuptias et banquetas (serm. quadr.*, sermon 24, fol. 130. For Metz, see *Chronique de Philippe de Vigneulles*, vol. 3, p. 117. for Arras, see Muchembled, *Popular Culture*, p. 123.

[26] M.-T. Lorcin, 'La prostituée des fabliaux est-elle intégrée ou exclue?', *Sénéfiance*, 1978, pp. 105–17.

the miraculous intervention of Our Lady, who sent she repentant harlot either to heaven or to the convent. She did not permit her to set up a home, however: 'Between the brothel and paradise, there was no middle ground. . . . The prostitute of the *fabliaux* was in the city but outside the family, from which she was forever excluded. The poets tended, consciously or unconsciously, to conjure away their fear of being duped by this woman who, even more than the legitimate spouse, wielded the weapon invincible in these tales: ruse.'

In the fifteenth century, marriage represented the end of a life of prostitution for public prostitutes, but it was also an ordinary civil status for many 'common prostitutes.' All the court cases, laws, ordinances (Paris 1427, Avignon 1441, Geneva 1459, Lyons 1478, Dijon, and so forth), speak of both unmarried and married prostitutes. The latter obviously provoked the 'indignation' of the municipal authorities – and above all of the religious authorities – at least at the beginning of the fifteenth century. In 1427 the authors of a sumptuary ordinance in Paris state that prostitutes took a husband in order to pass themselves off as respectable women so as to wear certain sorts of clothing. Prostitutes are thus accused of marrying to get around sumptuary ordinances, a simple inversion of the true situation. Let us say that married women occasionally prostituted themselves with the consent of their husband in order to add to the family coffers. During moments of crisis, many a wife of a journeyman was thus forced to work the 'twelfth hour' that Karl Marx speaks of. As the Metz chronicler put it, speaking of the food shortages of 1419, 'you could have four women for the price of an egg!'[27]

Frequently a prostitute would bind herself legally to her protector. Jean Favier cites a case emblematic of the mentality of Paris prostitutes around 1400: a prostitute could be reprimanded by her comrades if she lived with a man and 'kept him'. This was why this woman asked her companion – in vain – to marry her.[28]

In the cities of the south, the small number of *meretrices* in the municipal *prostibulum* aside, there were many prostitutes who lived conjugally, and there were also a number of intermediary arrangements between an 'honest' couple and an irregular arrangement. There is no reason to doubt the validity of such unions, however.

We must not forget that it was the city *quartier*, the neighbourhood community, that defined and recognized conjugality. For the ecclesiastical authorities these ambiguous fringes of the *ordo conjugatorum* represented a corruption they were powerless to combat. This is why, during the greater part of the fifteen century, prostitutes, married and

[27] La Chronique de Philippe de Vigneulles, vol. 2, p. 175.
[28] Favier, *Paris au XVe siècle*, p. 82.

unmarried, were invited to baptisms, marriages and funerals, to carnival dances, and to the festivities of St Valentine's Day or of the month of May.

Thirteenth-century literature made the prostitute an auxiliary to the family, but since it viewed her as marginal, it did not grant her the right to set up her own home. Two centuries later, city prostitutes, married and unmarried, found their place in civic space and in confraternal and familial gatherings. What had become of the epoch of St Louis?

6

A Victory for the Flesh: Theological Support for the Act of Creation

We need to seek out the roots and trace the development of this fundamental change in attitudes. The thinking of humble folk is nearly totally unknown, but by pursuing the thought of the clergy we can at least learn what they authorized people to think and to do.

When the twelfth-century goliardic poets sang of the beauty of young women, loudly proclaiming their rejection of the ascetic life and *contemptus mundi*, their eagerness for pleasures coincided with the liberty that young noblemen enjoyed and with the optimism that led the schoolmen of Chartres to return creation to its place in the divine scheme and give man back his body. But the Chartres school was only an avant-garde, and the goliards were merely marginal.[1] After 1200 they slowly disappeared, not through persecution, but because – in the university at Paris at least – their protest had lost its *raison d'être*.

Throughout the thirteenth century, in fact, teachers gradually incorporated what they could of the innovators' thought into the traditional teaching of the Church. In increasing measure, according to Georges Duby, the new school offered man happiness. Two major works crowned this long effort, Thomas Aquinas' *Summa theologica* and the second part of the *Roman de la Rose*. Jean de Meun tendered a passionate invitation to his readers to obey Nature unreservedly. As for St Thomas, he denounced 'all who fail to remember that they are men' and all who, like

---

[1] See J. Le Goff, *Les intellectuels au Moyen-âge* (Paris, 1960), pp. 35, 53. Nobles, if Guibert de Nogent is to be believed, lived surrounded by prostitutes; Jean of Soissons responded to a priest, 'I have been told by wiser people than you that women should be common property and that the sin you speak of is of no consequence' (see G. Duby, *The Knight, the Lady, and the Priest: The Making of Modern Marriage in Medieval France*, trans. B. Bray, New York, 1984, p. 156).

the heretics, refused to believe in the natural union of body and soul. He also recalled that the inner life does not develop in isolation from things, and that humanity inscribes its laws into the order of Nature.

The principal corollaries of this dual teaching were that henceforth:

1 Theologians and canonists drew a clearer distinction between spiritual sins and carnal sins. The spiritual were judged more severely than the carnal, since they lodged in the mind, not in concupiscence, and they were a graver offence to God;[2]

2 the defenders of orthodoxy admitted that it is difficult indeed to resist powerful natural impulses. The 'naturalists' forbade all resistance. Both groups agreed, however, in condemning unconditionally unnatural acts, which were denounced with increasing urgency in treatises and sermons. This tendency resulted in a lessened emphasis on sins qualified as natural;[3]

3 the re-evaluation of nature, and hence of the flesh, led to a relative devaluation of chastity: the 'naturalists' considered chastity as hypocrisy; St Thomas judged it a shared responsibility, for 'each accomplishes his mission for the safeguard of all'. Hence, even though Thomas placed the chaste on a higher plane of virtue, he reduced the distance that had been established between the abstinent and the rest of mankind.

This 'readjustment' was of course tied, in the theologians' minds, to the triumph of sacramental marriage. Where Jean de Meun states that man's 'natural labour' and his appetite for pleasure were justified by the fruit of the union, even outside all marriage bonds, St Thomas and his disciples insisted that it was within the framework of marriage, and hence within the limits of a sexuality under the control of the faithful, ritualized by the laws, and sacralized by its intentions, that the act of the flesh was rehabilitated.

[2] Thomas, *Summa theologica*, Ia IIae quest. 73 art. 5. Where possible, quotations from the *Summa* will be given from *The Summa theologica of St Thomas Aquinas*, trans. Fathers of the English Dominican Province, rev. D. J. Sullivan, Great Books of the Western World 19 and 20 (20 vols, Chicago, 1952).

[3] Ibid. 'The sin of lust . . . is of the greatest adhesion, and man can only with difficulty be withdrawn from it, for the desire of pleasure is insatiable' (ibid., Ia IIae. quest. 74 art. 3). Obviously, the distinction between natural and unnatural sins had not been ignored by earlier authors, but it was more emphasized in thirteenth-century theology and philosophy. This is the context within which chapters on the sexual act in treatises on medicine and surgery should be read. Arnaud de Villeneuve, for example, describes several procedures for making a deflowered girl appear a virgin, for tightening the vulva and narrowing the mouth of the uterus, and for increasing desire and enjoyment in sexual relations so that the woman takes pleasure in the sex act, and so forth (*De ornatu mulieris*, Lyons, 1586, in fol., p. 270, col. 2). Similarly, Henri de Mondeville, surgeon to Philippe le Bel, devotes a long chapter to 'L'embellissement des femmes' in his treatise on surgery, *Doctrine* (vol. 1, chap. 13).

All the same, the frontiers of orthodoxy became extremely blurred. This is why Etienne Tempier could draw from the teachings of St Thomas, the Averroists, and progressive circles to create a blend of propositions – 'chastity is not in itself a virtue', 'total abstention from the work of the flesh corrupts virtue and the species' – that he intended to condemn.[4]

Thomas's disciples held firmly to their master's ideas, in spite of condemnations, exploiting their inherent possibilities in matters pertaining to the flesh as in other questions. The new perspectives offered by the thought of William of Ockham were to reinforce these tendencies still further in the thirteenth century. It was not by coincidence that Durand de Saint-Pourçain, whose reasoning was solid in this domain, rallied to the Ockhamist position.

Three works of morality or spirituality written between 1270 and 1320 enjoyed a remarkable influence throughout the century. The *Speculum humanae salvationis*, written in the Dominican monastery in Strasbourg during the sombre decade of the 1320s by a brother of Saxon origin, were, not surprisingly, exceedingly austere and showed no concessions to the new ideas. But around 1275 P. d'Abernam was writing somewhat differently on the subject of sins of the flesh in his *Lumiere az lais*: 'Of the capital sins there are five spiritual and two carnal; vice of the flesh comes from nature, thus it seems that the carnal sins are the least grave. . . . Avarice is worse than debauchery, which does not prevent people from loving their neighbour (even Our Lord) or from spending generously. Furthermore, the lascivious man is more apt to repent than the miser.'[5] And what were the teachings of brother Laurent, director of conscience to the children of Philippe le Hardi, whose *Somme le roy* was translated throughout the western world after 1280? 'There are some branches [of sins of the flesh] that are in no way mortal sins, as are many impulses of the flesh that one cannot avoid. . . . provided, however, that one does not feed these impulses by drink, bad thoughts, etc.' An enumeration of sins follows, arranged in an order that was to continue, immutable, in later works: 'Three faults are absolutely to be avoided: the sin against nature on one's person or on another; lusting after one's neighbour's wife; and dishonest practices within marriage.'[6]

---

[4] Such notions had already been combined by clerics who belonged to none of these tendencies, however.

[5] Cited in C. V. Langlois, *La vie en France au Moyen-âge*, new and rev. edn (4 vols, Paris, 1926–9) vol. 4, chap. 5, 'La vie spirituelle', p. 89. Preachers echoed this reading up to the sixteenth century. According to Michel Menot, avarice is the third and final rampart of Jericho (*Sermones quadragesimales*, Paris, 1519, third Sunday, fol. 33; see also fer. quart. passion, fol. 69v).

[6] Cited in Langlois, *La vie en France*, vol. 4, p. 144.

In this manner, the grandchildren of St Louis learned that they really ought not to masturbate (a practice that was still not clearly condemned), and that their joyous abandon in the arms of a prostitute ought not to worry them too much. They would not die of it (in a spiritual sense, that is). On the other hand, they were strictly obliged to respect due conjugal moderation.

Georges Duby has recently shown how, when the *inconjugamento* of Christian peoples had been accomplished, these two moralities were obliged to admit reciprocal concessions within the bosom of the institution of marriage, the seat of social and spiritual order.[7] The domain of the sacred had been extended to marriage without eliminating its carnality, and the positive values attributed to conjugality were gradually transferred to conjugal relations as well. The most obvious changes in ecclesiastical moral attitudes can be seen towards the end of the thirteenth century. Richard Middleton saw moderate pleasure as an acceptable aim in sexual intercourse. For him, as for St Thomas (after Aristotle), sexual pleasure is good when it is sought in a good end. Better: such pleasure can contribute to the equilibrium of the individual and of society, and thus it can bear some of the virtue of the conjugal state. These theologians, then, in an attempt to help the faithful avoid fornication, adultery or other frowned-upon practices, presented conjugal relations as licit even without the end of procreation.[8] (This notion will prove to be important later for the process of the institutionalization of prostitution.) These concessions soon found their limits: churchmen and solid citizens alike kept watch over the security of the conjugal bond, ever threatened by lust, passion and social unrest.

The husband who shows his wife too much ardour is adulterous and defiles the conjugal bed. All the moralists reiterated that abandon is a graver fault within marriage than without. The man who lusts after another man's wife is adulterous as well: he shatters the public peace and adds injustice to his lust. When a married man commits such a sin (even in thought alone), it is far more dangerous than fornication; when a wife does so it becomes abominable. This sort of reasoning explains why female adultery was always very vigorously punished either by fines or banishment, running the town, or flogging when the guilty party was unable to pay.[9]

[7] Duby, *The Knight*, p. 212.

[8] J.-L. Flandrin, *L'Eglise et le contrôle des naissances* (Paris, 1970), pp. 65, 89; J.-L. Flandrin, *Le sexe et l'Occident* (Paris, 1981), pp. 193ff.

[9] See J.-L. Flandrin, *Un temps pour embrasser: Aux origines de la morale sexuelle occidentale* (Paris, 1983), pp. 115ff.; Duby, *The Knight*. As early as Burchard, the unreasonably insistent husband was pictured as four times more guilty than the bachelor taking his pleasure. The theme is reiterated by all the moralists; by Jean Gerson, for

Women's nature was weak, the argument went, which is why they respond to solicitation or consent to brutality. Women were long considered fair game for young nobles, who proudly recounted their exploits. In the thirteenth century this sport was to some extent sublimated and transformed to the realm of symbolism by the literature of courtly love. Violence remained a part of the fantasies of the young men of noble houses, however, and *courtoisie* and fornication were parallel routes on a common itinerary. On the lower road the student encountered the 'free maidens' who satisfied his desires; on the other road there were fairy queens to be taken by force, but who none the less lent the conquering hero their protection. Practice in the princely courts showed a similar shift in social behaviour: the game of love was played in my lady's chambers, where women were desired but respected; in the palace cellars and kitchens, desires were satisfied with servant girls or whores. The woman always bore the greater responsibility in sins of the flesh, no matter what the circumstances were. Thomas Aquinas makes the memorable and terrible statement that 'the victim of forcible seduction, if she is not wed by the seducer, will find it more difficult to marry. She may be led to give herself to debauchery, from which her modesty, intact up to then, had kept her.' These women tricked into providing momentary pleasure and mocked by all the males about provided pitiful figures for bawdy tales.[10]

Other unmarried youths in both town and country ritualized their conduct, but more often it was through sexual violence. Even in the villages of the valleys of the Ariège such as Montaillou, girls ran high risks, and in the smaller cities of Haute-Provence in the early fourteenth century studied by R. Lavoye, rape accounted for 25 per cent of sex-related cases brought before the courts. In urban centres during the fourteenth century the behaviour of males was not very different from

---

example, in the early fifteenth century. See appendix 1, 'The Evolution of Mores and Literary Translations: the Quarrel of the *Roman de la Rose*'.

In the thirteenth and fourteenth centuries, secular and ecclesiastical morality seemed in total agreement on the need to punish female adultery severely, since it was held to be a public crime. The most humiliating strictures remained on the books and were on occasion applied: running the town and public flogging occurred in Alès, Villeneuve-lez-Avignon and Manosque. In Salon-de-Provence, those who had knowledge of a case of adultery and who failed to report it risked heavy fines. See P. Pansier, *Les courtisanes et la vie galante à Avignon du XIIIe au XVIIIe siècle*, Bibliothèque Calvet, MS 5691, chap. 5; C. J. B. Giraud, *Essai sur l'histoire du droit français au Moyen âge*, 2 vols (Paris, 1846), vol. 2, pp. 251, 258; R. Lavoye, 'Criminalité et sexualité à Manosque (vers 1240–vers 1340)', paper presented to the seminar of Georges Duby, Aix en Provence, 22 June 1977.

[10] See Duby, *The Knight*, pp. 212, 67.

that of the young men of Dijon in the fifteenth century or the roisterous 'hunting parties' in Venice described by Elisabeth Pavan.[11]

Nevertheless, the triumph of marriage as a sacrament had given the clergy an opportunity to refine their reflections concerning fornication. This time, they distinguish categories and cases with precision. To 'qualified fornication' (which stood for the sin of lust consummated and included such public crimes as kidnapping for sex, adultery, incest, and 'crimes against nature') canonists and theologians opposed 'simple fornication' – a sin, to be sure, but severely disapproved only when unreasonably frequent. What is more, the most recent theology regarding marriage arrived at the point where it contributed, paradoxically, to freeing 'simple fornication' from the maledictions that had so long beset it. It was, in fact, defined as *copula soluti cum soluta ex mutuo consensu*. This act, committed by two persons free of all ties and consenting to a transitory union, was not, according to Thomas, of the odious nature of errors against the theological virtues. It threatened the rights of man directly, but, since the fornicator was seeking pleasure, and not to do ill, it threatened the Supreme Legislator only through its consequences. It is not considered criminal and it imperils only the regularity of the status of a potential and unborn Christian. Furthermore (the good doctor had concubinage particularly in mind), its consequences can be put right from both the moral and the material point of view.

It is in fact obvious that for the theologians fornication covered a range of very different circumstances and relationships. Until the conjugal model had been firmly established among the faithful of Christendom, moralists could do little more than condemn fornication with great severity, since it included concubinage. Thomas says at the outset of his argument (Ia IIae qest. 73 art. 7) that 'fornication is the intercourse of a man with one who is not his wife.' With reform put into effect and concubinage curbed, 'simple fornication' seemed to the doctors of the Church infinitely less dangerous, at least when it was committed by unmarried men with women who were truly free of all ties, for otherwise the young man was exposing himself to grave sin. This is why brother Laurent, reasoning somewhat theoretically in his *Somme*, teaches that carnal sin outside marriage is graver when it is committed with 'common women' than with entirely free, ordinary women, 'because such women

[11] Lavoye, 'Criminalité et sexualité'. Gang rape committed by youths goes practically unpunished. E. Le Roy Ladurie, *Montaillou: The Promised Land of Error*, trans. B. Bray (New York, 1978), p. 150 also shows rape as not very severely punished. For Venice, see E. Pavan, 'Police des moeurs, société et politique à Venise à la fin du Moyen âge', *Revue historique* 264 (1980), pp. 241–88.

[e.g. prostitutes] are never married nor of the religious life and refuse neither he nor his brother, cousin, son, or father'.[12]

This passage, which at first glance seems paradoxical, dates from a period in which the distinctive symbols designating public prostitutes may not yet have been imposed everywhere or had been imposed without great discernment, 'dishonest' women wore no coif, but such 'debauched females' may have included wives, itinerant nuns, and others. What was needed was a way to recognize the real public prostitutes. Once they had been set apart, 'simple fornication' consisted, to repeat Thomas's formula, in intercourse with a woman who was indeed not one's own wife, but who was also known for certain to be common property. The theorists of organized prostitution set up several criteria (more strictly defined by clergy than by laity) to define the woman reputed to be 'public'. She must rent out her body for gain and not lend it for pleasure (more on that subject to come); she must be free of all bonds, hence, in theory, must be a stranger in the city in which she plied her trade; and she must be either unmarried or widowed. This is the reason for the high proportion of foreigners still among the ranks of public prostitutes in the fifteenth century in Florence, Dijon, Avignon or Tarascon. This also explains why those who protested about the setting up of a house of toleration in Lyons in 1478 complain in particular that the proprietors carried out no preliminary interview with the women. This inquiry – one of the most important tasks of the 'abbess' – guaranteed that the girls admitted to the *prostibulum* were indeed free of ties, which thus protected the clients from committing the sin of consummated lust. It was to this same end that at the end of the thirteenth century the wearing of a red armband was imposed on public prostitutes, the only ones recognized by civic authorities. Rahab, 'harlot of Jericho', was told to place a red cord at her window as a sign of allegiance (Joshua 2:18). The sign of Rahab was ambivalent: not only did it separate the woman who wore it from the community of the pure; it also served as proof to fornicators that the consequences of their visits to a companion of the moment would not be serious. The *aiguillette* thus functioned somewhat like the prostitute's identity card in a regulation-prone France of the beginning of the current century, but where the latter brought theoretical protection from venereal disease, the former promised protection from 'qualified fornication'.

When this ideological and moral framework had been set in place, theorists were able to state that simple fornication with public prostitutes involved no grave spiritual consequences.

This means that one or two questions might legitimately be posed regarding the sentiments of Montaillou peasants (see E. Le Roy Ladurie,

---

[12] Cited in Langlois, *Vie spirituelle*, chap. 5, p. 163.

Montaillou, The Promised Land of Error, p. 149). The men of these villages and towns seem persuaded that the sexual act is innocent under two conditions: first, it must be pleasing to both partners. When this is true, the pleasure by itself is without sin, as it is agreeable to the couple, and not disagreeable in God's eyes. Second, if this is not the case, it must be paid for: 'To pay for one's pleasure was to be without sin.' Le Roy Ladurie notes that Bartolomé Bennassar has found this same belief on the Iberian peninsula in the modern period.

The high valleys of the Ariège – former heretical lands – had been reconquered by orthodoxy; the propagandizing of the mendicant friars had been intense there and had produced lasting results. Do these reactions, recorded at the dawn of the fourteenth century, really testify to an ancient fund of popular peasant wisdom? Are they not perhaps instead the results of the mendicants' catechizing, or of the individuals' caution before the inquisitors?

Durand de Saint-Pourçain, doctor of theology and Master of the Sacred Palace under Clement V and John XXII, wrote a 'Commentary on Sentences' that enjoyed considerable success. This *doctor resolutissimus* states in it that 'in natural law simple fornication constitutes only a venial sin; if [the sin] is considered mortal, it is a result of the sanctions of positive law'. In those times of the intellectual exaltation of Nature, when natural law and positive law were paired and contrasted, the latter came off second best. This judgement offers an excellent example of the shifting borderline between mortal sin and venial sin.[13]

Men on the fringes of orthodoxy – beghards and Brothers of the Free Spirit – drew radical conclusions from this sort of analysis,[14] but

[13] *Dictionnaire Théologique Catholique*, s.v. 'fornication'. B. Guénée (*L'Occident aux XIVe et XVe siècles: Les Etats*, Paris, 1971, p. 104) gives the following definitions: 'Natural law governs the relations between all human beings. It is a set of precepts dictated by reason to the human conscience. ... Positive law ... is the set of laws or customs that govern precisely the life of a people. Whereas eternal laws (divine law) and natural law are immutable, positive law, to the contrary, varies according to time and place. It is even perfectible: changes can be brought to it to correct its defects and make it respond better to the demands of natural law.'

[14] The Council of Vienne condemned the following opinion attributed to the Brethren of the Free Spirit: 'Mulieri osculum cum ad hoc natura non inclinat est mortale peccatum, actum autem carnis cum ad hoc natura inclinat peccatum non est.'

On the modification of theologians' and jurists' judgement of these questions, see C. Chauvin, *Eglise et prostitution*, thèse de 3e cycle, University of Strasbourg, 1973; C. Chauvin, *Les chrétiens et la prostitution* (Paris, 1983), is more readily available. Although his treatment of medieval prostitution is summary, Chauvin nevertheless notes that at the dawn of the fourteenth century it was no longer held to be a social crime (ibid., p. 63).

This marked change in Christian morality, which represented the first great shift before that of the 1400s, was the result of theological concessions and acquisitions and should be seen in relation to the condemnations of masturbation and sodomy.

beginning with the early fourteenth century, many theologians no longer considered simple fornication to be a major transgression. This is why it · often was no longer reserved to the jurisdiction of the bishop or his penitencer.[15] For further confirmation, we can turn to Jean Gerson, an austere theologian who, what is more, lived during a time of troubles when the institution of marriage seemed threatened. He writes in his *Miroir de l'âme* on the seventh commandment: 'Here is forbidden, under pain of mortal sin, all carnal company of man and woman together outside loyal marriage, and to say the contrary is an error of the faith.' This insistence is absent when he discusses the other commandments, which appear undisputed, and it may perhaps reflect an opinion that had even spread to the ranks of the clergy. Did Gerson himself condemn it? Let us turn to his *Confessional*. When he speaks of the sin of lust, he raises many questions, but they all concern unnatural acts or 'qualified fornication'. Once more, it seems (to the reader or to the penitent sinner) that the gravity of the sin of simple fornication is highly attenuated, and that it approaches the limits of venial sin.[16]

All preachers, Olivier Maillard and Michel Menot included, were obliged to explain that lust was illicit, contrary to what many people thought, would lead to many woes, and would weaken a man's energies and shorten his days. Menot's attacks include shades of difference, however, and, like his predecessors, he distinguishes four sorts of lust: simple fornication, incest, sacrilege and sodomy. In other words, when the sermon had ended, the hearer might have understood and remembered that lust was much more of a danger for the woman than for the man or for the clergy than for the laity; that fornication was not one of the gravest dangers and that God judged fornication much less severely than pride or avarice; and that it was excusable if it were not too frequently indulged in. And this during a period of moral reaction.

This is why intellectuals made such wide use of Augustine's opinion: 'Remove prostitutes from human affairs, and you will unsettle everything on account of lusts. . . . This class of people is by its own mode of life most unchaste in its morals; and by the law of order, it is most vile in social condition.' Furthermore, it is because the common good implies the existence of evil that Thomas Aquinas develops the principle of tolerance in his *Summa*. Thomas's confessor, Ptolomy of Lucca, goes a good deal further: he popularizes the principle of the lesser evil by referring conjointly to Aristotle and to a gloss of Augustine. According to

[15] As was the case in the diocese of Cambrai in the early fourteenth century (see Flandrin, *Le sexe et l'Occident*, pp. 114–15).

[16] J. Gerson, *Oeuvres complètes*, ed. B. Glorieux 10 vols (Paris, New York 1960–73), vol. 7, p. 201 (for the *Miroir de l'âme*) and p. 398. See also his *Poenitemini* sermons for Advent 1402 (ibid., pp. 86ff.).

Aristotle, 'if soldiers have no women, they abuse men'. The interlinear gloss of Augustine, which appeared during the thirteenth century and was often cited subsequently, says, 'the public woman is in society what bilge is in [a ship at] sea and the sewer pit in a palace. Remove this sewer and the entire palace will be contaminated.' This provided an authoritative reference of capital importance for anyone charged with the governance of a city. It justified public prostitution – vile as it was – allowed it to be established and to function, and promoted its practice to the status of a trade (*ministerium*).[17]

In this manner, prostitution had been ordained for the common good. It was a social necessity. There was no need to make matters worse: everyone knew that women were by nature fornicators, lustful and insatiable. They sold themselves or they offered themselves. Even when taken by force, they were to be held as guilty; when they were kidnapped, raped or forcibly seduced (as Thomas Aquinas notes, following Jacques de Vitry), they led men into debauchery, and their pride in their beauty made them all the more sinful.[18]

Furthermore, professional prostitutes had to be beautiful, for if one wanted the common good of the *ordo conjugatorum*, one had to work towards focusing the desires of unmarried men and widowers on 'beautiful and titillating' prostitutes. Did it not lessen the fornicator's sin

[17] The passage from Augustine (*De Ordine* II, IV, 12) is cited in Chauvin, *Les chrétiens*, p. 57 and given here from *Divine Providence and the Problem of Evil, a translation of St. Augustine's De Ordine* with annotations by R. P. Russell (New York, 1942), p. 95. The first mention of fornication in Thomas is in Ia IIae. quest. 10 art. 11: 'God permits evils to be produced in the universe; he lets them remain for fear that if they were eliminated, greater goods would be [eliminated] as well, or worse evil might ensue.'

Charles Chauvin has the merit of having restored what Augustine had written and of separating out the glossator's contributions, and he is correct in attributing the phrase cited to the jurist. The author of the *City of God* speaks in quite different terms and states that *lupanars* are a tolerance on the part of the terrestrial city. It is perhaps exaggerated to write that, for him, 'Christianity and prostitution were incompatible. There is not the slightest trace of tolerance' (Chauvin, *Les chrétiens*, p. 60).

Thomas uses *De Ordine* as a patristic proof: 'He is more Roman than Augustinian.' It is no wonder that the pseudo-Augustinian gloss was frequently utilized during the latter thirteenth century, when theologians and moralists were beginning to integrate prostitution into their models for society. *De Ordine* and its gloss reappeared constantly during the fourteenth and fifteenth centuries in the briefs of bathhouse operators' or procuresses' lawyers (as in Lyons in 1478).

The notion of the 'palace' and its 'sewer' was the basis for presenting the prostitute as the guardian of order. This is how Boccaccio presents her in the four novellas of the *Decameron* about Calandrino, which, as R. Zapperi has noted, make up four acts of the same comedy. In this comedy the four accomplices, who represent institutions charged with maintaining the order of society, are the tax-collector, the priest, the physician and the whore (R. Zapperi, *L'homme enceint*, Paris, 1983, pp. 157ff.).

[18] Duby, *The Knight*, pp. 212, 67.

when the woman's body was seductive? Alain de Lille had already said
that one should ask whether the woman with whom the sin was
committed was beautiful, adding that if she were, the penance should be
reduced. Thomas echoes this judgement: 'Because the greater a sin's
cause, the more forcibly it moves to sin, and so the more difficult it is to
resist. But sin is lessened by the fact that it is difficult to resist.' The very
sight of accessible feminine beauty stimulates nature, augments desire,
weakens judgement, and, by that very token, lessens the sin.[19]

Thomas's reflections on sin contain two propositions that caught the
attention of those (clergy and laity alike) charged with organizing or
controlling prostitution:

1 'The greater or lesser gravity of a sin, in respect of the person
   sinned against' depends to a degree on 'the condition of the
   person against whom it was committed'. Further, 'a sin is the
   more grievous according as it is committed against a person more
   closely united to God by reason of personal sanctity, or official
   status.'[20] Thus the sin of the fornicating city-dweller was, once
   again, attenuated, since the prostitute was considered at the very
   bottom of society, and it was scarcely appropriate, in her case, to
   speak of her virtue.

2 'On the part of his neighbour, a man sins the more grievously
   according as his sin affects more persons, so that a sin committed
   against a public personage, for example a king or prince who
   stands in the place of the whole people, is more grievous than a
   sin committed against a private person.'[21] The prostitute was
   believed to have broken with her family by her fall from virtue.
   As a public prostitute, she was necessarily and by definition free
   of all ties and accessible to all comers. The public prostitute, then,
   was, to put it in Thomist terminology, a publicly available private
   person.

But she was also available for pay: she was waged. As it happens, as
early as the end of the twelfth century, theologians, preachers and jurists
in Paris grouped around Peter the Cantor had perfected what Jacques Le
Goff has called 'the doctrinal *aggiornamento* of the new society founded
in work'.[22] They justified the remuneration of lawyers, professors and

[19] Alain de Lille's query is cited in Duby, *The Knight*, p. 261. For St Thomas, see *Summa*
Ia IIae quest. 73 art. 6 ('but sin is lessened by the fact that it is difficult to resist'); quest. 73
art. 9.

[20] Ibid., Ia IIae quest. 73 art. 9.

[21] Ibid.

[22] J. Le Goff, 'Le travail dans la France médiévale', *Encyclopédie de la Pléiade: La France
et les Français* (Paris, 1972), p. 317.

merchants. One of these intellectuals, Thomas of Chobham, a canon of the cathedral of Notre Dame, wrote a *summa confessorum*, one of the first of the genre. In it he discusses a problem that the canons had already had to debate in the past:[23] When the prostitutes decided to offer a stained glass window to the cathedral, were the canons obliged to accept their gift? Thomas opines that if the women prostitute themselves for pleasure and offer their bodies out of a simple desire for carnal enjoyment, they accomplished no work, in which case their earnings are as abject as their debauchery and the shameful offering ought to be refused.

Thomas, however, is more interested in the case of other women, who he realizes are in the majority, who sell themselves out of need. He does not hesitate: 'they rent their body and furnish work.' Still carefully weighing the worth of the offering and thus of the prostitutes' earnings, the canon pauses to discuss the quality of the work involved: Had the *meretrix* earned this money well or ill? Had she deceived the client about her beauty through the artifice of clothing or make-up? If her appearance and her behaviour conformed to the client's expectations, then she deserved her pay.

Our canon thus subjects prostitution to rules of good professional conduct. He returns at the end of his discussion to the shameful nature of this work and he concludes, prudently, that 'if they repent, they can keep the profits of prostitution to give alms.' But – and this is at the heart of the matter – Chobham none the less includes Parisian prostitutes among the working population. He subjects their profession to moral standards. Jacques Le Goff notes that this was a borderline case: it may well have been true in 1200, but Paris intellectuals of sixty years later, St Thomas first among them, picked up this 'case of conscience' again, and they show less reticence than Thomas of Chobham. St Thomas says that although 'a woman's profits from whoredom' are 'filthy lucre properly so called, because the practice of whoredom is filthy and against the Law of God, yet the woman does not act unjustly in taking money. Consequently it is lawful to keep and to give in alms what is thus acquired by an unlawful action.'[24] Whether they liked it or not, then, the thirteenth-century 'sociologists' began to attribute some degree of positive value to this

[23] This 'case of conscience' has often been cited by historians, for example, by Jacques Le Goff, 'Le travail', p. 317, or B. Geremek, *Les marginaux parisiens aux XIVe et XVe siècles*, trans. D. Beauvois (Paris, 1976), p. 259.

[24] Was this a case of conscience? Certainly, but we need to remember that those guilty of theft, robbery and lending at interest had to restore their ill-gotten gains. Simoniacs had to give all they possessed in alms.

St Thomas takes up these problems in IIa IIae quest. 32 art. 7, and in Ia IIae quest. 101 art. 1 of the *Summa*. The prostitute cannot offer her possessions to the Church *propter scandalum*. The Church had to avoid seeming to approve her sin as it took in the earnings it procured as an offering. Thomas concludes that the earnings can be tolerated and the alms 'shameful trade'. This necessary evil was no longer seen as totally lacking in virtues, since the professional morality that justified its earnings emanated from the common good. Some of the 'smells from the palace' penetrated into the 'sewer' as well as the other way around.

In accepting the prostitute's alms, the Church recognized that she had acted out of necessity. This working woman could be counted among the poor. Victim of human misery and of human frailty that she was, could she not serve as an example to others? The calendar of saints had long been enriched by the edifying inclusion of reformed prostitutes – St Pelagia, St Mary the Egyptian, St Afra, and others – who, following the example of Mary Magdalene, had saved their souls through repentance. It was because poor women who took to prostitution, voluntarily or by force of circumstance, tortured the conscience of the Church that Pope Innocent III taught that one of the greatest works of charity was to remove prostitutes from the public brothels and that marrying a prostitute was a work of piety. The Gospel clearly stated that the sinner's infamy was not irremediable.

When they were not haunted by eschatological concerns or preoccupied with taking collections, the teams of mendicant friars who soon overran the western world recalled that Jesus forgave fallen women and welcomed them into the Kingdom of his Father. They were even more attentive to the fate of their Magdalenes when demographic expansion reached its limit, the poor proliferated, and there were some who loudly proclaimed that poverty was not natural, that God listened to the complaints of the poor, and that justice was due them on this earth.

Jean de Meun offers a vivid portrait of Poverty:

> She wore only a skimpy, aged sack, miserably patched, that was both her cloak and her dress, and she had only that to cover herself, hence she often trembled. She crouched at a short distance from the others and was curled up like a poor dog, for anyone who is poor, whoever he may be, is always sad and shamed. Cursed be the hour when the poor man was conceived, for he will never be well fed, nor well dressed, nor well shod. Nor will he be beloved nor reach high places.[25]

are legitimate. It goes without saying that the repentant prostitute's offering of her possessions as an oblation posed no problems.

A new stage opened when, in 1337, the Maréchal of the Roman court of Avignon demanded a tribute from women of disorderly conduct and from their associates. Innocent VI forbade this traffic in 1358 (see Pansier, *Les courtisanes*, p. 20). As for the municipalities, they fairly frequently subjected the managers of bawdy houses to the tallage during the fourteenth century.

[25] Some preachers – Taddeo Dini, for example – went well beyond the traditional schemata in treating the justice due the poor (see M. Mollat, *Les pauvres au Moyen âge: Etude sociale*, Paris, 1978, p. 223).

How many people shared the new ideas that were being expressed by a few theologians and a handful of philosophers, students and friars? Such notions made some progress, but extremely slowly. It was only at the very end of the fourteenth century that they suddenly permeated the entire fabric of society, transforming daily practice and ways of thinking in less than two generations.

7

Nature Besieged by War and Pestilence: Visions of the Parousia

At the turn of the fifteenth century, the cause of 'Nature' was defended with a vigour hitherto unknown, and this time, men in positions of responsibility and concerned about the destiny of their city joined the fray.

The population of Western Europe plummetted between 1400 and 1440. Waves of pestilence, and above all, recurrences of the plague, had produced catastrophic death rates everywhere. The epidemic in 1400 was the worst Lille saw during the entire Burgundian period; it wiped out between one-third and one-half of the population of Périgueux; it took more than 12,000 victims in Florence. Contemporaries note that certain of these recurrent waves of plague struck children and young people particularly hard: the *parva mortalitas* of 1361–3 had already been dubbed 'the children's plague' in England and Italy alike. The same was true of the Paris epidemic of 1418, and we know that two years later in the small city of Valréas one-third of the adults and three-quarters of the young children died within a few months. For contemporaries, this long-standing torment appeared as a series of sudden collapses and disasters. They were fully aware of this precipitous population decline: they gazed on their depopulated cities and saw illustrious families disappear. The author of a chronicle of Montpellier written in 1395 states, 'A long time ago the city of Montpellier was a notable city in which there usually were at least ten thousand households. It is now so reduced that it probably contains scarcely eight hundred.' The capitouls of Toulouse state in 1408 that 'once the city was so thickly inhabited that a great many of the citizens were obliged to lodge in the suburbs. . . . Today it has become most ruinous.' In 1396 the syndics of Tarascon proposed to fight against the depopulation of their city and 'the danger of total destruction that may ensue'.[1] Other examples abound.

When population levels were high at the beginning of the fourteenth century, wars and epidemics were held to be natural phenomena tending to limit an infinite and dangerous propagation of the species, and some intellectuals had judged that calamities, on a moderate scale, were gifts of Mother Nature. Marsilius of Padua, observing that the world is divided into rival or warring nations, writes, 'One must see in this the influence of a celestial cause tending to limit the indefinite propagation of the human species. One might, in fact, consider that nature intended to limit this propagation by fomenting wars or epidemics.' This explanation is repeated a generation later by Jean Buridan, at a moment when the consequences of the first waves of plague were not yet clearly apparent and the population losses seemed easily replaceable. In *Le songe du vergier*, a knight holds it impossible for a father to feed too many children, and a priest replies that this is why virginity is held as a virtue.[2] As time passed and recurrences of the plague worsened, notables everywhere were persuaded that such phenomena ran counter to Nature and that attacks on Nature of this sort were unparalleled in history. Many thought it important to come to her aid to save both the city and Christendom before they were overwhelmed. The concern of city notables over depopulation was of course accentuated by the fiscal demands of princes and monarchs. In order to defend themselves they had to take censuses; like it or not, municipalities wrote their history, and it seemed to them terrifying.

City fathers were not alone in their consciousness of the problem of depopulation: it also concerned men who had a larger vision of Christendom. Weakened by wars, the Schism, and epidemics, Christendom appeared unable to resist the advancing infidel forces. We need to remember that the Turks seemed an even greater threat after the battle of

---

[1] On all these questions see, for France, G. Duby (gen. ed.), *Histoire de la France urbaine*, 5 vols (Paris, 1980–5), vol. 2; J. Le Goff et al., *La ville médiévale* (Paris, 1980), pp. 413–24 (cities' losses), 583–5 (awareness of depopulation). For Italy, see D. Herlihy and C. Klapisch-Zuber, *Tuscans and their Families: A Study of the Florentine Catasto of 1427* (New Haven, Connecticut, 1985). The population of Pistoia was reduced by more than two-thirds between 1340 and the early 1400s; San Gimignano at that later date retained only 14 per cent of the number of households that it had had in 1332; Prato lost four-fifths of its population in a hundred years, and so forth. For Tarascon, see M. Hébert, *Tarascon au XIVe siècle: Histoire d'une communauté urbaine provençal* (La Calande, 1979), p. 120, n. 123.

[2] These statements are cited in M. Mollat, *Genèse médiévale de la France moderne XIV–XVe siècles* (Paris, 1970), p. 120. Mental attitudes changed thirty years or so later, when virginity and population found themselves in opposed camps.

Nicopolis (1396). In western opinion this disaster roughly coincided with the terrible recurrence of the plague in 1398–1401.[3]

Culture took on the task. It was during this period that private journals proliferated in France and became a veritable literary genre in Italy in the *ricordanze*. Works on the family as well reached a richness of analysis unequalled since classical antiquity.[4] Authors of such works were more interested in safeguarding the *res publica* than they were in imitating the ancients. The objectives and the themes of this literature are well known: it is a hymn to the ancestors written for the enlightenment of children; an exaltation of marriage, which is presented as the foundation of the active life, the source of natural love, and the cement of social peace and civic harmony. It teaches the persuasion of the young to the conjugal state, how to make love in order to increase the chances of engendering male offspring, how to avoid producing malformed children, how to make children more robust, and so forth.

This translated into social terms in the municipalities' encouragement of marriage and the begetting of children and in measures regarding citizenship, access to the magistracy, and the reduction of dowries and wedding expenses, among others. On occasion preachers came to the aid of the city governments: Bernardino of Siena advises young men to 'take a wife, a handsome woman, big, good, and wise, who will bear a lot of children. A man's life is a sad one if he remains alone.' Propaganda in favour of marriage and the measures taken by the Italian cities are well known. Similar measures may perhaps have been adopted in some French cities.[5]

It was not enough, however, to encourage procreation, to show concern for the physical and moral health of the young by enrolling them in confraternal organizations, or to offer them the model of the good citizen and the steady worker fertilizing the conjugal terrain. The dangers that threatened the species must be warded of as well. Three 'crimes against nature' – sodomy, masturbation and chastity – were denounced more strongly than ever. Let us take them up in that order.

(1) As early as the end of the thirteenth century, theologians had considered 'the sin against nature' (homosexuality, for the most part) the

---

[3] Honoré Bonet, in his *Apparicion Maistre Jean de Meun* (1396) presents a prolific Saracen who lives on little or nothing; Guillaume Saignet, in his *Lamentatio* (see below), deplores the humiliation of the West by the Muslims; the Bourgeois of Paris incessantly uses the term 'Saracen'; and Gerson speaks of the great 'carnality' of the infidels.

[4] On these questions see Herlihy and Klapisch-Zuber, *The Tuscans*, pp. 332f., 345ff.

[5] The Bourgeois of Paris notes the terms of an ordinance of the provost and the Parlement in 1427 (hence at a demographic low point) obliging all sergeants, mounted police or tipstaffs, to marry before the next Ascension Day or loose their charge (*Journal d'un Bourgeois de Paris, 1405–1449*, ed. A. Tuetey, Paris, 1881).

worst of the sexual sins. The Church never slackened its severity, and it was encouraged to redouble its vigilance by municipal authorities, particularly in Italy, where the peril was thought to have reached disturbing proportions. In the 1400s, city fathers in the Italian peninsula renewed their efforts to curb this 'enormous crime, offence to God, peril to the city, contrary to the propagation of the human race', to quote the terms of the signori of Venice as they launched a systematic repression. In 1418 the search for 'sodomites' had become one of the state's chief tasks and was entrusted to a *collegium sodomitarum* that set up surveillance in all the suspect places (schools of dance, music, or fencing), rewarded informers, and increased the penalties, even for minors. In April 1403 in Florence, abhorrence of 'the filth of the evil, abominable and counter to nature, and the enormous crime that is the vice of homosexuality' led to an attempt to root it out by instituting the office of the *Onestà*. In December 1415, when the Florentine clergy launched a pamphlet and sermon campaign against homosexuality, the city government backed its efforts and in 1432, still in the interests of pursuing homosexuals, it created the Office of the Night. Popular preachers throughout Italy joined in to denounce an evil that was thought to be rampant throughout the land, to be enrolling more and more converts, and to be turning young men away from marriage. The Venetian magistrates stated baldly that it contributed to depopulation.[6]

Elsewhere in Western Europe, particularly in France, men in positions of political responsibility were usually more concerned about all the 'sodomitic' acts thought to lead to homosexuality, masturbation among them.

(2) If we look at penitential literature, it is difficult to see that masturbation was considered a grave sin; it appears, in any event, to be considered much less serious than fornication.[7] Theologians of course

---

[6] On Venice, see E. Pavan, 'Police des moeurs, société et politique à Venise à la fin du Moyen age', *Revue historique*, vol. 264 no. 536 (1980), pp. 241–88. It was after 1400 – after 1406 in particular – that homosexuality was regularly prosecuted, and in 1418 the *collegium sodomitarum* was given pre-eminence over all other city councils. For Florence see R. C. Trexler, 'La prostitution florentine au XVe siècle: patronages et clientèles', *Annales ESC* (1981), pp. 983–1015, esp. p. 984.

[7] Nicole Grevy-Pons, *Célibat et nature, une controverse médiévale: A propos d'un traité du début du XVe siècle* (Paris, 1975), p. 29, speaks of a 'certain erotic candour' in poems of the twelfth century addressed to handsome adolescents as well as to young women: 'pederasty does not have the scandalous character that one might think,' she concludes. It acquired this quality at the end of the thirteenth century. The famous trials of the 1300s (that of the Templars, for example) illustrate this. In Avignon in 1320 an old man was burned alive for having had relations with a youth (see P. Pansier, *Les courtisanes et la vie galante à Avignon du XIIIe au XVIIIe siècle*, Bibliothèque Calvet MS 5691). The incubus of the

modified their opinions during the thirteenth century, and they came to consider masturbation a form of sin against nature, and hence a crime. None the less, this new and theoretical severity was only slowly translated into punitive penitential measures. This 'pollution' was long excused among young children in particular. As late as 1300 in the diocese of Cambrai, sins against nature and the 'sin of weakness' in children up to the age of fourteen (for boys) and twenty-five (for girls) still fell under the jurisdiction of the parish priest.[8]

Towards 1300, however, denunciations of masturbation became widespread and violent. In his *Doctrinal de sapience*, written in 1388, the archbishop of Sens, Guy de Roye, wrote, 'The first branch [of the sin against nature] is when man or woman by him or herself, alone and aware of the fact and awake, falls into the filth of the sin for which simple priests cannot give absolution: for by its gravity it is given to the bishops or to their lieutenants or penitencers.'[9]

Several years later Jean Gerson, who had just devoted an entire book – the first treatise of the sort in didactic literature – to the problem of 'daytime pollution', noted in his *Confessional*: 'it is a greater sin against nature than having company with a woman or, for a woman, with a man, and is reserved to the prelate.' Similarly, in his *Examen de conscience selon les péchés capitaux*, the first questions posed regarding lasciviousness are aimed at masturbation and 'pollution' – 'abominable and horrid sin that is said to be against nature [and] is reserved, whether it is done by oneself alone . . . or with other persons.' He adds, 'and such sins are worse than eating flesh on Good Friday and must be confessed expressly, under pain of damnation.' Confessors were to question children and young people most carefully on this point and to warn them of the terrible risks they would run. Gerson is quite clear: 'Unmarried young men and young girls must be well informed about these matters . . . for there are few of them who, when they come of age, do not commit nasty and abominable sins if they are not married young.' Many of them, Gerson continues in his *Confessional*, 'dared not confess the dissolute acts they had committed at the age of nine, ten, eleven, or twelve years of age with their brothers and sisters when as children they slept together'. Following Gerson,

---

spread of homosexuality is perceptible at the very end of the fourteenth century, though it is not as clear as in Italy (see the responses of Christine de Pisan to the 'naturalists'). In the treatise of Burchard of Worms, male masturbation practised alone is very lightly punished – with ten days of mild penance, to be tripled if practised between two people. (See G. Duby, *The Knight, the Lady, and the Priest*, trans. B. Bray (New York, 1984), p. 67.)

[8] J.-L. Flandrin, *Le sexe et l'Occident* (Paris, 1981), pp. 114–15.

[9] Ibid., p. 259. Contemporary synodal statutes (1387) of the diocese of Nantes are equally severe.

homosexual or heterosexual relations between children, masturbation included, became the constant nightmare that haunted educators.[10]

If masturbation seemed so dangerous, it was because of its consequences: Gerson fails to say so, but he certainly believed, like everyone else, that sperm is blood of an extremely pure sort that descends from the brain and turns white when it goes through the veins. Thus ejaculation was the equivalent of being bled. The adolescent, who had not yet acquired the robust physique of an adult and was not constrained by the discipline of a life of work, risked by his incontinence falling into lassitude or idiocy.[11]

Furthermore, habits contracted in adolescence were not easily shaken off: 'Even in marriage, young people commit many nasty excesses.' Gerson advises confessors to put the same questions to older men and women. He accuses masturbation (according to Jean-Louis Flandrin, on this point Gerson once again agrees with modern sexologists) of encouraging other sorts of abnormal behaviour: 'And he who becomes accustomed to it and is obstinate in it, the devil lightly makes him stumble into several other villanous and terrible sins, which no one should name or write.'

It is clear, then, that for moralists of the 1400s nothing, not even the innocence of the child, excused this detestable vice that led to further crimes. 'By the horrid pleasure that it procures' it threatened to turn men away from marriage and from the act of procreation.[12]

(3) The populationist argument was openly advanced several years later. In 1418 Guillaume Saignet, sénéchal of Beaucaire, wrote his

[10] M. Rouche, *Histoire de l'éducation* (Paris, 1982), vol. 1, p. 550 deals well with Gerson's concern with these problems. See also J. Gerson, *Oeuvres complètes*, ed. B. Glorieux, 10 vols (Paris and New York, 1960–73), vol. 7, p. 398; Flandrin, *Le sexe et l'Occident*, pp. 256ff.

[11] All medical writers, echoing classical authors, agreed on this point (see R. Zapperi, *L'homme enceint*, Paris, 1983, pp. 29, 139).

[12] The famous doctor Tissot invented nothing: all his arguments can be found in the treatises of fifteenth-century moralists. The 'contemporary sexologists' who, according to Jean-Louis Flandrin, have so much in common with Gerson (an interesting remark, which is more flattering to Gerson than to the sexologists) have not yet totally got rid of such arguments.

Gerson's immediate concern here is by no means the continuation of the species, as we shall soon see. Nevertheless, his attacks on masturbation cannot be understood outside the vast naturalist movement that developed between 1390 and 1430. Gerson was perhaps the partially involuntary instrument of a populationist mentality on this point, as in his positions on carnal pleasure in marriage. As a person intensely concerned about children, he could not have forgotten the masses of innocent lives wiped out by the recent recurrences of the plague. Furthermore, 'naturalist' propaganda coincided in this domain with the teachings of the Church.

Lamentatio humanae nature attacking the celibacy of the clergy.[13] The author, who had a law degree and served as counsellor to the dauphin and to the house of Anjou and was later Chancellor of Provence, wrote his treatise in middle age. The reform of the Church, to which he claimed his work contributed, seems not to have been his prime concern, but simply one possible way to defend a Nature sorely in need of aid. He proclaims himself a child of Nature even before declaring himself a faithful follower of the Church.[14] If Nature was in his day in such a lamentable state, it was because she was being attacked by an ecclesiastical law that was absurd, contrary to reason, and without legitimate authority, since God had ordained that the living should increase and multiply. Like all his contemporaries, Saignet makes use of dream and allegory. Nature, Nobility, and Christian Faith are assailed near the Fountain of Vaucluse by two frightful harpies, Pestilence and War, accompanied by a maiden of virtuous appearance but shameful behaviour, Chastity. Nature, on the verge of surrendering, asks Pestilence and War for a truce, and they refer the matter to Chastity, thus setting off the disputation.

The allegory is unequivocal: in this new combat of the virtues and the vices, the author, by associating chastity with pestilence and war, imposes on his readers the association of chastity with famine (pestilence, war and famine having long been grouped together in prayer). Indeed, famine causes death, and those who suffer hunger's pangs are unable to participate in the eminently natural act of eating. The sexual act is thus implicitly compared to nourishment (a philosophical and theological reference to the thirteenth-century doctors who raised questions concerning the hypothetical sinfulness of a natural act). Continence and famine have similar consequences: the depopulation of Christendom. This is why, in Saignet's allegory, Nature can no longer hold out against her other enemies, War and Pestilence, whereas the infidels (Muslims), who follow their own laws, multiply at will. Celibacy is thus against nature, and her victims, whose vows are pronounced as children, incapable of resisting the pricks of carnal desire when they come of age, risk falling into sodomy or fornication.

We need to pause a moment here to consider a passage that Alfred Coville quite rightly judged to be essential but on which he does not comment. Nicole Grevy-Pons does no more than refer to the parable of the sower as a possible source of inspiration for Saignet (Matt. 13:4). I think it useful to reproduce the passage here, as it contains images that were, somewhat later, adopted by the Italian preachers.

[13] On Saignet, see A. Coville, *La vie intellectuelle dans les domaines d'Anjou-Provence* (Paris, 1941), pp. 319–57; Grevy-Pons, *Célibat et nature*, pp. 59–73.

[14] 'Inter Nature filios minimus et ecclesie sancte Dei servus et fidelis'; cited in Grevy-Pons, *Célibat et nature*, p. 138.

Alii enim granum super lapidum non in terram emittent, alii seminatum granum submergunt, alii terram satam non irrigant neque colunt, sed avibus dimittunt, alii cum ad maturitatem pervenit metere negligunt ac presumunt vel ardent, alii in horreo putrido exponentes illud perdunt, alii bene custodiunt sed inde farinam non eliciunt, sed raro vel nunquam de tali grano ad bonum panem attingere possunt.

All the sex-related crimes are enumerated here: Saignet denounces those who spill their seed on stone and not in the earth (*coitus interruptus?* masturbation?); those who make the woman use abortifacients (*submergunt*); others who neither irrigate nor cultivate the seeded earth, but abandon the land to birds (fornicators who make use of common prostitutes, the birds being the other lovers); others who neglect to harvest or who harvest too soon (abortion) or who burn the grain (infanticide?); others who do not bother to take in the harvest of ripe grain (who abandon the mother and child?); others who throw out the grain shaken from the stalk (infanticide? masturbation?); others who leave their grain in a putrid granary and thus spoil it (sodomites); others who store their grain but fail to make flour of it, and even less, good bread (who fail to supervise the upbringing of their offspring).

Saignet is by no means an extremist; he is part of the right-wing forces in Nature's battle and certainly does not embrace all the positions expressed in the *Roman de la Rose*, since the scene he chooses for his combat of the virtues and the vices is the highly symbolic space of the Fountain of Vaucluse. Love comes to its rendez-vous with Nature accompanied not only by the delights of the flesh, but also by its principles of joy and virtuous full blossoming (Petrarch's fountain is quite obviously a source of life). Saignet makes it clear that he is fighting on the side not of fornication but of the sacrament of marriage: *fornicationem non, sed matrimonii sacramentum.*[15]

The work finds its place, in a long debate. But is it true, as Grevy-Pons states, that it is 'only a passing issue in a quarrel that seems never to have died down'? Assuredly not. The work appeared in 1418, at a moment when the plague had just struck anew; it takes up an idea advanced not only by heretical groups (the Lollards denounced celibacy as a source of immorality and sodomy) but also by members of the Catholic hierarchy at the councils of Constance and of Basel. Its point carried all the more forcefully since Christians could see the proliferation of priests and ecclesiastics in their decimated cities. Many observers denounced the

---

[15] Ibid., p. 144.

immorality of this proliferation, and some saw in it a clear warning of danger for the human species in such distressful times.[16]

Saignet's treatise should thus be taken as one element in a vast whole (the fight against sodomy, against masturbation as prelude or accompaniment to homosexuality, against celibacy, and so forth) that embraced a number of treatises and laws directed at the regeneration of mankind.

During this struggle to safeguard mankind, the guardians of orthodoxy adopted certain ideas that had hitherto been defended only by innovatory thinkers. Chancellor Gerson asks, in this regard, 'Does a married person who seeks only his pleasure in the carnal act sin mortally? I hold that he does not, if he has no desire to seek such enjoyment outside of marriage and if he maintains the honesty of marriage.'[17] Gerson is unequivocal: in an attempt to make marriage attractive to the young and to turn them away from practices he thought to be spreading dangerously, he legitimizes natural pleasures of the flesh sought in marriage but without a procreative end. He thus repeats the idea of Richard Middleton that was so revolutionary in his day (1275). This notion thus did not lie dormant two centuries without an echo, as Jean-Louis Flandrin once believed.[18] It was the adoption of this progressive line of thinking on the part of the 'centrists' of moral theology that explains the extremely liberal commentaries of fifteenth-century theologians Martin le Maître (1432–81) and Denis the Carthusian. For the latter, conjugal love was enriched by many

---

[16] In 1370 St Brigitte rose up against an archbishop who had declared that if he were pope he would give total liberty to clerics and priests to contract marriage, thinking that God would find this more agreeable than the dissolute life they were leading. At least they would avoid more serious sins. At the Council of Constance this idea was expressed frequently, even in the entourage of the council's president, cardinal Zabarella. Zabarella states that 'it would be better to permit priests to marry than to tolerate their concubinage'. (He does not breathe a word about fornication with prostitutes, however.) In Basel, the Bishop of Lubeck demanded the abolition of obligatory celibacy. Was this a 'repetitive quarrel that reappeared at every critical period of the Church' (Grevy-Pons, *Célibat et nature*, p. 53)? If you like, on the condition that we admit that the reiterations were particularly numerous and violent between 1370 and 1440 (see below on the propositions attacked by the 'anti-Rose' faction). We must also wait for the reign of Sixtus IV to find another treatise demanding the abolition of the rule of celibacy – that is, between 1471 and 1484, a logical moment, for the reformers vigorously attacked clerical mores, especially fornication and concubinage.

Recent studies show, what is more, that during this period of demographic lows (1350–1450), the number of tonsured clerics, priests and mendicant friars increased until it reached 2 to 7 per cent of the civilian population. Guillaume Saignet, who had been the royal judge at Nîmes before becoming Sénéchal of Beaucaire, must have been well aware of the population decline in his own district.

[17] Gerson, *Confessional*, in his *Oeuvres complètes*, vol. 7, p. 819.

[18] J.-L. Flandrin, *L'Eglise et le contrôle des naissances* (Paris, 1970), p. 65.

currents and included carnal love founded in 'the sensual delights' and in 'worldly consolations'.[19]

When moderate ecclesiastics rallied to these opinions, the consequences were of capital importance. Men close to the episcopate could proclaim at the councils of Constance and Basel, without causing a scandal, that ejaculation was a healthy occurrence, indispensable to sound physiological equilibrium. Thus there was implicit recognition that fornication was not only inevitable in unmarried men but necessary.[20]

Conjointly, an increasing number of voices were raised even in the bosom of the Church in favour of the marriage of priests, who were thought to be incapable of respecting their vow of chastity. The hierarchy resisted: however, since it was fully aware of the risks of celibacy and equally firm in its opposition to marriage for the clergy, concubinage, and unnatural acts, it admitted that clerical fornication with *public* prostitutes represented a lesser evil for ecclesiastical discipline.[21]

[19] Martin le Maître writes, 'is it not admissible to seek pleasure, not as an ultimate end but as an intermediate end; as a means, in sum, to reaching legitimate ends?' Flandrin believed that this thesis contradicted a millennial tradition and that it was to encounter general hostility for the next century.

However, Martin le Maître – who was writing in the 1460s, a high point in 'lay' morality – was merely repeating ideas admitted by theologians of the early fifteenth century, Jean Gerson, the most eminent among them, in particular. It was also at this time that Denis the Carthusian developed the theme of a conjugal love that was also spiritual, natural, sensual and carnal. Denis (1402–71) was, however, generally prone to severity, notably in his sermons.

In this same line of thought, St Antoninus of Florence, in the mid-fifteenth century, authorized married couples to indulge in caresses and in *amplexus reservatus* (intercourse with withdrawal before orgasm but without ejaculation) and 'came close to separating the sexual debt and claim of marriage from procreation' (Herlihy and Klapisch-Zuber, *The Tuscans*, p. 253).

Needless to say, these men, Gerson in particular (though not St Antoninus), condemn absolutely voluntary contraception or any form of abortion. Furthermore, beginning with the fifteenth century, one can find theologians who hold it illicit for a man to demand conjugal duty of a nursing wife, as it was feared that conception could be fatal to the nursing baby. 'No one had supported this opinion between the seventh century and the late fourteenth, and several theologians had even held the contrary opinion in the thirteenth and fourteenth centuries,' Jean-Louis Flandrin remarks (*Le sexe et l'Occident*, p. 195). This observation supports the theses developed here.

[20] Thus in 1440 the Polish physician and humanist Jan de Ludzisko, speaking in the name of the University of Krakow, harangued the ambassadors assembled at the Council of Basel. He demanded the abrogation of the rule of celibacy, using the physiological argument that it is good to expel the 'superfluities of seminal liquids' that the blood constantly produces and that irrigate all the body's members (cited in Grevy-Pons, *Célibat et nature*, pp. 53, 57 n. 21).

[21] It was concubinage that the reformers pursued so vigorously, not fornication with public prostitutes and their like. Olivier Maillard and Michel Menot remained discreet or hesitant on this point, as we have seen.

As a consequence, the bishops who held civil jurisdiction followed a policy comparable to that of the city governments, and they relaxed restraints, gradually eliminating the systems of social segregation that still afflicted public prostitutes.

After Gerson, theologians and moralists either used great discretion in their attacks in this domain or they denounced sexual desire in terms so general that their condemnation lost its thrust. It is apparently paradoxical, but in the long run totally logical, to hear Bernardino of Siena thunder against marriages 'pledged to the Devil' but say not a word about Siena's and Florence's recently opened municipal brothels.[22] The flamboyant preachers may have castigated female vanities and luxury with extreme violence, but they were a good deal less loquacious about prostitutes, saving their attacks for the procuresses. Furthermore, faithful to a set of priorities discernible as early as the thirteenth century, they devote entire sermons to pride and to avarice, but not to lasciviousness (in the male, at any event), provided that it is renounced in this world. The lustful man had time for contrition in his old age – unless of course he met a sudden or accidental death – whereas the miser was pictured in his final hour still refusing to disclose where he had hidden his treasure.[23]

This is why persons in positions of responsibility were able to build brothels or directly control or develop prostitution without coming into conflict with the clergy. After the late fourteenth century, the signori of the Great Council in Venice held that prostitution was necessary to public health, and when the Florentines created the tribunal of the *Onestà* in 1403, they charged it with encouraging public prostitution and 'from the start established a positive relation between [prostitution] and the system of civic values'.[24] In the cities of south-east France, prostitution worked not only to protect women of higher social status from the aggression of young males, but also to turn the latter away from practices leading to damnation. The same was true in Florence: lascivious women at liberty to reveal some of their charms were thought to encourage young men to natural 'efforts' and eventually to marriage – particularly youths of the lower strata, who had no access to servant girls or women slaves and were not wealthy enough to frequent prostitutes in private

---

[22] Trexler, 'La prostitution florentine', p. 1007 n. 5.

[23] According to the Bourgeois of Paris, Friar Richard hardly touched on the problem in his sermons in Paris and, as Michel Menot said at the beginning of the fifteenth century, 'Peccatum luxurie successive consumitur iuvenis cui vir et mulier qui tempore iuventutis vixerunt luxuriose desinunt hujusmodi opus; gulosus qui nunquan unam diem voluerit ienivare quando habebit mortem inter dentes non poterit comedere sed hec maledicta avaritia hominum prosequit usque ad tumulum et quando certus est de morte sua adhuc timet et recusat revelare thesaurum' (*Sermones quadragesimales*, sermon 3, 3rd Sunday of Lent, fol. 331.

[24] Trexler, 'La prostitution florentine', p. 984.

brothels. Thus they could do their apprenticeship for conjugal life through venal amours with beautiful foreigners.[25]

This policy was backed up by propaganda. Jacques Heers has rightly remarked[26] that it was around 1400 that the oversexed image of the fool, sketched out as early as the beginning of the fourteenth century, fully crystallized into his grey costume, ass's ears (the ass was an animal of proverbial vigour and lewdness), the erect cock's comb that became a yellow and green pointed hat decorated with jingle bells for the dance. Fools often led the 'joyous companies'. At this time, at least in a vast area stretching from the Mediterranean to Flanders, the joyous companies that recruited their members from the more affluent levels of society became institutionalized, and the major 'principalities', 'kingdoms' and 'abbeys' charged with the organization of festivities at Carnival, but also throughout the year, had the right to receive aid from the municipal governments. I now think that the sudden solicitude that the city magistrates showed these principalities and youth abbeys in great part originated in a desire to spread these recently admitted ideas. The exaltation of Nature by 'monks' of good family must have contributed to the regeneration of morality, marriage and the population.[27]

These shifts in attitude made for no radical or sudden changes in habits of thought or social behaviour, however. Around 1400 several things retarded the spread of the new morality for at least a generation.

First of all, it is clear that the debates in which both partisans and adversaries of 'naturalism' were so passionately involved were not restricted to scholars, nor to courtiers in search of a pleasurable pastime. The 'quarrel' was not about the Roman de la Rose; it was aimed at important tenets of social morality. The naturalist ideology overflowed the milieux that had traditionally been its own; the notables took it on and admitted Dame Venus into the same neighbourhood as their own town house. Male morality, with this backing, quickly bargained away female dignity and condemned virginity. It is hardly surprising, then, to find Christine de Pisan, Jean Gerson, and a handful of nostalgic or

---

[25] In the urban world of the later Middle Ages, no social activity was conceivable without preliminary apprenticeship. Conjugality required apprenticeship for men, first, because procreation was considered essentially if not exclusively the man's doing (see Zapperi, L'homme enceint, pp. 29, 97); secondly, for the governance of the conjugal family, which implied male initiative and experience.

[26] See J. Heers, Fêtes, jeux et joutes dans les sociétés d'Occident à la fin du Moyen-âge (Montreal and Paris, 1971), pp. 127ff.; J. Heers, Fêtes des fous et carnavals (Paris, 1983).

[27] See J. Rossiaud, 'Fraternités de jeunesse et niveaux de culture dans les villes du Sud Est à la fin du Moyen âge', Cahiers d'histoire, 1–2 (1976), pp. 67–102. The idea expressed here does not exclude my original hypothesis.

frivolous courtiers allied albeit temporarily for motives that were, obviously, quite different.[28]

In both her *Apologie au dieu d'amour* and her *Dit de la Rose* Christine de Pisan expressed the same thoughts as Marguerite Chasserat, Gontier Col's wife:

> Thus we innocent women will forever be cursed by men, who think themselves permitted everything and above the laws, while nothing is due us. They are carried away by a vagabond depravity and as for us, if we so much as turn aside our glance we are accused of adultery. We are not spouses and companions, but captives taken from the enemy. . . . On the streetcorners and in taverns and dishonest places whose name I will not mention they bite into us, tear us apart, curse us, accuse us, demanding of us often what they never offer to us. . . . They are iniquitous judges.[29]

Apart from a few women of the aristocracy and the patrician class, townswomen of the time were in no position to defend themselves. Christine de Pisan's protestations did not die without an echo, however. They earned the assent of many who remained faithful to the tradition of courtly love and they aroused the interest of princely circles. The great Court of Love instituted in February 1401 at the demand of the Dukes of Burgundy and Bourbon, in which it was forbidden to attack female honour and women judged amorous suits and distributed prizes, was a pretext for worldly entertainment. There were men there who, like Boucicaut, sincerely defended female honour and preferred to 'bow low to ten common prostitutes than to fail [to honour] a respectable woman'. Then again, there were others who attacked the ideas of Christine de Pisan in their writing or their comportment. Nevertheless, these princely courts of love of the 1400s were not as frivolous as Johan Huizinga believed.[30] They served as models for the patrician joyous abbeys, which, as we have seen, acquired a certain stability and instigated rituals that, fifty years later, were to some extent to permit women to escape the constraints imposed upon them.

Jean Gerson, of course, came over immediately to Christine de Pisan's point of view. He wrote his treatise against the *Roman de la Rose* in May 1402 and gave major sermons on the subject in December of that year.

---

[28] See appendix 1: The Evolution of Mores and Literary Translations: the Quarrel of the *Roman de la Rose*.

[29] See A. Coville, *Gontier et Pierre Col et l'humanisme en France au temps de Charles VI* (Paris, 1934), pp. 64–5.

[30] Huizinga speaks of the 'pompous and grave apparatus of a graceful amusement' in connection with the courts of love (*The Waning of the Middle Ages*, Anchor Books (Garden City, New York, 1934), p. 116.)

What seemed to him of prime importance was to condemn the 'veritable pestilence' of unbridled pleasure, and although he proposed to his own sisters an ideal of chastity, he conceded a good deal to other women. In June 1423, when he had retired to the monastery of the Celestines in Lyons, Gerson, out of a sense of duty and of discipline, took on the task of refuting Saignet's work. He did so clumsily,[31] since in his efforts to defend the rule of celibacy he advances arguments of convenience and the purity of the cult, but by implication he concedes that chastity had little worth when divorced from divine ends. This dialogue – the *Apologeticus pro celibatu ecclesiasticorum* – was intended to express the point of view of order and tradition. In spite of this, in both its hesitations and in what it leaves unsaid, it bears the marks of the new spirit. It was a weak bastion that provided little help for attacking the enemy.

The members of the secular hierarchy who defended Chastity, or rather Appearance (who embodied courtly love), had very little influence on the mass of townspeople. On the other hand, the same phenomena that incited some to rush to the aid of a dying Nature were interpreted by others as signs and portents of the end of the world. Even the least extremist of the mass preachers had no hesitation in enumerating recent divine punishments for execrable human conduct.

Fear of the Parousia grew: from the 1390s on, eschatalogical anxieties were spread everywhere by zealots of popular preaching. Jean de Varennes, Vincent Ferrier, Manfred of Verceil, Thomas Conette, Friar Richard and their imitators who ranged the western world between 1390 and 1430, preached before millions, and on their rostrums there appeared the disquieting silhouettes of the Messiah and the Four Horsemen of the Apocalypse. As late as 1431, the Dominican inquisitor who had come to Paris for a public justification of the execution of Joan of Arc took pains to specify to his auditors that the four demons in female form who had recently appeared were really four horsewomen in male dress.[32]

For those who held the world in contempt, new modes of behaviour were the source of all evils. Many of those who listened to Vincent

[31] Gerson had already tackled the problem in 1402 (see E. Hicks (ed.), *Le débat sur le Roman de la Rose*, Paris, 1977, pp. 184–5). Alfred Coville (*La vie intellectuelle*, pp. 350ff.) imputes the lack of conviction in Gerson's argument to his melancholy life and his disappointments. Nicole Grevy-Pons (*Célibat et nature*, p. 109) reiterates this notion. But Gerson had already presented somewhat qualified praise of chastity in 1402 (see appendix 1). For more than twenty years he had been torn between his allegiance to order and discipline and a sense of duty to defend celibacy, on the one hand, and a deep-seated scepticism concerning the clergy's respect of chastity and equally deep-seated 'naturalist' ideas, on the other.

[32] J. Delumeau, *La peur en Occident XIVe–XVIIIe siècles* (Paris, 1978), pp. 196–231; *Journal d'un Bourgeois de Paris*.

Ferrier, Friar Richard or Manfred had read or heard the passage from the old and austere *Speculum humanae salvationis* that declared:

> When charity and truth falter
> Pride, avarice and lasciviousness rule
> Every day God's anger rises against the world
> Because of these three scourges.

Thus God was portrayed as punishing cities, collectively, for the crimes committed in them. It was with the aim of imploring God for respite or of ransoming the sins of the world that the penitential movements were occasionally so violent. Those who took part in them were not, for the most part, 'apocalyptical fanatics'; they simply believed that divine wrath would be appeased by the offering of their blood.[33]

After 1400 activities of this sort were taken in hand by the Church, but the fact remains that mass preaching always involved not only collective acts of contrition and mortification, but a major rite of social purgation: the offering of symbols of indecency on a pyre bearing the arms of Satan.[34]

All the ceremonies of public penance were aimed at remedying public sins; it was seen as the only way to save innocent people from punishment. It is clear that apocalyptic preaching revived the idea of collective responsibility, and even the more moderate preachers, joining St Thomas on this point, concluded that although each sinner is punished for his or her own transgressions, there is nothing to prevent sinners from being struck down by a salutary punishment for someone else's sin and chastised with him if they had tolerated or given consent to the sin.[35] Thus God might punish the family, the neighbourhood, or the vast family of the city, and he might loose the *male mort* (foul and violent death) for the crimes or the backsliding of a few. This severely limited the consequences that were beginning to be drawn from the theology of

[33] N. R. Cohn, *The Pursuit of the Millennium: Revolutionary Millenarians and Mystical Anarchists of the Middle Ages* (rev. and expanded, New York and Oxford, 1970) insists perhaps too much on the millenarian nature of flagellants' processions and he occasionally accepts suspect testimony, that of those who tried and condemned the flagellants, among others.

[34] In Paris with Friar Richard, in the north of France with Thomas Conette, in Italy with Bernardino, etc.

[35] They refer to Exodus 20:5: 'I the Lord thy God am a jealous God, visiting the iniquity of the fathers upon the children unto the third and fourth generation of them that hate me'. Thomas Aquinas writes: 'Those who are near of kin are said to be punished, rather than outsiders, for the sins of others, both because the punishment of kindred overflows somewhat upon those who sinned, ... in so far as the child is the father's property, and because the examples and the punishments that occur in one's own household are more moving' (*Summa* Ia IIae quest. 87 art. 8).

purgatory.[36] Of course, the mendicant orders had long taught the means to a 'good death', and the 'Arts of Dying' unveiled the way to salvation through confidence in Christ's mercy, but a 'good death' – a natural death within the faith – demanded preparation. In death against Nature the sinner risked eternal damnation.

This is why even those whose social status enabled them to pay scant attention to the clergy, who were able to comprehend all the implications of the new devotion, and who had the means to make offerings or bequests were not exempt from anxiety when they obeyed Nature's call.[37]

Thus it was a simple matter for those who held to the older morality to rally the common people by railing at the 'debauchery from which all evils come'. The monks of Saint Denis were not alone in stigmatizing the occasions for wantonness and the dissolute dancing that were reported to have sullied the princely jousting matches in Saint Denis in 1389, and denunciations of the Court of Dame Venus were repeatedly and publicly made for moral and political ends.[38] This propaganda reached serious-minded bourgeois circles in Paris that offer a good many points of comparison with the Florentine milieux of 'civic humanism'. Matteo Palmieri, for example, said, speaking of the sexual act, 'in its end, the act of generation is necessary to the conservation of the human species, but in itself it is the most hideous thing imaginable.'[39] And when Guillaume Saignet engaged in combat against the celibacy of the clergy, he did his best to remain within the main stream of traditional teaching: 'Marriage is a good thing, for it permits the multiplication of men at the same time as it

[36] See below, pp. 121–2.

[37] Gaston Phoebus confided to God in his book of hours: 'I have an evil, Lord, even worse than all the other evils in me; in childhood, in adolescence, and in youth it always multiplied in me and still refuses to let me go. This evil, Lord, is delectation of the flesh, a tempest of lustfulness that in too many ways has wounded me and taken me from your grace. Most sweet and most benign God, I show myself before Your omnipotence still enflamed by filthy thoughts' (cited in Mollat, *Genèse de la France médiévale*, p. 208). It remains to be seen just to how great an extent he was indeed governed by *immondes cogitations* and *tempêtes de luxure*!

[38] Jean Juvenal des Ursins wrote: 'And it was common knowledge that the said jousts were accompanied by indecent things in the way of flirtations (*amourettes*), from which many evils have since come.' In the early fifteenth century the Augustinian monk, Jacobus Magnus, preached at the Hôtel Royal, declaring, 'the goddess Venus reigns at your court; drunkenness and debauchery serve as her suite and turn night into day amid the most dissolute dancing. People everywhere are talking of this disorderly conduct.' Monks who supported reforms and the Burgundian cause contributed much to publicizing such behaviour.

[39] M. Palmieri, *Della vita civile*, ed. F. Battaglia (Bologna, 1944), bk 4, cited in C. M. de la Roncière, P. Contamine and R. Delort, *L'Europe au Moyen âge, documents expliqués* (Paris, 1969–71), vol. 3, p. 228.

avoids fornication.'[40] Among these 'moderate naturalists' concern for conservation of the species were still mixed with older values. According to them, municipally-backed fornication (which they themselves organized) was to be reserved to the young and the unmarried. Although it preserved public welfare, it was imperfectly integrated into society. What is more, fear was still great, in those uncertain times, that prostitution would spread its 'gangrene' throughout the body social.

When intellectuals debated Nature in the 1300s, they appear as privileged figures in a world crushed by poverty.[41] The situation changed after 1350, but the social trend, which varied in its duration, its rhythms and its extent, led first to a decline of the great fortunes, in particular those based on landed estates. Crises, civil struggles and quarrels over inheritance led to a weakening of lineages, occasionally to a veritable slaughter among the patriciate. Those men who found themselves in greatly reduced straits experienced poverty as a dishonour. It was at the moment of the great turmoil in landed fortunes, between 1360 and 1390, that the expression *pauperes verecundi* first appeared in Lyons.[42]

If the rich had become poor, those with scanter resources had even less chance of coming out of the crises unscathed. Immediately after the plague wages shot up: master workers' nominal wages had doubled and day labourers' had increased by 150 per cent. The *anni mirabiles* were few everywhere in the West, however. From 1360–70 on, stagnation preceded a recession that was due not so much to the taxation of wages as it was to a large increase in reserves in the workforce, a rise in the price of foodstuffs, and, here and there, severe devaluations that encouraged economic activity but generated poverty. Nor should we forget the fiscal burden or the wheat shortages. In Tuscany, the years 1371–6 had been particularly harsh, indebtedness had grown, and only unmarried workers escaped serious hardship.[43] In France, exacerbated by war, the generation of disillusioned workers of 1380 was followed by the one of pauperized workers of 1420. Florence had a host of the wretchedly poor. Even for those who benefited from the economic conditions of the day – food distributors, men of law, servants to the princes or the municipalities – the road to social success was still founded on widespread poverty and had traps and snares. 'Fortune operated by chance,' the Bourgeois of Paris observes. He adds, 'the great hated one another, the middling were

---

[40] See Grevy-Pons, *Célibat et nature*, pp. 144ff.

[41] In French cities, at least. All the fiscal documents of the time show a concentration of wealth that worked to the detriment of the less fortunate, who often made up more than 60 per cent of taxable households (see Duby, *Histoire de la France urbaine*, pp. 410ff.).

[42] N. Gonthier, *Lyon et ses pauvres au Moyen âge (1350–1500)* (Lyons, 1978), pp. 73ff.

[43] C. M. de la Roncière, 'Pauvres et pauvreté à Florence au XIVe siècle', in *Etudes sur l'histoire de la pauvreté*, ed. M. Mollat (Paris, 1974), vol. 2, pp. 661–745.

overburdened with taxes, and the poorest found no means of earning a living.'[44] Only a very few could count themselves sheltered from misfortune.

This is why prostitution was still held to be odious by many of the more vulnerable townspeople. All were aware that pauperization and hard times were leading thousands of women to sell themselves or to live in dishonour. Only the wealthier citizens of the princely cities, or the cities that were enjoying a relative expansion could, without enormous scruples and between recurrences of the plague or waves of apocalyptic fervour, indulge in dalliance in the baths or the new municipal brothels.[45]

Around 1440, however, when the preachers of penitence had moved on and the plague returned less often, men who held civic responsibilities could once more advise their children and their domestics, echoing with almost no reservations the famous admonition of Genius: 'labour, barons, labour and repair your vineyards.' They could also assert that the brothel had been 'ordained for the service of the commonality'.[46] and they could sponsor the decoration of a bronze baptistry door on which the triumphant nude body of Eve surges forth into joy.[47]

[44] *Journal d'un Bourgeois de Paris.*

[45] 'At this time [Metz, 1419] many women went so cheaply that you could have four of them for one egg' (*La Chronique de Philippe de Vigneulles*, ed. C. Bruneau, facsim. ed. 4 vols, Metz, 1927–33, vol. 2, p. 175).

[46] A. Rigaudière, 'Saint-Flour à la fin du Moyen-âge', typewritten thesis, p. 518.

[47] Between 1425 and 1447 the citizens of Florence could contemplate Eve, newly created and held aloft by angels, on the new door of the baptistry of San Giovanni. Georges Duby devotes a passage of fine writing to this detail of Ghiberti's 'Doors of Paradise' in his *The Age of the Cathedrals: Art and Society, 980–1420*, trans. E. Levieux and B. Thompson (Chicago, 1981), p. 306. The fathers of the Florentine republic had approved the sketches after careful reflection and examination of all the figures in it. These were the same men who, only a few years before, had voted to open the public house of prostitution in the Chiasso de' Buoi, two steps from the baptistry.

8

The 'Cult of the Good Time' and the Theme of the Compassionate Christ

If men of the late fourteenth century trembled as they caressed the whores, as Georges Duby has said, their grandsons in the 1450s had a steadier hand. Young working men in Lyons, Burgundy or Provence tell us that they go to the bordello 'to have a good time' (*s'ébattre*), to 'stir up some fun' (*mener joie*), to 'take their pleasure'; they do so because 'nature moves them' or 'nature impels them'. These phrases spring spontaneously to their lips; they are not, as I once wrote, just a distant echo of learned works or shreds of naturist morality spread by young law clerks familiar with learned authors and with the goliardic tradition. They illustrate and reflect one of the central values in urban culture after the first decade of the 1400s, and they are the fruit of civic propaganda carried on by notables and heads of household.

That young men frequented the brothel and bathhouses seemed, in fact, proof of their normality. Not only their companions, but their parents as well egged them on to fornication: 'You give your sons money and permission to go to the brothel, to the bathhouses, and to the taverns', Olivier Maillard and Michel Menot thunder, but they do not seem really shocked, and they also reprimand young artisans for exhorting their friends to accompany them to the brothel of a Sunday. These two men preached, for the most part, in the north and the west of France, so we can conclude that social practices among the young (and the less young) were the same in the Île-de-France, the cities of Normandy and the Artois as they were in Dijon at the very end of the century.[1]

---

[1] See O. Maillard, *Sermones de adventu quadragesimales dominicales* (Lyons, Et. Gueygnard, 1503); O. Maillard, *Quadragesimale opus Parisius predicatum* (Paris, J. Petit,

Thus fathers provided money for wine and women, the tavern and the bawdy house. Phrases such as these crop up frequently in the sermons, and they show that this custom was quite obviously not limited to south-east France. Almost as frequently, the preachers harangue the fathers for going to the brothel and the tavern themselves.

Young men were given permission to use the services of the public prostitutes from about sixteen to eighteen years of age. We know little of the rules of social morality in later childhood (between twelve and sixteen years of age, for example), but there is good reason to believe that male masturbation was tolerated, and children were aware at an early age of parental 'familiarities' in the home. When they were old enough to frequent the brothel, they took their carnal pleasures with scarcely an afterthought, persuaded that God would forgive them, since lust was only a venial fault in a young man, a simple natural sin hardly likely to provoke the wrath of Jesus.[2]

As we have seen, the clientele of the Dijon brothel, in the fifteenth

---

1511); M. Menot, *Sermones quadragesimales ab ipso olim Turonis declamati* (Paris, Claude Chevallon, 1525); M. Menot, *Sermones quadragesimales Michaelis Menoti Parisius impulsi* (Paris, Claude Chevallon, 1519). The references that follow are to the Gueygnard edition of Maillard and the 1525 Chevallon edition of Menot.

'Vos domini burgenses datis eis cordam dampnationis eorum' (Maillard, *Serm. quadr.*, sermon 5, fol. 96); 'vos iuvenes . . . quando estis in lupanari' (Maillard, *Sermones de adventu*, sermon 23 fol. 51); 'vos patres qui dimittitis filios ire ad lupanaria et ad loca inhonesta' (ibid., sermon 22, fol. 49); 'you young artisans who on Sunday incite your companions to accompany you to the brothel' (ibid., sermon 4, fols 10 and 36); 'you give your sons money and freedom to go to the brothel, to the baths, and to the taverns' (Maillard, *Serm. quadr.*, fol. 66v); 'drunken husbands who strike your wives when you return from the brothel' (Maillard, *Sermones de adventu*, fol. 57), and so forth.

[2] Olivier Maillard reprimands young men who claimed that they would do penance later in life after taking their pleasures during their youth, for 'iuventutem difficilis ad transeundum' (*Serm. quadr.*, sermon 15, fol. 115; sermon 19, fol. 120). 'Iuventus est dura ad transeundum et iuventus excusat nos Deus miserebitur nostri propter fragilitatem nostram' (ibid., sermon 7, fol. 101); 'Nos summus iuvenes opportet transire et post modum in senectute concordabimus nos cum Deo' (*Sermones de adventu*, sermon 29, fol. 61).

Michel Menot repeats what he hears people say: lust is not a very infamous sin; young blades interested in seducing a girl say that simple fornication is not distasteful to God 'quia solutus cum soluta . . . Quia intervenit consensus amborum et quod est peccatum naturale et quod Deus non irrascitur inde . . . Audeo dicere quod hodie non est peccatum' (*Sermones quadragesimales*, 2nd sermon for the third Sunday of Lent, fol. 77).

God's assent seemed to some so sure that they portrayed Paradise as a place of more than spiritual delights. Menot reprimands those who wallow in voluptuous pleasures in this world and fully expect Paradise to be a continuation of their way of life. 'May malediction fall on their heads!' he exclaims (*Sermones quadragesimales . . . Parisius*, sermon 6, fol. 7). Was Menot exaggerating? This is what a Dijon weaver had to say in 1528 on his return from his daughter-in-law's funeral: 'She was a real goer [*avait besoigné*] in this world and is doing the same in the other world, for the angels of Paradise give it to women there' (AD Côte-d'Or, B 11 360/29). We can deduce from these words that women who have *bien besoigné* in this world are admitted to Paradise and that our Dijon weaver wasted no time on century at least, did not include youths under eighteen years of age, and in all probability the public prostitutes had orders to refuse underage youths. The savage night-time bands of roving youths had few members under eighteen. There was still tolerated and clandestine prostitution, of course, and the servant girls. I believe that male masturbation was allowed by social morality precisely because the moralists of the early fifteenth century turned their efforts to uprooting it, this 'sin' was difficult to control, the Church had long held it to be a minor transgression, and fathers had good reason to let their young children indulge in it. Female masturbation, on the other hand, seems to have been roundly condemned. In Dijon in 1486 a woman accused of having prostituted a very young girl whom she said she had kept as a servant claimed that when the girl was less than thirteen years old she had found her one day 'putting her fingers in her nature'. When the girl was asked why, she answered, 'to enlarge myself'. The mistress beat her and sent her packing. There does not seem to be any reason to doubt the truth of this incident. The girl's response seems to indicate a refusal to recognize masturbation, and it is likely that the mistress was not fooled by the reason given and that it was because her servant was masturbating that she dismissed her. Masturbation constituted proof of serious immorality in her line of reasoning.[3]

The young of the Dijon elite carried their privileges quite far, and young law clerks in festive dress, wearing a headdress in the form of a cock's comb, drew a face on a level with their genitals – a remote and excessive echo of the celebrated admonition, 'you have forgotten that you are men'. This behaviour proclaimed to all that the soul, the mind and the flesh were indissolubly united; it abolished any hierarchy between the higher and the lower body; it rehabilitated sexual pleasure, as did the phallephoric marchers in processions in Albi and other cities of south-west France.[4]

---

subtle arguments about the sex of angels: they are bisexual, for he is also sure that men will not lack partners in their heavenly abode.

These portrayals of a joyous afterworld are perhaps not anomalous, as attested by François Garin's descriptions (on which more below), where the Kingdom of Heaven is a place in which courtesy rules; a high city in which knights and their ladies, surrounded by troubadors, group around the angelic host. This palace of 'sovereign nobility' is not very far removed from the green pastures on which the elect were to dance, according to Martin Luther.

Sermons on resurrection of the flesh or on the glorious bodies of the just, admitted to Paradise at their prime and without their physical deformities, are related to this image. The Dijon weaver merely translates this teaching into its 'naturalist' and perhaps socially humbler form.

[3] See AD Côte-d'Or, B 11 360/15.

[4] See J. Rossiaud, 'Fraternités de jeunesse et niveaux de culture dans les villes du Sud Est à la fin du Moyen âge', Cahiers d'histoire, 1–2 (1976), p. 91. The procession illustrated had been organized by a 'king of love' elected by the law clerks.

Around 1460 a Lyons merchant named François Garin wrote an extremely lengthy *Complainte* in verse intended as a treatise on moral and social doctrine 'for the education of his children' (or at least using this aim as a pretext).[5] Garin had on several occasions been master of the changers' and drapers' guilds, and he had even been a member of Lyons' consulate in 1459. A victim of financial reverses and a man inclined to *contemptus mundi*, he is a faithful reflection of mental attitudes in a relatively conservative milieu attached to the traditions of good governance in the city and the family alike. He does not lack cultural baggage, but what he knows comes out of his grammar school years. As a bard of decent mediocrity with a penchant for proverbial maxims, François Garin shows us how a large portion of the bourgeoisie of Lyons viewed the world.

The entire second part of his work is a warning of the many dangers that lie in wait for young men. And what is his chief bit of advice, which his sons are to observe strictly?

> There is no law that can do ought
> Against the power of nature
> Dominating all creatures.[6]

The powers of the senses are superior to all human laws; all the same,

---

[5] *La complainte de François Garin, marchand de Lyon, 1460* (Lyons, 1978). This long poem (2316 lines) is the only known literary work from Lyons in the fifteenth century. It happens that the author was neither very cultivated nor very original: he had frequented the grammar school and knew Boethius, Cato, Alain Chartier and Jean de Meun, plus a few 'histories', the titles of which he does not reveal. Garin's mental framework was in all probability typical of the merchant bourgeoisie of Lyons. A banker (*changeur*), he states that he wrote his *Complainte* after a commercial failure that prompted him to warn his children of worldly perils. Garin's latterday editors exaggerate his discomfiture, however, and in particular the influence of financial setbacks on the nature of his work.

Historians of Lyons have brought little modification to what Jean Déniau had to say nearly fifty years ago: Garin was a good merchant, solidly egotistic, who preached mediocrity and prudence (see J. Déniau, *La commune de Lyon et la guerre bourguignonne, 1417–1435*, Lyons, 1934, pp. 155ff.). The editors of the excellent 1978 edition, who seem somewhat short on knowledge of the social history of the fifteenth century, go so far as to say (*Complainte*, p. 21) that this merchant was retransmitting 'prefabricated ideas faithfully borrowed from the common fund of naturalism'. They state, more generally, that they 'search in vain for constructive advice' (which is, on the contrary, given in abundance). In reality, *contemptus mundi* is merely a flimsy backdrop for Garin, who lacks neither verve nor irony. Finely sensitive to social and moral change, he welcomes the maxims of 'popular wisdom' into his pages. The *Complainte* cannot be reduced to a litany of past misfortunes; it is intended as a lesson by means of which his sons could make a success of their lives. The spirit of this poem does not seem to me very different – talent and culture apart – from that of some of the Tuscan *ricordanze*. I shall return to Garin to show that he knew how to amuse his readers, he followed the major events of his time, and he was not as pessimistic as he may seem.

[6] *Complainte*, vv. 1898–900.

marriage – as we might have expected – requires long reflection and must be contracted with the father's advice. In the meantime, young men should work, serve loyally, shun drunkenness and sloth, and not abandon themselves to a 'bestial life of concupiscence', enemy to all the virtues. Above all, they must never overindulge in the reading of tales or poems. Garin never uses the term *luxure* (lust, lasciviousness) in connection with the young; he does not say a word against prostitutes, the bathhouses or fornication. Giving in to sentimentality (tied to the dangers of reading) seems to him infinitely more dangerous ('the ardent desire of youth often turns to sadness') than a weakness for carnal delights.

The conclusion implicit in this long moral poem are clear and they echo those of the various 'mirrors': it is useless to attempt to tame the impulses of the flesh. One must live in accordance with 'Nature' and become a good husband – somewhat later in life – by staying away from the dangerous games of love. This is why too much reading is harmful. What do the *romans* relate and the poets sing of? Love.

Although François Garin dissuades his sons from learning 'new sciences' (v. 1089), he lingers longer over the harmfulness of *ystoyres et beaulx livres* (tales and beautiful books) (vv. 1185ff.) that inebriate the reader and will make him unhappy. The allusion to *l'amour fol* (love's madness) is quite clear here.

François Garin clearly suggests that brothels and the bathhouses entered into the proper functioning of social and familiar order. By their own lascivity, prostitutes satisfied the body's impulses; they made multiple and fleeting unions possible; in making love banal, they saved the young from sensual follies and from conflict with their parents. Garin states simply, like a good Lyonnais merchant, what Lorenzo Valla strove to prove in his *De voluptate*: that the brothel is preferable to the convent, the courtesans to chaste virgins.

But did the brothels fulfil the expectations of their organizers and their champions? In other words, did they function as Nature's workshops, as training grounds for the duties of marriage?

It would be naive to suggest that all city-dwellers everywhere in Western Europe had identical sexual behaviour patterns. I shall limit my remarks to the cities of south-east France, venturing a comment or two on the situation in Italy.

In Dijon in the mid-fifteenth century, things seem to have happened very simply, in the municipal brothel, in the bathhouses known to be places of prostitution, and in the streets at night, when bands of youths *chassaient la garce* (went whoring). We can find information on the sexuality of young males in three sorts of documentation: transcripts of the interrogations of rape victims, which are extremely precise when the girl was young or when she was a virgin; the descriptions of the 'scandals', 'lewd activities' and 'depravities' of procuresses or bathhouse managers given by 'scandalized' neighbours; details on the habits or the demands of clients of the municipal brothel occasionally (in fact exceptionally) furnished by the prostitutes.

Let us begin with an essential element: the vocabulary used by humble folk. The verbs used are *chevaucher, rouir, labourer, jouter* (to ride, steep, plough, or joust the prostitute).

These terms express the fundamental law of male morality – it is the man who commands and takes the initiative – and they define the position normally adopted in intercourse. Out of twelve precise descriptions of erotic scenes, the 'normal' position is used in ten cases. Let me give two examples: a client in a public brothel (a law clerk, thus a young man who belonged to the milieu of the 'joyous companies') lay one Sunday in 1451 with Jeanne de la Fontaine. 'He had his pleasure of her and kept her *under* him [emphasis added] about an hour; and he so wore her out and worked her so hard that she could no more, and she dropped down beside the bed because this working overdistressed her so.' For the second example, Jeanne Saignant is given as having been found *soubz un prebstre* (under a priest).[7]

Two cases in this group refer to 'abnormal' positions. In one, the amorous couple are standing (a position that the chance witnesses find scandalous). In the second (from a late period), the girl is lying on top of the man, but it may be because of her tender age – she was only twelve – that the carter who was 'working her' had chosen this position.[8]

Clearly, then, in France the position *mulier super virum* seems not to have been characteristic of venal amours. The figure of the 'erotic horse' had been denounced by theologians of the thirteenth century as hindering or even preventing conception. The position, forbidden by the Church, permitted sexual relations with a pregnant woman without endangering the foetus. When François Villon speaks of fat Margot astride him it is, he clarifies, 'so she would not spoil her fruit'. The position of the woman on top was quite possibly used with greater frequency by adulterous lovers or by concubines than by prostitutes and their clients.[9]

---

[7] AD Côte-d'Or, B 11 360/4 (22 May 1449 and 6 January 1450).

[8] Ibid., B 11 360/8 (1460) and B 11 360/31 (1533).

[9] See R. Zapperi, *L'homme enceint* (Paris, 1983), pp. 163ff. It is true that 'the phantasm of the woman astride haunts the theologians' dreams', and Zapperi is correct in drawing a comparison with the image of the witch riding her broomstick. This position was thought to upset the usual order of nature, to impede procreation, and so forth. In my opinion, women did not have the right to take the initiative, either in the bordello or in extramartial affairs. In theory, perhaps she did, but in the reality of practice she assuredly did not, at least in the city brothel. Both for 'technical' reasons (this position is more tiring for the woman and its contraceptive efficacy is dubious to say the least) and, above all, for 'moral' reasons, clients observed the necessary hierarchy between the sexes.

I think that if religious iconography and, on occasion, civic iconography beginning in the thirteenth century illustrate fornication by pic-
turing the woman astride the man, it is probably for propagandistic ends.
At the beginning of the century the Church still took a severe stand on
fornication and was attempting to persuade the mass of its flock to accept
the Lombard ideology of marriage. It was thought good tactics to
associate venal love, adulterous love and free love (hence prostitution and
concubinage) with a reversal of the hierarchy of the sexes as Providence
had established it. The 'erotic horse' was thus at first a 'battle horse' for
the clergy, who made use of it and of the young woman astride a he-goat,
another version of the theme, to condemn conduct contrary to Church
teachings and for that reason classified with unnatural sins.

In the chambers of the brothel or the bathhouse there is every
indication that Dijon youths carried on, as they proclaimed, 'according to
nature'. The mistress of the bathhouse in the parish of St Philibert was in
the habit of going into the rooms to contemplate these 'works of nature'.
Never does a woman raped by a band of young working men denounce
them for committing sodomitic acts, even when she is in an advanced
stage of pregnancy.[10] Nor does a prostitute in the city brothel ever
mention such demands on the part of her clients. There is one exception,
but it seems to confirm the rule. In 1453 Jeanne de la Fontaine, a
well-known boarder in the city house, gave testimony in favour of a
prostitute who had been beaten by a hosemaker named Guillaume
l'Enragé who seems to have deserved his name. Jeanne may well have had
her own reasons for accusing the man before Jean Rabustel, the city's
procureur. Guillaume headed a band of thugs whom we find implicated
in a number of cases of battery and rape. He of course frequented the
public brothel, coming there at night, and, Jeanne says, 'when he is there,
he causes a great disturbance and has company with the girls where he
wants to on them (où bon luy semble d'icelles) and does not pay them
what they deserve'. The allusion seems clear: Enragé demanded sodomy
of them and perhaps fellatio. Jeanne, who wanted him banned from the
house, accused him of serious practices that apparently transgressed
accepted custom.[11]

Unnatural acts were not unknown in Dijon, but they seem to have been
infrequent and disapproved or even refused by the public prostitutes.
Practice within the world of prostitution most probably reflects practice

---

To be sure, as Zapperi remarks, in depictions of adultery or fornication in miniatures, the
woman is always shown on top of the man. The position is even to be found in the early
fifteenth century in the frescoes of the Palazzo della Ragione in Padua, but I would be
willing to believe that there the iconographic motif is an archaism.

[10] For example, the chambermaid of a priest gives birth only a few days after she was the
victim of a rapist (AD Côte-d'Or, B 11 360/12, 4 January 1473).

[11] Ibid., B 11 360/5 (6 January 1453).

in other spheres as well. Heterosexual sodomy seems even more infrequent than bestiality, at least in the lower and middle strata of Dijon society.[12]

'Works of nature' did not preclude preliminaries of varying duration expressed by such terms as *expériences, gracieuses contenances*, and *tastement et esbattemens*. Jeanne Saignant had her girls undress so the guests could choose their companion judiciously, *en connaissance de corps*, and couples were often nude in the rooms. This nudity seemed to some almost scandalous.[13]

In other words, the places of public or tolerated prostitution seem not to have been dens of vice. François Villon describes prostitutes in the Paris streets 'showing their breasts in order to get more clients'. This is also the way things were in the society of the *fabliaux* and in the daily reality of the small provincial towns studied by R. Lavoye.[14]

In Manosque, Lavoye tells us, the sex acts involved in sexual crimes seem to be absolutely orthodox, although it is true that the cases present the testimony of the accused. There is no trace of homosexuality, perversion, bestiality or masturbation. It is the male who performs or imposes the foreplay that precedes the sex act. This is a curious orthodoxy, which results from the nature of the sources. The Dijon archives are less suspect, for there the accusers often denounce the 'depravity and scandals' they have chanced to witness or of which they have knowledge. As it happens, they reveal little fantasy, probably because the facts themselves, without being monotonous, seem to reflect a lack of imagination. All the Dijon court records give the same impression of an untroubled and hearty sexuality that corresponds to the eroticism of the collections of obscene riddles compiled in the mid-fifteenth century in Burgundian lands.[15] In the long run, Bernardino was

[12] There are two cases of bestiality: a vintner with a cow (ibid., B 11 360/8, 1463) and a foreign journeyman who committed the crime several times with a she-ass, a horse, a mare, and so forth (ibid., B 11 360/9, 1464).

[13] Ibid., B 11 360/8, p. 986, inquiry regarding Jeanne Saignant (1460).

[14] See R. Lavoye, 'Criminalité et sexualité à Manosque (vers 1240–vers 1340)', paper read in the seminar of G. Duby at Aix-en-Provence, 22 June 1977.

[15] See B. Roy, 'L'humour érotique au XVe siècle', in *L'Erotisme au Moyen âge* (Montreal, 1977), an analysis based on 575 riddles taken from four fifteenth-century anthologies. Certain of these riddles are older (from the eleventh century or even earlier), but the date of their compilation permits Roy to regard them as indications of fifteenth-century 'humour'. Out of 391 mentions of parts of the human body, 200 (or 51 per cent) concern sexual parts. Male genitalia receive more metaphoric (hence veiled) mentions than female, which is logical, given that the riddles were written by men. Roy notes that 'their interest is reduced to female genitalia, neglecting the breasts'. This may very well be so, but he is on less certain ground when he deduces from this that 'there is no transfer of the man's erotic interest to the breasts or to orality' because the breasts or the mouth were not considered 'shameful' parts of the body. Although anality is expressed preponderantly in the *devinettes*, it is far from always being connected to sexuality.

probably right when he advised Tuscans to follow the example of the peoples beyond the Alps, the French in particular, whom he thought unscathed by sodomy.[16]

Was the situation very different in the Italian cities? City-dwellers on the Italian peninsula, to be sure, had evaded the constraints of clerical morality earlier, and male homosexuality, at least in some circles, was a more than marginal phenomenon. But when Panormita, in the *Hermaphroditus* dedicated to Cosimo de' Medici, celebrates the triumphant obscenity of the Florentine bordello, what does he describe? Nudity, dancing and masturbation – and nothing more. It would be incorrect, then, to deduce from this virtuoso piece that sodomy frequently took place among the customers of the red-light district.[17]

What is more, the Florentine public prostitutes, their madams, procuresses and male 'protectors' were, until around 1470, overwhelmingly of foreign origin. They came from Flanders, from the Rhine valley, or from northern France.

According to a 1436 census, 36.6 per cent of Florentine prostitutes came from the Low Countries; 22.5 per cent were from Germany, 9.8 per cent from France, and 1.4 per cent from England. Thus foreigners from northern Europe accounted for 70.3 per cent of the population of the municipal brothel. Tuscan women almost never appear among them.[18] The ethnic characteristics of this group calls for two remarks.

1 As I have noted in connection with public brothels of the Rhône valley, a large proportion of the women came from northern lands (Artois, Picardy, Flanders, lower Rhine valley). These regions had been through sorely trying times, but it is also probable that the high proportion of northern women was due to Mediterranean men's taste for women physically different from the women they dealt with every day. Their reputation may also have entered into the picture, and several travellers, Pero Tafur or Hieronymus Münzer, for example, speak of the sensuality of Flemish women.

2 More important: this ethnic structure of *public* prostitution in Florence proves that the city fathers who organized the brothel in the early fifteenth century not only paid careful attention to the

---

[16] D. Herlihy and C. Klapisch-Zuber, *The Tuscans and their Families: A Study of the Florentine Catasto of 1427* (New Haven, Connecticut, 1985).

[17] 'Here you can say and do all that is obscene/Never will you suffer a refusal to make you blush/Here what you are able to, what you burn to do [you can do] to satiety' (cited in R. C. Trexler, 'La prostitution florentine au XVe siècle: patronages et clientèles', *Annales ESC* (1981), pp. 983–1015, esp. p. 1009. I shall attempt to explain the significance of this text below.

[18] Ibid., p. 986.

teachings of the Church, but saw to it that the *prostibulum* functioned smoothly and to the profit of Florentines. The clients ran no risk of committing an act of qualified fornication when the women were foreigners from outside Tuscany. Transgressing ties of spiritual parentage (the godparental relationship, for example) or committing incest were made impossible as well, and the city officials avoided subjecting local girls to the sin of lust. The prostitutes in private prostitution, who did not fall under the jurisdiction of the *Onestà*, may easily have had quite different geographical origins.

Were clients able to impose special demands on the women, supposing them to have had any? Wealthy Florentines who felt themselves less bound by religious prohibitions frequented other sorts of places, and it was the common people who used the public houses. It often happened that a Florentine prostitute was found wearing men's clothing and sentenced for doing so by the court of the *Onestà*. But female transvestitism did not necessarily constitute an invitation or an incitement to behaviour 'against nature'. Far from it. Men's dress enabled a prostitute to enter into 'honest' places unnoticed (as it enabled respectable young women to enter gambling establishments). It was a convenient disguise for the women and their accomplices. Furthermore, Richard Trexler found only one instance before the early sixteenth century (in 1474) of a man accused of acts 'against nature' with a prostitute, although in the later period the women did not hesitate to complain of their customers' demands. The situation was basically the same in Venice, where until 1470, according to Elisabeth Pavan, prostitutes, both public and private, were almost never – once again, there is one exception – involved in trials for sodomy.[19]

---

[19] In Dijon transvestitism was frequent among women who wanted to go to the baths run by Jeanne Saignant without being recognized. The citizens of Dijon attacking her speak of 'women and girls dressed and garbed in the guise and habit of clerics', 'the greatest women of estate of the city disguised', and so forth (AD Côte-d'Or, B 11 360/8, fols 15, 21, etc.).

Richard Trexler notes twenty-four cases of transvestitism among the ascertainable misdemeanours committed by Florentine city prostitutes ('La prostitution florentine', p. 998), and he concludes that 'transvestitism was just another form of "sodomy"' (ibid., p. 995). Fair enough, if he is speaking allegorically. Moreover, these cases of transvestitism occurred after 1476.

It does not seem to me – and this is my only aim in this commentary – that sodomitic acts were more widespread in relations with public prostitutes than they were between heterosexual couples in Tuscany. I am aware that St Antoninus of Florence invited the faithful not to assume the responsibility of bringing more children into the world than they could properly care for and that Leone Battista Alberti says that two sons (or two children?) are enough. But is this any reason why Florentine couples should have had to have recourse

In short, for two or three generations before the end of the fifteenth century the public brothel seems to have fulfilled the hopes that city governments in both Italy and France had placed in it. It was intended above all to be Nature's workshop.

Moreover, the presence of the municipal house in the centre of the city seemed to carry no dangers for the body social. I should note that in France – and the same seems to have been roughly true in the rest of Western Europe – the 1440s were years in which population reached its lowest point, a relative equilibrium existed between urban and rural wages, and competition was down in the hiring markets. It was after 1440 that the real wages of journeyman artisans and, even more, of day labourers reached a new peak: the nominal increases of the preceding thirty years had not been wiped out by the economic recovery and cereal prices reached their lowest point. In Tours in 1450 a master mason earned half again what his predecessor of 1380–1420 had earned, and day labourers in the city were in an even more favourable position. In the cities of the North – Lille, for example – day labourers in 1460 could purchase enough wheat for a year with twenty days' work, and the only truly poor among them were the heads of household with the most children. At the time, domestic servants in Provence ate white bread, and the barley with which their ancesters had had to be satisfied went to make dogmeal.[20] For all common labourers (at least, for the citizens of the city, who had the benefit of hiring priority in its workplaces), and for journeymen or apprentices who ate at the master's table, this new affluence was enhanced by better opportunities for professional advancement, since apprenticeship was not costly and positions as master craftsmen remained by and large available.

Prosperity was not evenly distributed, though. Newcomers with few skills, the widows of journeymen, or girls with no strong family ties continued to swell the ranks of the poor, which were contained, however, by the charitable institutions or by mutual assistance networks.

---

to contraceptive practices (*coitus interruptus* or 'unnatural acts') that they then put aside (and for what reason?) at the end of the fourteenth century? Is it because the preachers denounced sodomy? I shall explain below why their testimony seems to me unreliable.

I am not attempting to minimize the incidence of homosexuality or heterosexual sodomy; I simply believe that up to the end of the fifteenth century such practices were not widespread among humble folk. As Savonarola said, Florence's notoriety in this domain 'comes perhaps from the fact that you discuss and chatter so much among you about this vice. For perhaps it is not as widespread as people say' (cited in Trexler, 'La prostitution florentine', p. 1006).

[20] On the evolution of the standard of living, see G. Duby (gen. ed.), *Histoire de la France urbaine* (5 vols, Paris 1980–8), vol. 2, pp. 491ff.; on the food supply, see L. Stouff, *Ravitaillement et alimentation en Provence aux XIVe et XVe siècles* (Paris and The Hague, 1970), p. 47.

This 'golden age' for waged workers was brief, but for nearly a century it had slowly been spreading throughout the social strata (beginning with the better-off of the middle stratum, the *mediocres-majores*), and it lasted long enough (one generation in Paris or in Flanders, much longer in Montpellier, Lyons or Tours) to allow the new ways of living to take firm root. As business was good, there was work for all the people, and the mechanisms for assistance functioned efficiently, the widows or daughters of artisans seemed in no danger of falling into prostitution, and public prostitutes offered no threat of corruption to the body social. There were some prostitutes whose earnings were greater than domestic servants or washerwomen, but only a few among them – the courtesans of noble or high-placed men – could challenge 'decency' with impunity. They had only very recently emerged from the red-light district, and their social status was precarious. As for the others, the more numerous recruits in the battalions of public or tolerated prostitution, fines and arbitrary levies (the price they had to pay for the protection of the city or the neighbourhood) kept their rise within narrow limits, unless marriage or abandonment of the profession crowned their 'conversion' and rehabilitation.

Moreover, the body social had means of defence that had never been as numerous or as efficient. It was from the mid-fifteenth century on that professionally and geographically defined fraternal organizations proliferated, until they eventually formed a dense network. Their objectives went well beyond the defence of their interests. The brotherhoods were structures for bringing people together, but they also were intended to be institutions for harmony, for mutual assistance, and for settling conflicts within the group. Their statutes dictated models for social and cultural conduct. During the period of reconstruction and repopulation, it was the minor notables of every neighbourhood and every confraternity who determined attitudes, exalted labour, celebrated the life forces, recognized or rejected the conjugality of a couple new to the area, and traced the frontier between the licit and the illicit in matters pertaining to mores. In short, they set the tone and defined morality.[21]

They had no intention of letting others meddle in their affairs, what is more. The police? It intervened only on presentation of a complaint. The privilege accorded by Paul II to the citizens of Avignon serves as a good example: The officers of the civil court could not, from that moment on, enter a house in order to confirm cases of adultery, fornication or

---

[21] This was true of France, at least, but I might also observe that confraternal organizations, for so long kept in check by the Signoria in Florence, seemed to blossom before the mid-fifteenth century. It was around 1440 that we see the first *potenze* (powers) charged with organizing festivities and based in the immediate neighbourhood (see R. C. Trexler, *Public Life in Renaissance Florence*, New York, 1980, pp. 399ff.).

concubinage except on written complaint of the neighbours or of relatives of the persons involved. Thus adultery and concubinage were only considered public crimes if the neighbourhood thought them so![22]

This concession is obviously neither aberrant nor extraordinary. The Sovereign Pontiff ratified a *de facto* situation known to exist in other cities. The male membership of neighbourhood associations had the right, officially recognized, to define their own social practices; by the same token, if the law courts or the Church abandoned any serious control over the signs or the places of prostitution, it was not through the weakness or the acquiescence of any official or provost, but because they recognized the status quo.[23]

The 'joyous abbeys', an outgrowth of fraternal organizations, had the precise task in the sexual domain of exercising powers delegated by the group at large to discipline unruly young women or bad wives, deciding what form to give to a charivari, organizing burlesque cavalcades, and in general celebrating the life forces. Channelled into theatrical forms, these activities no longer endangered the peace of the neighbourhood and loudly proclaimed the group's values and collective rights.[24]

The Church conceded much to the 'customs of the place'. Its best energies were absorbed by other and urgent missions: reconstructing its temporal power, healing the wounds opened by the Schism and the confrontations that had taken place at the councils, and reconquering lands and souls won over to heresy. Many ecclesiastics tacitly accepted the recent changes in social morality. Others knew they were powerless to oppose laymen who considered priests or monks, in Georges Duby's term, 'administrators of the sacred' and who put their works into the hands of God or their systems of spiritual insurance.

Rigorist ecclesiastics who attempted to intervene in matters of morality to condemn evils were met with a prompt response in anti-clericalism and an untroubled insistence on a right to obscenity.

Anti-clericalism was not a new phenomenon, but that is no reason to underestimate its effects. It crops up, good-natured or acid-tongued, in street-corner gossip, songs, farces and *sotties*. Artisans in Dijon who were prone to taking potshots at parish priests or monks did not think twice before repeating a good story. Although making a priest swear 'by my virginity' always aroused laughter, joking about fornicating clergy was anything but hostile. It legitimized and even incited breaking the rule of

---

[22] P. Pansier, *Les courtisanes et la vie galante à Avignon du XIIIe au XVIIIe siècle*, Bibliothèque Calvet MS 5691, added p. 19, p. 354, citing AM Avignon, box 11, item 20.

[23] The phenomenon was universal; see Florence, Venice, Metz, Paris or Lyons (discussed above).

[24] It is apparently around the mid-fifteenth century that the rites of control borrow from the customs of the major abbeys (see Rossiaud, 'Fraternités de jeunesse', pp. 96ff.).

celibacy, and thus aided integration into the social community for the rectors or the chaplains whose conduct was in accord with the prevailing morality. Jean-Claude Aubailly assures us that criticism of the clergy

> was not destined to satirize a class comportment by emphasizing the inobservance of vows, in particular, the vow of chastity. The choice of a character of the sort [the *curé* or the friar] is better explained by the desire to find a type of trickster whose social function at first makes him seem above suspicion. Above all, he is type-cast as the lover in the vaudeville trio inherited from the *fabliau*.[25]

This remains to be seen. The cleric was unmarried, he belonged to a hierarchy, and he held power. Other sorts of lover – the student or the *damoiseau* (esquire), for example – could serve the purpose of comedy just as well. The testimony of the judicial sources and of François Garin concur to show that the authors of *fabliaux* and, later, of farces made this choice on the basis of social response.

As Marie-Thérèse Lorcin has rightly remarked,[26] the *fabliaux* portray two aspects of the priest. The first is reassuring: he is good-natured and 'just a little ridiculous'. This is the parish priest who minds his own business. The other face of the priest is disquieting and elusive, perhaps disreputable; he is a *beau parlier* (fast-talker) who enjoys the sensual aspects of life. But although in the *fabliaux* the lecherous *curé* is usually punished, and in ways that border on the sadistic, in farce he gets his own way and comes out of his amorous adventures with honour – a noticeable difference in treatment that Aubailly mentions but on which he fails to comment.

The explanation that I propose is this: The *fabliaux* evolved at a time when there was still a strong contrast between clerical and lay culture. Even in these earlier works, however, the satire is ambivalent: the good priest, by definition, does not meddle in the (conjugal) affairs of his parishioners. The other sort of priest, who represses and seduces, is cruelly beaten. The farces were composed two centuries later in a radically different intellectual context. Discreet or lecherous but moralizing priests still existed, but public opinion, turned 'naturalist' or, more generally, lay-oriented, no longer believed in the virtue of chastity, and they came out in favour of marriage for priests. So authors were not about to show a fornicating parish priest being beaten: it was all to the good if he behaved like this. He achieved his ends thanks to the dull wit of the

---

[25] J.-C. Aubailly, *Le théâtre médiéval profane et comique: La naissance d'un art* (Paris, 1975), p. 186.

[26] M.-T. Lorcin, *Façons de sentir et de penser: les Fabliaux français* (Paris, 1979), pp. 181ff.

cuckolded husband. The lesson was addressed primarily to complacent or slow-witted heads of household, since they were the butt of the joke.

In real life, hatred is discernible only regarding concubinary clergy or preaching friars, as the examples from Dijon show. In my opinion, these violent feelings were consciously encouraged after 1470 by the reformers (Olivier Maillard and Michel Menot, for example), and were perhaps less intense between 1430 and 1470. In one telling incident in 1434, a priest attached to the collegial church of St Paul in Lyons had his illegitimate son baptized publicly and even boasted about it, inviting passers-by to join him for a drink at the tavern, 'to the great scandal of all', as the *Actes capitulaires* of the church report. This seems questionable, as the act is scarcely comprehensible without the complicity of the parish. Other writings, on the other hand, were intentionally savage. They were aimed at concubinary clergy, who could on another occasion seduce someone's wife or daughter, or at *maistres frères foutards* and their *jacobines* (lecherous friars and their doxies), portrayed as having a ready store of money and as lascivious, hypocritical and – the last straw – pious moralizers.[27]

But let us leave the streets of Dijon and return to François Garin, who writes page after page warning his son against the wiles of the clergy. These people, he says, are not all bad, to be sure, but the good ones are few and far between. The moral is 'It is good to be wary of them all/Out of suspicion of the bad ones.'[28] Wild with lust (this is the only occurrence of the term *luxure* in the *Complainte*), they endanger marital stability and prove too attractive to women. As 'popular' wisdom put it: *sous umbre de la sainte messe, bonne femme devient prêtresse* (under cover of the holy mass, the good wife becomes the priest's woman). Even worse, by using the pretext of confession, Garin says, priests try to get women to talk

[27] See Déniau, *La commune de Lyon*, p. 160 and J. Rossiaud, 'Prostitution, sexualité, société dans les villes françaises au XVe siècle', *Communications* 35, 'Sexualités occidentales' (1982), p. 323.

[28] *Complainte*, vv. 953–4. For Garin, it was above all the clergy's fault that mores and the state of marriage were degenerating: 'those who shame women the most/defile the bed in which they lie' (ibid., vv. 1501–2). Priests, he claims, cannot live in chastity; most live a merry life; they should be married, and many who 'gnaw at' the people should be dismissed. The prince should become aware of all this, and 'should take such income/to relieve the people a little'.

The proverb that Garin cites is similar to another contemporary maxim: 'the good Christian woman is the one who dares not go to bed without the priest' (A. Montaiglon (ed.), *Recueil de poésies françoises des 15e et 16e siècles* (13 vols, Paris, 1855–78), n. 45).

Some citizens of Dijon, hostile to the moralizing claims of the mendicant orders, went as far as deliberate provocation (even in the middle of a period of reform). March 15 1523, several journeyman vintners erected a gallows in front of the Franciscan church of the Cordeliers, and that Sunday, during the sermon, they roasted a carp on it. The allusion needs no comment. (AD Côte-d'Or, B 11 360/27).

about their marital 'secrets', a domain into which they have no business venturing.

It is for reasons such as these that it would be imprudent to take too seriously the attacks on conjugal mores of certain preachers who hammered away at marriages 'consecrated to the devil' or berated couples 'plunged into a dismal ignorance like pigs in a trough of mud'. Were these allusions to contraceptive practices or unnatural acts? More simply, conjugal relations were pictured as consecrated to the devil because they were not reported to the confessor. Was it not Bernardino of Siena who said that sermons on marriage were 'as rare as a bird on the barrens'? The best of the bishops urged parish priests to extreme caution on these treacherous paths. When some of them inveighed against marital sex, they aimed at instilling a sense of guilt in couples who indulged in carefree intercourse and who had no intention of telling the *curé* about it.[29]

It seems evident to me that verbal obscenity was part and parcel of this social reaction to the threat of rigorist control. French humanists of the early fifteenth century had already demanded the right to speak in natural terms of natural matters, to call a spade a spade.[30] 'Blue' language and

[29] It is true that Bernardino denounces husbands who have 'unnatural' relations with their wives. He also cites the example of one beautiful young wife who remained a virgin for six years after her marriage, living in a most grave state of sin against nature. I could also cite the sermons of Fra Cherubino in which he denounces, in explicit terms, husbands who practise *coitus interruptus* (they 'sow their seed on stone and not in the earth'). But the very fact that Fra Cherubino repeats Bernardino's example of the lovely young bride sodomized for six years leads me to think that his discourse is out of touch with reality. Guillaume Saignet has already condemned 'those who sow their seed on stone' in nearly the same terms in his *Lamentatio*. And one hundred years earlier, the Pisan preacher, Giordano da Rivalto (d. 1311) said, '"out of 100 persons there was not one" who acted in marriage "according to nature, as God wishes"' (Herlihy and Klapisch-Zuber, *The Tuscans*, p. 252).

The refusal of the faithful to report on their sexual behaviour is explicit in one of Bernardino's sermons: 'Often a foolish woman will say to her husband, in order to seem modest, "the priest interrogated me on that disgusting thing, and he wanted to know what I do with you", and the foolish husband will be scandalized by the priest's question.' Bernardino adds, 'They have become like mute hounds' (see J.-L. Flandrin, *L'Eglise et le contrôle des naissances*, Paris, 1970, pp. 56, 60). Jean Gerson shows discretion in this domain: he advises women to confess their husband's sins only to a priest unacquainted with him. Gerson intended by this to mitigate hostile reactions that he knew to be widespread. Such reactions were not a recent phenomenon. Georges Duby notes the rancour of twelfth-century husbands toward directors of conscience who challenged the husband's power over his wife and who 'encourage their wives to be frigid' (G. Duby, *The Knight, the Lady, and the Priest*, trans. B. Bray, New York, 1984, p. 159). He further notes (ibid., p. 175) that at that time 'many ecclesiastics on the fringes of orthodoxy were always saying how unseemly it was for clerics to concern themselves with such essentially carnal matters'. This attitude must have persisted into the succeeding centuries. On the other hand, there were probably even more priests who did not care to venture into this dangerous domain in confession, either out of connivance or, more often, out of prudence.

[30] This problem is central to the literary dispute concerning the *Roman de la Rose*: see Appendix 1.

precise terms invade nearly all literary genres. Collections of obscene couplets or riddles circulated in Burgundy and in Flanders at the very time that Antoine de La Sale was recounting the complicated adventures of La Dame des Belles Cousins and that the *novellieri* in Italy – who delighted in slashing at priests and monks – were cultivating obscenity.

This movement had long been established in Italy, but it spread a good deal more widely in the fifteenth century. Following the example of Boccaccio, Martino Scarfi, Niccolò Carmignano and Poggio Bracciolini delighted in composing manuals of erotica inspired by classical antiquity. Panormita rejuvenated and added piquancy to the satire, and the *Hermaphroditus* figured in all major private libraries.

In France, the *Cent nouvelles nouvelles* and the *Quinze joies de mariage*, the works of Antoine de La Sale, and, even more, songs bear the mark of this spirit and this inclination for pornography. Even François Garin takes delight in recounting how in olden times, when the Sultan of Egypt cut off only the testicles of his harem guards, they still managed to *fourgonner* ('poke up the fire') with what remained.

> Which is why the law ordained
> To cut off everything and leave not a thing
> > (*Complainte*, vv. 1851–3)

This movement was so sweeping and this language seemed so nearly natural that somewhat later even the severest preachers – men such as Olivier Maillard and Michel Menot – made concessions to it.

So much for form. The works cited seem to me unequivocal. Antoine de La Sale was, after all, a judge, and he held the post of *viguier* in Arles. Thus he was perfectly familiar with the customs and the hierarchical structure of the youth abbeys. The *Histoire et plaisante chronique du petit Jehan de Saintré et de la jeune dame des Belles Cousines* was written in 1456. In it the young widow pushes the hero into extravagant adventures. To my knowledge, insufficient attention has been paid to the lesson given the lady by the physician, master Hue de Fiesol (*eu de folie* – born of a mad mother). The good doctor decides to send the lady to her native haunts to breathe the airs. The widow consents. She is welcomed into an abbey that she holds *in commendam* by Damp Abbé, a large, stalwart and hairy monk bursting with lusty sensuality, precursor to Rabelais's Friar Jean des Entommeurs. The lord abbot is amusing, agreeable and insistent, and the lady succumbs to his charms. Damp Abbé quite obviously represents the youth abbey, which recalls the laws of nature and acts in accordance with them. The adventures that follow (in particular, the grotesque combats between the monk and the lady) evoke the rites of those fraternal organizations, which accorded as much to Nature as to *Courtoisie* in the mid-fifteenth century. Antoine de La Sale's intention is clear and the moral of the story is not very favourable to the knight.

In the *Paradis de la reine Sybille*[31] we learn that anyone can enjoy the sulphurous pleasures of the kingdom of Sybille, the realm of all sensual delights, with impunity if he is wise enough to leave them in good time – in this case, after 330 days, since the adventure is set in the time-frame of the passage through the kingdom of the dead symbolic of life's pilgrimage and long believed to require one year. The function of the Church was to pardon: it is because the knight's pontifical absolution is delayed that he returns to the underground kingdom.

In other words, salacious or pornographic discourse was not invented by an aristocratic society dissatisfied with the codes of courtly love.[32] It expressed recent directions in a social morality in appearance dissociated from the control of priests. Men wanted to speak freely of the body and of pleasure. Some – Panormita, for example – invented refinements. There were few, however, who, like Poliziano, refused to be shocked by anything and attempted simply to record facts, believing that 'in this world, the only thing to do is to experiment and to live.'[33]

The young people whom Maillard or Menot encountered thought that their fornications were free of sin or involved only venial sin. For those who worried about their eternal salvation and still believed such acts sinful, there were new portrayals of the other world and recently established systems of spiritual insurance to restore their peace of mind.

Jacques Le Goff has recently shown that at the doctrinal level, Purgatory had triumphed at the turn of the thirteenth century.[34] This intermediary space represented hope; it liberated from Hell a good number of sinners who previously, through the nature or the gravity of their sins or by their estate alone, would have been seen as having very little chance of escape. Now the process of penitence, and thus the hope of salvation, became possible even beyond the passage of death. This

[31] *Paradis de la reine Sybille*, eds F. Mora Lebrun and D. Poirion (Paris, 1983).

[32] According to Roy, 'L'humour érotique'. Remarking that the collections of riddles also contain examples of highly sophisticated amorous casuistry, Roy explains (after Evans-Pritchard) that obscenity made its appearance when the code of courtesy was perceived as operating in a void, at which point it was necessary to liberate erotic tension verbally. 'It is at that moment that certain aristocratic milieux sought in children's folklore and in the discourse of the tavern and the bordello a store of terms that until then no one had thought to put into writing.' Roy also points out, however, that for some time the code of courtesy had coexisted peacefully with carnal pleasures, and that many writers – obscenity's militants – cared not a fig for *courtoisie*. The current of obscenity was not exclusively aristocratic, and so forth.

[33] Cited in Zapperi, *L'homme enceint*, p. 193.

[34] J. Le Goff, *The Birth of Purgatory*, trans. A. Goldhammer (Chicago, 1984), esp. pp. 289ff.

period of penitence was proportional to the sins committed on this earth, but whatever their gravity, deathbed contrition permitted escape from damnation and entry into this space of expectation and hope. Dying the 'good death' and salvation through Purgatory opened the door to living well. Le Goff rightly suggests that the system of Purgatory necessarily influenced behaviour in this world; it made it possible to see shades of good or bad in people's actions. Hence it facilitated an evolution in mores.[35]

These theoretical schemata were diffused during the thirteenth century, but only among the narrow cultural circles of the upper clergy. A good deal of time was needed before Purgatory was embraced by all levels of society and even the lowest ranks in the ecclesiastical hierarchy became aware of all the possibilities, temporal and spiritual, that it offered.[36]

We can observe this slow evolution in the Comtat Venaissin, now that Jacques Chiffoleau has provided us with a rigorous chronological analysis of that region.[37] Chiffoleau finds the first socially significant mentions of bequests to the souls in Purgatory in testaments of the laity only in the mid-fourteenth century, and only in the bigger cities. It was not until the next fifty years that the cult spread, socially and geographically, and not until 1450 that parishes in all towns and villages took up collections to this effect as part of their good works. At the time, both village assemblies and urban parishes, acting collectively, had masses said 'for the souls in Purgatory', who, as everyone was not persuaded, interceded in their turn for the salvation of the living.

In other words, it was not until the mid-fifteenth century that Purgatory became a widespread belief and 'received the material consecration of iconographic representation'.[38] In short, that it became part and parcel of humble folk's stock of images and thus fully fulfilled its spiritual and moral functions. At the same time, the ramification and diversification of the various confraternal networks of temporal and spiritual assistance, aided by increased prosperity, facilitated preparation for a 'good death'. In times of intense poverty, pestilence and war, not only was its opposite, *la male mort*, frequent, but *la bonne mort* was inaccessible to all but a few. It took money to organize the soul's passage to the next world. At the mid-century all could afford masses, both

[35] Ibid., p. 305.
[36] P. Chaunu, *Le temps des réformes* (Paris, 1975), pp. 192ff., 'La théologie du troisième lieu à travers l'image'. Chaunu rightly emphasizes the official stamp that the Council of Florence gave in 1439 to the immediate judgement of souls after death: 'the minute it was preached regularly, it was welcomed with enthusiasm by popular piety'.
[37] J. Chiffoleau, *La comptabilité de l'au-delà; les hommes, la mort et la religion dans la région d'Avignon à la fin du Moyen âge* (Rome, 1980), pp. 389ff.
[38] Ibid., p. 420.

'retail' and 'cumulative',[39] and confraternal services supplemented individually-funded masses. By this time, an occasional monk might well recall that extramarital acts of the flesh should be held as mortal sins, but city-dwellers knew they were not about to be condemned to Hell for that reason alone.

It would be mistaken, however, to reduce all widely-shared attitudes to one level. Many who had sung the praises of Nature in their youth became more serious-minded as they grew older. The city fathers, who organized the brothels and recruited the prostitutes, knew well that they were taking poor girls driven by violence or by poverty and subjecting them to the sin of lust. They might have asked themselves if they were not thus accomplices to public crimes. But they also knew that the city whose fortunes they safeguarded was producing nuns as well as whores. They themselves presided over this dual process. In order to marry some of their daughters, they made eternal virgins of others by inducing them to live in community as a lay nun in a béguinage, to serve in the hospitals, or to lead a life of prayer in the cloister. Two groups of women – the only women who had a collective identity – coexisted in any city worthy of the name: nuns and whores. If the prostitutes were crushed by the vice of lust, the nuns were equally crushed by the virtue of chastity, for everyone thought that virginity could be maintained only at the price of inhuman suffering.[40] This was why God, master of Nature and respectful of its laws, surely accords particular attention to the prayers of virgins. Thus these small communities were seen as capable of interceding for the remission of sins committed thanks to the efforts of the city fathers, who felt themselves responsible for the greater urban family much as each head of household did for those under his charge.

This close relationship between the domains of sin and intercession is not often expressed, but occasionally it becomes extremely clear. I offer two examples, the first from Lyons. Friar P. Mulat abandoned family business matters when he entered the order of the Prêcheurs in 1446, but he retained ownership of the baths of Sabliz, one of the city's larger centres of tolerated prostitution. Fortunately, the house made an annual offering of twelve oil lamps to the church of St Romain, where prayers were said on behalf of all the inhabitants of the parish. The second example comes from Sisteron, where public prostitutes arriving in the city had to pay an entry tax, a 'welcome', which went to the convent of the Poor Claires. The virgins cloistered there were invited to believe, as the

[39] Ibid.; M.-T. Lorcin, *Vivre et mourir en Lyonnais à la fin du Moyen âge* (Lyons 1981), pp. 135ff.

[40] Gerson had admitted earlier that chastity required heroism, and François Garin depicts cloistered virgins thus: 'The little birds sings in his cage/ever yearning for the wood;/woman curses all her kin/when thrust out of the world' (*Complainte*, vv. 1837–40).

notables of the city had taught them, that these fallen women thus in part protected their purity (God, the Virgin and St Claire aiding) from the carnal desire of men. Praying for the prostitutes was thus a duty, since the municipal government necessarily profited from such saving prayers.[41]

The longest-lasting and most explicit condemnation of fornication, however (in St Thomas, for example) was related to the social turmoil to which it led when the resulting offspring were abandoned or their upbringing was neglected. Here I would like to venture a hypothesis: the city fathers chose to believe that the public prostitutes and their clients were operating according to Nature, hence the rules that for several generations had been admitted in marriage were at this point applied to the boarders of the municipal brothel. Some of the women continued to practise their trade there when they became pregnant, and did so without reservation, given that the clergy had admitted that intercourse with a pregnant woman was not a mortal sin, as long as the life of the foetus was not endangered. It was for that reason that the *retro* position had been made licit.

It was widely held that public prostitutes were not very fertile, since sterility was thought to involve either black magic or the couple's sins, it was considered normal that fornicating couples could not conceive. Gerson repeats this old belief: 'women become barren and sterile when they are too abandoned to men'; 'all the ills that come by carnal sin outside marriage, like sterility and malediction . . .'; 'a woman bears children better by one man than by several'[42]

Furthermore, the image of the fecund woman with a well-rounded abdomen quite probably did not predominate in iconography for moral reasons alone: erotic painting and sculpture produced for the aristocracy portray woman in this fashion both in France and in the Burgundian lands until close to 1450. Thus the canons of beauty implicitly referred to the silhouette of a pregnant woman, and she could be the object of male desire just as easily as any other woman. The existence of pregnant prostitutes in the public brothel was thus normal on two counts, and it comforted the conscience of the organizers of municipal fornication.

Public prostitutes had long made use of contraceptives and abortifacients. The measures they took may have been harmful, but they were not secret, as they were known even outside the world of illicit sex. If this

---

[41] For Lyons, see AM Lyon, CC 3 (1446), fol. 319; for Sisteron, see P. Dufour (pseud. P. Lacroix), *Histoire de la prostitution chez tous les peuples du monde* (1861 edn in 8 vols, Brussels), vol. 4, pp. 143ff.

[42] See J. Gerson, *Oeuvres complètes*, ed. B. Glorieux (10 vols, Paris and New York, 1960–73), vol. 4, pp. 385, 859, 866. The fact remains, however, that city governments knew very well that it was far from true that public prostitutes were all sterile.

were not so, why should Olivier Maillard speak of such matters so openly? 'There are women and priests', he exclaims, 'who say that women who take drugs to expel the matter in their uterus before the soul is introduced into it do not sin mortally. *Ha ha!* What a grave sin that is!'[43]

Canons of female beauty seem to have diverged from canons of morality after that date, and fashions accentuating a slim waist appeared. These fashions were bitterly attacked by the preachers, not only because they threatened harm to the fruit of the woman's womb, but also because they offered an image of the female body that failed to reflect the imperatives of Christian morality. This hypothesis, which is founded on a restricted sampling of miniatures and paintings, merits a more thorough iconographic analysis than I have been able to undertake.

Thus the extremely ancient idea that abortion was nearly licit before the quickening of the foetus had not been eliminated by the attacks of 'natural' morality.[44] The idea seems to have been held commonly and even admitted officially: in Dijon in 1455, to take one example, a public prostitute confided to the supervisor of the public brothel that she was expecting a child. Soon after she was involved in a brawl (real? staged? invented?) during which she was struck and 'made [i.e. aborted] her child', no subsequent trace of whom can be found. The city's public prosecutor investigated the incident – a proof that infanticide was as severely punished inside the public house as elsewhere – with the aid of several midwives sworn in for the occasion. Their findings are given in great detail: since the girl was only eight to ten weeks pregnant, murder was not involved. Thus, by implication, the abortion was legitimized by

---

[43] Maillard, *Sermones de adventu*, sermon 48, fol. 26.

[44] In penitential literature, abortion before forty days after conception involves only one year of penitence or less, whereas after 'quickening', the penalty rises to three to ten years (see Flandrin, *L'Eglise et le contrôle des naissances*, pp. 43ff.). The author of the *Lumière az lais* states that giving blows that result in spontaneous abortion constitutes homicide only if the child was fully formed and 'already had a reasonable soul' (see C. V. Langlois, *La vie en France au Moyen-âge*, new rev. edn, 4 vols, Paris, 1926–9, vol. 4, p. 102). In the *fabliaux*, 'contraceptive procedures are not presented as the exclusive domain of venal women. It seems taken for granted that they make use of them. If prostitutes know how to avoid an inconvenient maternity, they have no monopoly on deadly secrets.' The tale of the 'knight who caused talk' speaks at length of a vaginal 'tampon', and in this instance a married woman is involved (see Lorcin, *Façons de sentir*, p. 55). Bernardino accuses Sienese women of recourse to abortion and to contraceptive methods: 'they destroy [children] in their bodies', and Fra Cherubino, a generation later, returns to the question (see Herlihy and Klapisch-Zuber, *The Tuscans*, p. 251). See also J. T. Noonan, *Contraception: A History of its Treatment by the Catholic Theologians and Canonists* (Cambridge, Massachusetts, 1965), pp. 268–70, 343, 347f. On this question the 'moderates' in moral theology held firm, even at the height of the battle with the 'naturalists'. See Gerson, who condemns practices aimed at destroying the foetus (potions, dances, tight clothing, blows, etc.) in several of his sermons.

the testimony of the midwives before the highest city court. The leeway accorded to abortion seems extraordinary, as does the late 'quickening'.[45]

Some prostitutes bore their children, though how many we cannot know. When the mother was unable to raise her child herself or to entrust it to a nurse, the city government had two possible solutions to the problem. It could encourage the mother to marry, or take over responsibility for her child. Scholars have insufficiently noted that the founding of hospitals and hospices specializing in newborn infants was contemporary with the institutionalization of prostitution. I obviously do not intend to suggest a direct relationship between the foundling hospital and the city brothel; I am simply remarking that municipal governments had taken into their charge both public morality and public assistance.[46] The founding of such specialized institutions can be explained by the new attention paid to life forces and to childhood, and to some extent the construction of the city brothel reflects corresponding preoccupations. The foundling home, an element of a certain importance in the natural and spiritual economy of the city, seemed open to the possibility of taking in children born of illicit relations, and hence of abolishing or mitigating the harmful consequences of institutionalized 'disorder'.

I am well aware that Richard Trexler has found no mention of infants admitted to the Florentine Hospital of the Innocenti whose mother was given as a public prostitute.[47] The question does not seem to me unanswerable, however: could not another qualification – domestic servant, for example – have been entered for the mother out of charity for the child?

[45] AD Côte-d'Or, B 11 360/6, item 712. The timespan granted to abortive procedures is extended here from 56 to 70 days. St Thomas, following Aristotle and St Augustine, situated quickening at the 40th day for a male and the 90th for a female, perhaps adding the 6 extra days granted by St Augustine (making it the 46th and the 96th days, respectively). It is thus probable that the Dijon midwives consciously split the difference as they argued the question and reckoned quickening as occurring on the 65th day (40 + 90 ÷ 2). They probably adopted the second formula, since it was said that a woman who aborts at less than 10 weeks from conception (70 days) does not commit infanticide. The substitution of the term *fruit* for *child* in many instances is perhaps deliberate.

[46] For Florence, see R. C. Trexler, 'Infanticide in Florence: New Sources and First Results', *History of Childhood Quarterly*, 1973–4, pp. 98–116, 259–84. The city government of Florence voted to create a foundling home in 1419, but the hospital of the Innocenti was not actually opened until 1445.

[47] Trexler, 'La prostitution florentine', p. 1013, n. 103. Trexler finds no prostitutes among those involved in cases of infanticide, adding that 'the documents seem to indicate that prostitutes made love without having children'. This leads him to overestimate both the incidence of relations 'against nature' (although he does recognize that public prostitutes are not accused of sodomitic acts until the end of the century) and the efficacy of contraceptive techniques.

Even if the population of the urban hospices included only a very limited number of children born of fornication, as a group they were numerous enough to provide symbolic reassurance to the city fathers.

Finally, social assistance included the foundation, supervision and support of institutions to aid repentant prostitutes. In Abbeville, Amiens, Lyons, Avignon and Paris, such institutions, although they took in only an infinitely small proportion of the cities' public prostitutes, were protected and partially financed by the city. Former prostitutes, officially charged to play the penitent, participated in the salvation of the city as a whole by their prayers and their good works and they offered the notables peace of soul at a bargain price.[48]

To reiterate: gravity was out of fashion for the better part of city-dwellers between 1440 and 1480. God did not frown on mankind's happiness; that the plague had subsided and the harvests were good was proof of His pleasure. It is quite precisely between 1435 and 1480 that the theme of the Last Judgement declined in painting, replaced by the theme of Calvary and of Christ crucified – a compassionate Christ with his Mother at his side.[49]

The end of the world was not going to occur tomorrow. If anyone happened to depict it, the Apocalypse took on a novel cast. François Garin, in his latter years, ended his *Complainte* with a description of the last days of the world. The antichrist reigns, and he subverts Christians. How? By generous distributions of the gold and silver from the treasuries of which he had become master. Is this a millennium of fortune or misfortune? Garin sees it as corruption by desire. But the Lamb appears in triumph without being preceded by horsemen or by massacrers. Only the antichrist is punished; the Parousia is no longer apocalyptic.[50]

Thus it is money that corrupts the world. In spite of his own virulent anti-clericalism, our Lyons magistrate faithfully transmits the principal

[48] See above.
[49] R. Genaille, *la peinture des anciens Pays-Bas, de Van Eyck à Breugel* (Paris, 1954), p. 90.
[50] *Complainte de François Garin*, vv 2027–110. The end is near and the signs are clear; St Peter's keys have rusted and will no longer open the gates to the heavenly palace. The antichrist sends for the great treasures hidden under the seas and the earth. He distributes them so widely that the majority of Christians are corrupted (providing the only serious note in this long eschatological account: 'and any who refuse to believe in him/will die a martyr to have glory'). But immediately after this God removes the antichrist and all the devils and throws them to the bottom of a deep pit. The Jews are confounded and the Saracens and pagans cry for mercy; they are baptized and saved.
    This depiction of the antichrist and the last days should perhaps be seen in relation to the myth of Jason and the Golden Fleece that the Duke of Burgundy had brought back into fashion. With a touch of humour, Garin draws a comparison between Charles the Bold and the antichrist: like the latter, the duke subverts the entire world by the display of his wealth. But this wink in the direction of monarchical power is not the essence of this 'vision'.

theme of the friars' teaching: the world is dominated by money, and money leads to corruption. 'There is nothing that money cannot do', Arnould Gréban, deploring the neglect of works of charity, has one of his characters exclaim. But was this a question of money, or was it rather the conviction that Christ's mercy has no limits and paid intercession could accomplish all things?

9

Urban Disorder and the Preaching Missions: Poverty, Penitence and the Mortification of the Flesh

For half a century material, social and spiritual conditions in the cities had made possible the full expansion of the moral system described in chapter 8. With the period from 1480 to 1500, certain stabilizing factors disappeared, after which collective sensibilities changed slowly, leading up to the rupture of the 1560s.

From the mid-fifteenth century, throngs of immigrants continued to grow, but between 1450 and 1480 cities were able to welcome and to assimilate without inordinate difficulty all who arrived at their gates. Towards the end of the century the urban economy proved less able to absorb all comers. The gap had widened between urban wages, kept relatively high artificially, and rural wages, affected by demographic growth, and this imbalance pushed impoverished peasants towards the cities. Since most of the immigrants were recruited from the ranks of the poor, municipal authorities reacted by requiring security deposits and setting up rights of entry or of citizenship. Cities were willing to accept the resident penniless, but they reserved the benefits of charitable institutions to long-established townsfolk and they did not hesitate to expel newcomers when the need arose.[1]

Urban wages soon felt the effects of this shift. Nominally stable, they were gradually eroded by a rise in the price of basic foodstuffs (which occurred at differing rates from one place to another). In Rouen, wages

[1] On the evolution of society, see G. Duby (gen. ed.), *Histoire de la France urbaine* (5 vols. Paris, 1980–3), vol. 2, pp. 494–9. Italy seems to have undergone difficulties just as great: see J. Delumeau, *L'Italie de Botticelli à Bonaparte* (Paris, 1972). For Florence, see R. C. Trexler, *Public Life in Renaissance Florence* (New York, 1980).

declined by a quarter during the last third of the century; in Paris, a day labourer's purchasing power, in terms of grain, was reduced by half. Urban waged workers, day labourers at the head of the list, were the first losers in the reconstruction that was coming to an end. During the first decade of the 1500s, a manual labourer in Tours or Lyons had to devote 70 to 80 per cent of his earnings to feeding his family – and poorly at that. He no longer had the option of placing one of his sons in the world of more highly skilled workers; at the same time, artisans found the road to becoming master craftsmen gradually closing. Social distances increased between the beneficiaries of economic prosperity and its victims, between the elite and the common people. At this point, social tensions increased: within the sphere of the 'mechanical arts', when trade guilds proliferated; between leaders in the arts and crafts and oligarchs hostile to 'monopolies'; between tight groups of merchants who lacked access to profitable business ventures and the few large-scale merchants who controlled the tax farms and municipal offices. All who were 'established' and protected by territorial or professional solidarities shared an increased suspicion of the outsider as a dangerous rival, and a mixture of hostility and fear towards paupers and vagabonds.

Prostitution gained recruits nearly everywhere. It was not the first time that urban societies had seen these sombre cycles that brought to their gates and their hiring markets troops of penniless wretches and knots of women reduced to selling themselves. This time, however, the proliferation of vagabond, idle, uprooted women seemed uncontrollable. Moreover, it was clear that this 'gangrene' was reaching not only into the ranks of foreign day labourers, but was also affecting families newly settled in the city and on occasion even native citizens when they sank into poverty. The 1520s were terrible years in Avignon, Lyons and all the cities of the Rhône valley, and families that everyone knew were reduced to beggary by the hundreds.

In Paris, after the foundation in 1490 of the Refuge des filles de Paris (later known as the Refuge des filles pénitentes) by the Cordelier, Jean Tisserand, poor girls took to prostitution in order to be admitted and others, at their parents' suggestion, attempted to gain entry by declaring that they had lived by prostitution. In 1500, to counter this practice, candidates were first examined by midwives, then required to swear that they had not sold themselves in order to be admitted. By a paradoxical inversion of priorities, these women were asked, not to show proof of their repentance, but of their past debauchery. They were required to show proof of immorality![2]

[2] J. Rossiaud, 'Prostitution, sexualité, société dans les villes françaises au XVe siècle', *Communications* 35 (1982), p. 81.

Thus parents prostituted their daughters out of poverty, for which Olivier Maillard and Michel Menot roundly berated them. Mothers turned procuress, and charitable hospices became a danger to general morality. In a world in which wealth and poverty existed side by side, prostitution threatened to become a second source of income for a good many day labourers' or artisans' families. In Florence during this same period, foreigners had completely disappeared from the ranks of public prostitution, displaced by Lombard women, and Tuscan and even Florentine girls were recruited for private houses.[3]

Far from protecting the family, the old moral system tended to corrupt it. The poor were not the only ones endangered, for prostitution now had a new face. Thanks to long-standing permissiveness on the part of city councils and regional powers, prostitutes now formed a complex society. Prostitutes who had left the official red-light districts or had never lived in them gained access to a dignity unknown to the ordinary public prostitute. As Elisabeth Pavan has noted, they became courtesans.[4] Unevenness in the distribution of literary sources has limited to Italy a social type that quite evidently was common in many other lands of Western Europe. In France before the 1470s, the courtesan is little more than a shadowy figure appearing only rarely. By the end of the century, however, all moralists are taking pains to denounce her and distinguish her from the prostitute of the public brothel.[5] The courtesan was richly

[3] R. C. Trexler, 'La prostitution florentine au XVe siècle: patronages et clientèles', *Annales ESC* (1981), p. 986. Northern Italy accounted for only 26.9 per cent of public prostitutes in Florence between 1451 and 1461; it furnished 77.6 per cent between 1481 and 1491, and 96.2 per cent between 1511 and 1521. At that date, public prostitution had become a purely Italian affair, as tolerated or 'clandestine' prostitution had probably been for some time.

In France, preachers frequently returned to the theme of procuration in the family: 'habemus multas mulieres vendentes filias suas, et sunt lene filiarum suarum et faciunt eis lucrare matrimonium ad penam et sudorem sui corporis', Olivier Maillard declares (*Sermones de adventu quadragesimales dominicales*, Lyons, Et. Gueygnard, 1503, sermon 16, fol. 37; sermon 20, fol. 45; sermon 22, fol. 49, and so forth).

In Dijon, a general police ordinance repeating the wording of earlier edicts specifies: 'because the greater part of the said male children [of poor families] beg and for not knowing a trade or wanting to learn one, put themselves to theft and bad living so that they are often arrested, flogged, have their ears cut off, or are banished or hung; and several girls of the abovementioned sort put themselves to whoring, going to the bordello, and living idly' (AM Dijon I 142).

[4] See E. Pavan, 'Police des moeurs, société et politique à Venise à la fin du Moyen âge', *Revue historique* 264 (1980), pp. 241–88. See also P. Larivaille, *La vie quotidienne des courtisanes en Italie au temps de la Renaissance* (Paris, 1975). In the late fifteenth century the term *courtisane* signified *meretrix honesta*; use of the term spread rapidly, making it possible even to speak of an 'honest courtesan'.

[5] B. Chevallier, *Les bonnes villes de France du XIVe au XVIe siècle* (Paris, 1982), p. 297 states, somewhat hastily in my opinion, that 'the *courtisane de luxe* did not exist in our

attired and she lived in a respectable street; she rarely frequented the baths, and did not even keep a private bordello but received her admirers and paid 'visits' to important personages. Accompanied by her serving women or, on occasion, followed by a matronly lady's maid on her way to a sermon or a respectable inn, nothing in her bearing set her apart from a woman of estate. She was untouched by the violence of the young because she enjoyed effective protection. At ease in the company of the gilded youth of the town, she could permit herself the luxury of choosing her 'associates'. Far from being 'common to all', she was mistress or concubine to only a few, confounding the comfortable categories of traditional typology. She was held to be infinitely more dangerous than other women of easy virtue, and on several counts. First, as Guillaume Coquillart, Olivier Maillard and Michel Menot insist, returning incessantly to the theme, because she demanded ever more money and fine clothing. She was the ruin of young men of good family and embodied a threat even worse than dicing.

It is true that the courtesan's lovers asked a good deal of her. When

---

French cities'. Let us say more simply that she had not yet acquired an historiographic existence. From the early fifteenth century – at a time when prostitution was still contested – traces can be found of her presence in Paris. Some women of easy virtue wore sumptuous attire, went walking carrying their book of hours, and had a serving woman (see B Geremek, *Les marginaux parisiens aux XIVe et XVe siècles*, trans. D. Beauvois, Paris 1976, p. 267 n. 76 (for 1422)).

In Dijon in 1450, Jeanne Saignant resembled a courtesan, though she was a procuress. Important personages protected her, the notables frequented her bathhouse; she was *belle parlière* (a good conversationalist); her friends were well-born women, and she chose her lovers. Jeanne Jumelle, a well-known prostitute in Rennes in the early 1500s, slept with the city's dignitaries (see J. P. Leguay, 'Les villes bretonnes à la fin du Moyen âge', typewritten thesis, Bordeaux, 1976, p. 896). Private bordellos for the rich existed in Dijon around 1480, and in 1483 a complaint was registered against procuresses for 'seducing several women and girls, some of estate, saying they had been so charged by great personages' (AD Côte-d'Or, B 11 360/14). The Sybille who frequented King Charles VIII in Lyons was assuredly not a fortune-teller (as stated in Y. Labande-Mailfert, *Charles VIII et son milieu: 1470–1498: La jeunesse au pouvoir*, Paris, 1975, p. 142), but provided the king with the same services as Antoine de La Sale's hellish queen. Not to mention La Gigonne or La Passefilon, beloved of Louis XI, who inspired fashions (a jig named 'la Gigonne' and a hair style 'à la Passefilon').

On several occasions Guillaume Coquillart, a poet and government official, criticizes 'these luxury prostitutes who demand ten écus a time and insist on dressing in silks and on wearing miniver furs' (*Oeuvres de G. Coquillart*, ed. J. J. Freeman (Geneva, 1975), vol. 1, p. 126). Michel Menot also speaks of such women, whom he continues to call, on principle, *meretrices*: 'oportebit meretricum habere numerum tunicarum et cum veniet estas oportet habere duplicatur de serico et veluto' (M. Menot, *Sermones quadragesimales*, fol. 77).

These are thus kept women and they cost their lovers a pretty penny. We have no record of a French Imperia or Tullia, and we need to keep in mind differences in cultural milieu. All things considered, however, the luxury prostitutes of French cities of the Renaissance period have more in common with courtesans than they have with the prostitute of the municipal brothel.

Francis I, King of France, dedicated a quatrain to the memory of Agnès Sorel, thus coming to the rescue of the tradition that Agnès had inspired the reconquest of the kingdom, and when, before him, J. Chartier and Monstrelet had dared suggest that Agnès's liaison with the King was innocent and that 'the love that the king showed her was only for the follies, the playful delights, the joyous sports of polished language that were in her', they were adding several strokes to the portrait of the cultivated, refined courtesan and her 'good conversation'. The quatrain attributed to Francis (and if he did not write it, he surely knew of it) runs thus:

> Gentle Agnes, your merits [have] more honour
> The cause being to recover France
> Than can work inside a cloister
> Closed a nun or a devout hermit.[6]

These lines have an aim beyond that of explaining their supposed author's behaviour or justifying the love-affairs of Charles VII. They are saying that love is a source of strength and victory; they are addressed to the ecclesiastics who recalled that the reconquest of the kingdom had been achieved thanks to the efforts of a virgin (and many preachers made a bigot of Joan of Arc).

Thus both nature and culture presided over trysts, and it was probably in this highest circle of prostitution that practices somewhat remote from 'nature' were deliberately practised. Other prostitutes took the courtesans as their model, and after 1475 cases of transvestitism were no longer exceptional in Florence, while after 1500 the public prostitutes in that city began to make formal complaints about their clients' behaviour. In Venice after 1470 prostitutes, both official and freelance – meretrici and puttane – were fairly frequently implicated in cases of sodomy. No doubt sexual deviance developed at that time for a good many other reasons, but the example set by the highest level of prostitutes was perhaps not totally extraneous to its relative popularization in the world of venal amours.[7]

---

[6] Cited in P. Dufour (pseud. P. Lacroix), *Histoire de la prostitution chez tous les peuples* ... (Brussels, 1861 edn), vol. 5, p. 181.

[7] In Venice it was only after 1480 that prostitutes had mannish haircuts 'in order to seduce men better'; only from the early sixteenth century do the archives show mention of sodomitic acts committed with prostitutes. By that time, 'sodomy was far more widespread than the closed framework of men's societies, and it tended to become an essential element in Venetian sexual life' (Pavan, 'Police des moeurs'). In contemporary Florence prostitutes registered similar complaints and transvestitism was frequent (Trexler, 'La prostitution florentine', p. 998).

In France there are convergent indications of a diffusion of sodomy, to that point rare. In Dijon in 1518 two Flemish journeymen force an apprentice over a period of several weeks, having told him that they were demonstrating 'how good it was to mount whores' (AD

Finally, the courtesans knew how to make love – that is, above all, how to talk about it. They were no longer scorned by the scions of city families, who could on occasion be smitten with a passion for one of them. Olivier Maillard states that 'lust gives rise to disappointment. You vile *meretrices*, you afflict your lovers with torments and passions.'[8] This means that the upper echelon of prostitutes was guilty of a social crime just as serious as sodomy: that of encouraging infatuations.

As it happens, in just this period the daughters and wives of reputable townsfolk were demanding their right to break through traditional constraints, take part in such sports, and talk of love.

The cynical spectacles and cruel games that had been the stock in trade of fifteenth-century youth abbeys disappeared fairly soon from bourgeois circles, and the magistrates' sons who usually served as their officers no longer limited the organizations' activities to public dances, cavalcades or charivaris. 'Abbeys' and 'principalities' now also served as the setting for more refined social activities, and they added 'of love', 'of joy' or 'of joyous folly' to their names to express the ideal that inspired their membership. Dances and parties were arranged for *dames et damoiselles*, and the ladies also attended jousts, banquets, parades and poetry contests. At such events the unmarried young men of the *grant jovent* – the fashionable young – tried their skill at amorous games and learned to be *beaux parliers* as they expressed their preferences. In this way the major abbeys helped to modify collective behaviour to the benefit of the wives and daughters of the entire magisterial class, and these women in turn had access to a perhaps necessary education in manners. As ornaments of the

---

Côte-d'Or, B 11 360/25). In 1527 a fourteen-year-old servant girl is sodomized by her master's father (ibid., B 11 360/29). In Lyons a man is condemned to be burned alive as a sodomist in 1524 (AM Lyon, BB 41, fol. 171); in Montbéliard in 1539 a *ribaud* was tortured, flogged and banished permanently for roaming the streets in female attire (Lacroix Dufour, *Histoire de la prostitution* vol. 4. p. 179). In Avignon Antoine d'Arena, who studied law at the university around 1520, exclaims, 'Avignon, Oh happy, sumptuous city, noble, holy and populous! If you have a taste for beautiful women and pretty girls, you will find them in plenty! If you prefer young men, a thousand are there to please you' ('Ad suos compagnones studiantes', cited in P. Pansier, *Les courtisanes et la vie galante à Avignon du XIIIe au XVIIIe siècle*, Bibliothèque Calvet MS 5691). The tone of this lyrical flight seems strongly influenced by contemporary Italian works, however.

Once again, the case of Dijon leads to the conclusion that sodomy was no more practised in brothels than it was elsewhere. We must distinguish between two phenomena: First, there were some who sought 'amorous experiments' and erotic refinements with courtesans or luxury prostitutes. The second is more tied to hard times, to pauperization in particular. It is possible that lovers took to acts hitherto rare with the aim of avoiding conception. In any event, this emergence of sodomy in French documentary sources seems a logical result of the freedom of comportment observable after 1440.

[8] 'Estis hic viles meretrices que datis tot tormenta tot passiones amatoribus vestris' (O. Maillard, *Serm. quadr.*, sermon 14, fol. 114).

city, such women figured in the 'histories' offered to the prince and they were expected to accompany the city government when it appeared as a body in public and to dance and converse with official visitors. They met together more frequently than women of other social strata, and they were used to being in the company of the men of their circle. They enjoyed a relative freedom of action, and could walk through the streets with their 'gallants' without prompting scandal in their circles. It was in this milieu of the bourgeois youth abbeys that women slowly took a more active role in festivities and began to gad about the streets at night masked and take part in serenades and organized games. In Bourg-Saint-Andéol not long after 1500 (perhaps following the example of Avignon) the ladies of good family, married and unmarried, went as far as electing the youth group's 'abbot', an office at one time charged by males with the correction of female mores.[9] Certainly the practices of many of the parish-based 'misrule' groups remained faithful to tradition. Still, the abbeys, which sat in judgement on the orthodoxy of marriages, also facilitated unions, made it possible for young men to serenade their beloved under her window, and helped the valets and servant girls lingering in the square outside the neighbourhood abbey to learn the language of the noble 'principalities'. Ritualization authorized the expression of sentiments and gave rise to a moral code of joy and, on occasion, of shared pleasures.

These 'dangerous' tendencies found expression in the works of women authors of the early sixteenth century. Before comparing love to a

---

[9] J. Rossiaud, 'Fraternités de jeunesse et niveaux de culture dans les villes du Sud Est à la fin du Moyen âge', *Cahiers d'histoire*, 1–2 (1976), pp. 98–100. It would be an easy task to cite a great number of examples. In Avignon in 1477, on the occasion of the entry of the legate (Charles de Bourbon), the young men and women of the best social circles of the city danced the *moresque des singes* for his pleasure (see P. Pansier, 'Les débuts du théâtre à Avignon', *Annales d'Avignon et du Comtat*, 1919, p. 11); in princely courts the ladies danced in mummers' plays and sang (see G. Arnaud d'Agnel, *Les comptes du roi René*, 3 vols, Paris, 1908–10, vol. 3, pp. 44, 45, 50, 64–6, etc.). Before the mid-sixteenth century *moresques* were normally danced by mixed groups.

David Herlihy and Christiane Klapisch-Zuber have remarked on the attention that Tuscan mothers of good family devoted to the proper education of their daughters for religious and sociable ends. Paul Larivaille (*La vie quotidienne*) observes that 'the fair sex' directed social gatherings. A good many treatises and poems of the early sixteenth century attest to this female leadership – Baldassare Castiglione's *Book of the Courtier* being the most famous of them. Larivaille's conclusion is that social intercourse increased, but women's true condition remained the same: there was an 'over-evaluation of the woman-object'. This may well be so, although I have some doubt concerning the first half of the sixteenth century (see below). In any event, an 'over-evaluation' was better, from the woman's viewpoint, than the previous state of affairs.

What is important is the reality of female participation in festivities, dances, mummers' plays, games and masquerades. Without it, it would be difficult to grasp why reform should have been preached.

contagious disease that spreads like the plague and drives its victims insane, some women dared to write that passion was a natural emotion. 'The most joyous thing in this world is to share youthful love with a partner who is one's equal,' confides Hélisenne de Crenne. She adds, 'Take the greatest care, dear Ladies, not to offend true love, not to scorn heaven's dispositions and perfectly ordered causes in accordance with which young persons are meant to experience the warmth of love at the proper age.'[10]

It is this sort of atmosphere that enables us to understand the blossoming of female love poetry after 1500. Some of the authors of these hymns to sensuality and passion – Louise Labé, for example, or Pernette du Guillet – were married women; many others – Claudine and Sibylle Scève, for instance – frequented literary circles close to the major youth abbeys of Lyons.

A certain number of these poetical works have vanished; those that have come down to us, few as they are, attest to 'pernicious innovations' that were infiltrating and subverting 'conjugal order'. Italian influences most certainly had a part in this movement, but it is because Petrarchism found such fertile soil among the cities' young people that it enjoyed such a vigorous growth.

Equality in love; shared pleasures and sentiments: these demands sprang, for the most part, from two mutually supportive ideological and moral models that had consequences which their champions at first refused to envisage. When notables in the early fifteenth century had sung the virtues of marriage, some, Matteo Palmieri, for one, founded these virtues in mutual attraction and saw the stability of the conjugal union as reinforcing sentiments born spontaneously at the meeting of two people. In short, Palmieri was speaking (and he was not alone in this) of natural love.[11]

In like manner, ecclesiastics (as early as Gerson) were more and more clearly interested in respecting the doctrine of consent in marriage, and they recognized the *créantailles* and comparable vows of engagement, granting the promised couple – too generously, in the opinion of many laypersons – the dissolution of their union when both parties requested it. Jean-Louis Flandrin has described the uses to which young people could put these 'promises of marriage', either to foil their families' plans or to

[10] Cited in E. Sullerot, *Women On Love: Eight Centuries of Feminine Writing*, trans. H. R. Lane (Garden City, New York, 1979), p. 83.

[11] 'At its start, the drawing together of the man and the woman is a spontaneous thing, as is the mutual love they bear one another' (M. Palmieri, *Della vita civile*, bk. 4, cited in C. M. de la Roncière, P. Contamine and R. Delort (eds), *L'Europe au Moyen âge, documents expliqués*, Paris, 1971, vol. 3, p. 228). The notion of natural love, so defined, returns frequently in fifteenth-century letters of remission.

satisfy their own fickle amorous desires.[12] The preachers called such devices *truphes* – deceptions, swindles – and thundered away at them. What follies were not committed 'in expectation of marriage'? Olivier Maillard complains that engaged couples had no compunctions about embracing, adopting immodest attitudes, and sleeping together before their wedding day.[13] In fact, in Dijon, couples 'engaged by the priest's hand' could live together as man and wife if they had the consent of the neighbours and of the priest who had witnessed their engagement.

This was true in the case of Jean Chalopin, a thirty-year-old pin-maker, and Madeleine Viste, twenty-six years of age, who had lived together for four months when we hear of them in 1540. The engagement ceremony had been conducted by Father P. Le Sely, priest of the church of St Michel, in the presence of neighbours and of Madeleine's brothers and sisters. Jean's parents did not attend the ceremony as they disapproved of the marriage. We know of this affair because it ended tragically: Madeleine was most probably denounced by Jean's parents and the Dijon court intervened *ex officio*. She had been married before and had been abandoned by her husband four years earlier. She had heard that he had been murdered, but she could produce no proof of his death.

This affair is interesting as it occurs in a period of reform of morals and

---

[12] 'Promises of marriage served young people who had matrimonial plans that differed from their parents.' All they needed to do was to promise marriage to their beloved before their parents had had them contract another engagement, then bring their case before the ecclesiastical court of the *Officialité*, which would then annul the second engagement and 'condemn' the lovers to solemnize the marriage they had initiated. The records of the *Officialité* of Troyes show that parents were powerless in the face of this strategy (see J. -L. Flandrin, *Le sexe et l'Occident*, Paris, 1981, pp. 61–95, 'Les créantailles troyennes').

In spite of the difficulties of interpretation, the evolution of the rituals of engagement and marriage seem to support these facts. Engagement – *fiançailles* – was an obligatory prelude to marriage in the late fifteenth century, but did not necessarily take place in the church or even in the presence of a priest. What was essential was that the rite be public. When they took place, these *fiançailles par main de prêtre* (engagement by the priest's hand), as was said in Dijon, were of an extreme simplicity, the priest simply acting as witness. More important, the active, spoken 'giving' of the spouses to one another at the moment of the marriage rites seems to have won support in a majority of dioceses in France during the fourteenth and fifteenth centuries. At the beginning of the sixteenth century, no formula was said by the priest in half of these dioceses: 'the *ego conjugo* tended to appear as a simple sacramental formula' (see J. B. Molin and P. Mutembé, *Le rituel du mariage en France du XIIe au XVIe siècle*, Paris, 1974). The early fifteenth century was most probably an important moment in the evolution of these rites.

[13] Olivier Maillard says: 'Does not the fiancé visiting his promised bride give her kisses? Does he not permit himself immodest acts? Do not carnal relations ensue? All this, to hear you talk, in expectation of marriage' (*Sermones de adventu*, sermon 38, fol. 76). 'Before, people did not lie together before their wedding day' (ibid., sermon 48, fol. 26); 'Young women, do not allow this to happen. Afterward they will appraise you and will treat you like whores' (ibid.).

repression of concubinage. Still, the priest and the neighbours had given their assent to the couple living together, considering their age and that Madeleine was not a virgin. Forty years earlier, when the movement for reform was still limited, situations like this (especially less complex ones) must have been frequent.[14]

We need to avoid oversimplifications: between the two extremes of clandestine marriage and arranged marriages, a broad range of compromises developed, and even though the couples' parents or brothers still contracted for the marriage, in the first half of the sixteenth century they often had to take personal preferences into account.

On the lower levels of society, among working men or servants, the absence of kin or family fortunes greatly facilitated 'natural' unions.[15] Among the gilded youth, frequent and ritualized meetings permitted young men to approach girls and make their choices within the social circle acceptable to their family's matrimonial strategies. In Lyons around 1520, it even appears that a girl from the merchant bourgeoisie could make her own choice, and that this was not considered unusual. This sort of alliance, nearly inconceivable fifty years earlier, involved a certain penalty (her dowry was halved), but not the disinheritance of the girl. It was to the advantage of the male heirs – her brothers – to let their sisters marry as they wished, since their own share of the estate would increase.

Michel Menot says, 'Ecce multe dantur hodie ut virgines in matrimonio que tamen sunt meretrices' (*Sermones quadragesimales . . . parisius* (Paris: Claude Chevallon, 1519)), 6th sermon after Ash Wednesday, fol. 27v; 'et dicimus hodie, dames, quomodo fient matrimonia hodie Turonis? Sicut capiuntur equi on trial. Ecce dicit una aliqui domine, faciatis eo modo quo Yultis in the name of marriage' (ibid., fol. 103).

The subject of engagement rituals invariably returns in Maillard's and Menot's sermons on mores. The doggedness they show in denouncing the custom and the details they give seem to show: (1) that engaged couples were free to meet, and their 'immodesties' – that is, public expression of their mutual desires – were admitted in Paris, Normandy, and the west of France at the very end of the fifteenth century, as they were in Champagne in the seventeenth century or in Savoy somewhat later; (2) under cover of 'promises of marriage' couples formed and broke up, sometimes with their parents' assent and the agreement of the court of the Officiality.

By implication, what the reformers protested was the laxity of those who promoted these rites: the Officiality was reduced to registering decisions taken by the laity. Coquillart could not have been very severe in his post of Official of Rheims. We might have a right to question, in this connection, whether the nearly total disappearance of the records of the courts of the Officiality does not come of a desire on the part of the Catholic Church of the Reformation period to have all traces disappear of what was considered in the sixteenth and seventeenth centuries a scandalous weakness.

I shall return in note 26 below to the question of the trustworthiness of Maillard and Menot as witnesses.

[14] See AD Côte-d'Or, 11 360/33.

[15] As revealed by the regimen of *communauté universelle* – common law marriage – often adopted by couples of humble origin.

This concession on the part of the family brought a happy solution to the problem of the estate, and the girl paid for her (relative) liberty of choice.[16]

How far-reaching was this demand for liberty? In Avignon, the movement was widespread enough to drive fathers to the extreme solution of debating family problems in the city council: 'In recent times, the young women of Avignon have had the audacity to marry without the knowledge and consent of their fathers and mothers, which is a thing marvellously scandalous and injurious to the whole of public welfare.'[17] These words were pronounced 16 June 1546, ten years before the famous edict of Henry II on 'disorderly' marriage among children of good family!

Were these girls who had tasted freedom still capable of respecting their marriage vows?[18] Women young and old had a ready answer for men and for censors who stigmatized their conduct: they were victims of unequal treatment. 'We have the world against us', they protest to Olivier Maillard, demanding the rights of youth – their own youth – just like young men.[19]

---

[16] I return to this example because it seems to me fundamental: Jeronyme Meynier, a noted river trader, drew up a will dated 11 September 1538 in which he bequeathed 450 *livres* of dowry to his daughter Louise, prohibiting her from marrying without her mother's and her older brother's consent, and adding that should she marry without consulting them, she would receive only 200 *livres tournois*, a dress, and an overdress. Meynier figured among the *apparents* of the city; he had been prior of the confraternity of St Nicholas and of the bourgeois confraternity of the Trinity, and one of his sons was deacon of the city church of St Nizier. Meynier was an authoritarian man of wisdom and mature years who had always been involved in public life. His provision in no way runs counter to the customs of the wealthy bourgeoisie into which he had managed to rise (see AD Rhône 3 E 3 759 fol. 337). What is clearly visible here is how the normal middle-class system of marriage is upset when the father dies, since his widow or his son no longer has authority equal to his own. Competing interests enter into the picture, of course. Girls who had lost their father thus were among the first to break through the defences of tradition. But the example they provided in its turn influenced fathers, who adopted a solution that would devour their daughter's pennies should her choice be inappropriate. In Lyons at least, bourgeois fathers seem to have been unwilling to pack off their daughters to a convent (see M.-T. Lorcin, *Vivre et mourir en lyonnais à la fin du Moyen âge*, Lyons, 1981, p. 81). François Garin has already told us why. There were also understanding or 'weak' parents: Olivier Maillard surely had them in mind when he asks (and answers affirmatively) whether a father can deprive his daughter of her dowry if she gives herself to lascivious living or otherwise proves ungrateful (O. Maillard, *Serm. quadr.*, sermon 24, fol. 52v. See also Maillard, *Sermones de adventu*, sermon 36, fol. 76; sermon 48, fol. 26).

[17] Pansier, *Les courtisanes*, p. 166 (citing AM Avignon, BB).

[18] The reformers either call such women whores or let it be understood that they are not much better, which explains why the preachers use the word *meretrix* in such a broad sense.

[19] 'Nos habemus mundum qui militat adversus nos et iuventutem quod est difficilis ad transeundum et iuvenes mulieres dicunt quod oportet complacere maritis', Maillard, *Serm.*

Some women went further, however, to answer like Mary Magdalene to her sister Martha in the *Passion* of Jehan Michel:

> You will hear nothing but reproaches
> And will never see honour
> In a man who speaks poorly.
> If you abhor my pleasurable actions
> Run no risks for me:
> Look out for yourself, my sister.[20]

When preachers or city governments in the beginning of the fifteenth century protested that they could no longer distinguish honest women from prostitutes, they were still speaking of a simple confusion of clothing and of outward signs. A century later, this confusion seems to have run deeper, and in fact did. How was one to recognize the daughters of the patriciate, who now went about in public with men, wore a tunic laced at the side to show the under blouse, and talked of love with their admirers? How could one tell them from the courtesans frequented by the notables and their sons, coddled mistresses who served as models for some young women, something that had never been true of the city's public prostitutes?

This is why the figure of the Magdalene took on so much importance at the time, both in preaching and in religious drama. Olivier Maillard, Michel Menot and Jehan Michel in his *Mystère de la Passion* (which was staged in Angers in 1486) describe in detail the worldly activities of Mary Magdalene and the pleasures to which she abandoned herself. When all three men portray her in identical fashion, it is not out of convenience or respect for literary tradition, but out of didactic necessity.

To outline briefly the 'metamorphosis' of the figure of the Magdalene, Jacobus de Varagine saw her as sinful and headed for eternal damnation

---

quadr., sermon 19, fol. 120. This admirable phrase (which is not Maillard's own) confirms the influence of the mixed-sex groups of youths discussed above. Thus girls picked up the young males' arguments, and now they claimed the rights of youth!

[20] Since I have been unable to consult Jehan Michel's *Passion* in its edition by O. Jodogne (Gembloux, 1959), I have used *S'ensuyt le mistere de la Passion Nostre Seigneur Jesucrist nouvellement corrigée avec les aditions faictes par très éloquent et scientifique Me. Jehan Michel, lequel mistère fut ioué à Angiers et dernièrement à Paris* (Paris, Philippe le Noir, 1532), fols 74, 74v. This rejoinder seems to me of capital importance. Historians of the theatre have often cited it as appropriate to their interests and found in it similarities with *Le Tartuffe*. Jehan Michel had no intention of writing a brilliant speech, however. Between 1480 and 1486 he reworked the text of Arnould Gréban's *Passion*, and when he inserted this phrase it was in order to criticize frequently-heard notions. This was why he took the risk of presenting such ideas to an audience of thousands in Angers. Mary Magdalene's answer to her sister is revealing of a particular way of thinking involving personal responsibility, spritual assurances (by means of money or through the confraternities), and confidence in Christ's mercy.

before her conversion. By her profligate life, this noble young woman had sullied her body and lost her honour and even her family name. When she goes to the house of Simon the Leper, she does not dare mingle with the righteous, and the Pharisees call her unclean.[21] This is also how Eustache Mercadé depicts her in his *Passion*. She is a courtesan, but she does not sell her favours: 'In love I said no to money/All I needed was a fine friend [bel amy].' However, she granted so much to her innumerable admirers that she speaks of herself as a public woman:

> To all I am abandoned,
> To each one; Have no fear,
> Here is my body, which I present
> To all who want to have it.[22]

While Arnould Gréban, in the mid-fifteenth century, avoided depicting Mary Magdalene's errors, a brief generation later Olivier Maillard deliberately insisted on her life of sin. Maillard takes his text from Luke 7: '. . . A woman in the city, which was a sinner', and he immediately sows doubts in his listeners' minds: 'Was this sinner's sin committed in her heart alone, or also in action? Some say, in fact, that she was a virgin in body and flesh but only corrupt in spirit.' He concludes that she satisfied her libidinous instincts without modesty or reserve, but he goes on to explain that she also 'ate well, drank well, and slept late'. When Maillard calls her 'abandoned to men', it is because 'their love for her is vain and depraved'.[23]

Michel Menot, some thirty years later, may well state that 'evil rumours circulated about her because of her wanton life', but he does not dwell on her 'abandonments of the flesh', emphasizing instead the banquets she attended and her gaming, dancing and walking the streets in the company of her admirers.

Maillard's 1470 sermon on the Magdalene, given in Nantes, provided the model for all subsequent portraits. Was she a public prostitute? A venal courtesan? Some said she was and others denied it; Maillard decides that she was not, for she was of very high birth and was accustomed to living in opulence. At the death of her father, when she was only fifteen or sixteen years of age, she began to lead a worldly life, gave herself free rein, and without leaving her own home sank into all the delights of this world. Jehan Michel has her sister Martha say: 'You give in to all sins; You draw nigh to all unworthy acts.' But what exactly were these *vilain*

---

[21] Jacobus de Varagine, *La légende dorée*, tr. K. B. M. Roze, intro. R. P. H. Savon (Paris, 1967), vol. 1. pp. 456ff.

[22] *La Passion d'Eustache Mercadé*, ed. J. M. Richard (Arras, 1893).

[23] Maillard's 1470 Nantes sermon on the Magdalene is given in A. de la Borderie, *Oeuvres françaises d'O. Maillard* (Nantes, 1897), p. 129.

faits that dishonoured her? Fine clothing and cosmetics, the pleasures of the table, frivolous songs and salacious talk, and above all gaming and dancing in the company of young men, with whom she then perhaps abandoned herself to lovemaking. Thus Mary Magdalene *took on the semblance* of a courtesan before she ultimately gave herself 'to the handsomest of gallants'.[24]

Thus the moralists quite cleverly maintained the ambiguity of Mary Magdalene, and the figure they presented was so enigmatic that the spectators watching the *Passion* in Angers or the crowds listening to Olivier Maillard or Michel Menot could imagine her either as a courtesan or as a spoiled young woman who led a free life[25] for lack of family guidance. As all authors emphasize, the absence of a father is what lay behind such a life of abandon.

Morals would only be reformed by restricting the courtesan, by bringing insubordinate daughters into line, and by re-establishing order in the family.

* * *

After 1470 men scandalized by the new code of morality and persuaded that souls were being led to perdition took on the regeneration of the world.[26] They were few at the outset and they realized that their task

[24] Such changes in the portrayal of Mary Magdalene evidently arose from shifts in the moral teachings of the Church. Mercadé's *Passion d'Arras* was written towards the beginning of the fifteenth century (it was played in Metz in 1437), at a moment when carnal pleasures were the subject of bitter debate. Thus Mercadé depicts Mary Magdalene's 'abandons' in full detail. Gréban's text (in part based on Mercadé's) was written around 1450. Here Mary Magdalene first appears at the house of Simon the Leper, and her sins are known only through her repentance. Gréban was writing in the 'liberal' atmosphere of his generation. Jehan Michel's scenes concerning Mary Magdalene begin with Martha's reproaches to her sister, whom she finds in the company of Perusine and Pasiphae, her serving women, playing with jewels she takes from her coffers. Michel is assailing the habits of the richest women of inherited wealth, who also enjoyed the greatest liberty, and whose behaviour was taken as a model by others in society.

[25] The iconography of the worldly pleasures of the Magdalene is in this spirit: she is shown leaving for the hunt, a falcon perched on her fist, hunting deer with merry companions, or, more frequently, dancing to the sound of flute and drum (see L. Réau, *Iconographie de l'art chrétien* (3 vols, Paris, 1955–9).

[26] This movement for reform really began with Jan Standonck's arrival in Paris in 1469. At that time Standonck (who became rector of the university in 1485) wrote: 'Those who love God must apply all their energies to forming a new generation composed of the very youngest, to whom they will inculcate, along with knowledge, the love of a life of mortification, so that, scorning the pleasures and the ambitions of worldly life . . . [and] fortified by an honest conscience and a literary culture in accord with the purity of their mores, they may become faithful workers with God for the salvation of the souls sinking into perdition' (cited in M. Mollat, *Genèse médiévale de la France moderne*, Paris, 1970,

p. 324). This manifesto of the Catholic Reformation inspired certain of the decisions of the Synods of Sens (1485) and Tours (1493), but above all it served as a model for the preachers' sermons and an encouragement for efforts for the instruction of the young.

Standonck asserts that the body social is corrupt and that the world can be saved only by innocent beings, duly formed by and habituated to mortification of the flesh. Savonarola's vision of things was not too different from this, nor was that of the learned Observants who sermonized throughout France at the time.

Olivier Maillard and Michel Menot were among these. Between 1470 and 1502 Maillard criss-crossed the better part of Western Europe, as did Menot (nicknamed 'the Golden Tongue') until his death in 1518. These two men, by far the leading preachers of their day, lent inspiration to the pulpit in France at least through the mid-sixteenth century. Their sermons, printed in Paris and Lyons, were extraordinarily widely read, and all less prominent preachers dipped into them for inspiration and examples.

We need to be careful not to misunderstand the spirit behind their catechetics. Augustin Renaudet (*Préréforme et humanisme à Paris pendant les premières guerres d'Italie, (1494–1517)*, Paris, 1916, pp. 163ff.) emphasizes Maillard's influence, but says almost nothing about his moral theology. He claims that Maillard was 'loved by the crowds for his rough manners and brutal frankness' and his 'vulgar, insulting and cynical' language. Undoubtedly Maillard, the 'outspoken monk' knew well, as did Menot, how to amuse an audience with his acid criticisms of the wealthy or the high clergy. This was a well-known and successful formula, but let us not confuse demagogues and democrats.

It would be kinder to ignore the highly unlikely conclusions of Pierre Darmon (*Mythologie de la femme dans l'ancienne France, XIVe–XIXe siècle*, Paris, 1983, pp. 74ff.), who is beguiled by the colourful language of the two men and goes so far as to write that they 'pronounced equivocal sermons before the still loutish (*mal dégrossies*) populations of the environs' (this in the church of St Jean en Grève in Paris!) and that they revelled in spicy anecdotes and stimulated the sexual ardours of their parish audiences.

It is hard to believe one's eyes. Either Darmon has not read these sermons or he has not understood them. The fact that in 1566 Henri Estienne found their language unseemly is hardly surprising. A Protestant reformer, Estienne was totally incapable of understanding the world in which Maillard and Menot had moved. It is even more astonishing that the author of a work denouncing the misogyny of traditional civilization in the West should transform into merry roisterers with a strong appreciation for women two men who contributed greatly to the social subjection of women.

H. Martin, on the other hand, comments on Maillard's sermon on the Magdalene (in *Les ordres mendiants en Bretagne*, Paris, 1975, pp. 330ff.), calling it an intimist sermon 'that aims at prompting individual action among the men, and above all the women, listening to it'. Martin sees the discourse as 'aimed in particular at the dominant strata' of society, and the vices mentioned as 'specifically noble and patrician' (the late morning rising that Maillard denounces is not, Martin writes, a sin the people could afford). In my opinion, this reflection is true only in part, and before affirming that this teaching is 'well adapted to the urban bourgeoisie, desirous above all of *honnêteté* and *bonne tenue*', we need to define what values we are talking about and to know more about the mores of this bourgeoisie that Maillard and Menot so admirably flattered or stigmatized, according to the circumstances.

How valid is the testimony of these preachers? Are their portraits caricatures? Were they the victims of their own phantasms? These men often preached to an audience of thousands. They could not expose themselves to public ridicule by stating, for example, that the banners of prostitution fluttered in every city street if the situation were radically different. One can see by perusing the notes that follow that every item in these friars' denunciations corresponded to a real situation or practice in society. The statements they attribute to

would be a long one and that they needed to take a good many precautions if they wanted to be understood. It is hardly surprising, then, to hear Olivier Maillard affirm that St Nicholas did not lead young women into a life of lasciviousness, that St Albert did not spend his days embracing young ladies, and that the Virgin did not scurry about soliciting invitations to banquets.[27]

Maillard, Menot and their kind avoided a direct attack on the male moral code. They denounced lust, of course, and they did their best to prove that, contrary to what many thought, fornication had never been held as licit. They took pains to associate lust with a host of other sins and to include fornicators in a more imposing flock of lost sheep (misers, blasphemers, gamblers, and so forth). On this level, then, they remained within the traditional purviews.[28]

What were the most important tasks at hand? In a Lenten sermon given in Tours, Menot first condemns punitive excommunications and then goes on to enumerate the criminals who, since their sin was mortal and public, must of necessity be condemned. They are the procuresses 'who have led twenty, thirty, or forty girls into perdition and have no other trade'; gallants 'who maintain *meretrices* with board and lodging (*à pain et à pot*)'; married men who keep a concubine; and all who abandon their legitimate spouse or are public adulterers or blasphemers.[29]

The preachers (and the other sermons follow this model) did not attack prostitution itself, but only the abuses to which it led. Women who were 'vile' – the poor, lepers or prostitutes – did not risk exclusion from the spiritual community. Moreover, since prostitution was a public function, prostitutes were rarely ridiculed or taken to task for their conduct. Although Olivier Maillard calls the brothels 'the most ignoble and filthy

---

young people or heads of family are by no means invented: I have found their like documented from the mouths of craftsmen or burghers. Similarly, the vision of the other world and of the stock of images of humbler folk are faithfully evoked.

The preachers occasionally may have been carried away by their own eloquence and exaggerated. Thus Maillard exclaims, 'There are more whores in Paris than there are honest women, and more usurers than merchants of probity' (*Sermones de adventu*, sermon 18. fol. 43v). But perhaps Maillard himself did not feel he was stretching the truth, since he includes under the category of *ribaudes* elegant women who permitted themselves laughter in public.

If the veracity of these preachers' testimony has been doubted, it is because their critics were insufficiently versed – on occasion, by choice – in urban mores of the 1470s. As we shall soon see, these men did their utmost to transform those mores.

[27] Maillard, *Sermones de adventu*, sermon 16, fol. 35v; sermon 26, fol. 56v; sermon 34, fol. 70.

[28] Menot, *Sermones quadragesimales ... parisius*, sermon 5, fol. 11v, is addressed to 'blasphematores lusores, luxuriosos'. Moreover, its accusations are so global that its impact is weakened for Paris 'id est dedita lubricitatis' (ibid., fol. 26).

[29] Ibid., fol. 100.

places there could be',[30] he does not demand they be closed. What they all clamour for is a clear delineation between the prostitutes and the temporal community through a revival of the old prohibitions modelled on the edicts of St Louis.[31] In the meantime, prostitution should not be advertised in the heart of the city, near schools and churches, and prostitutes must not join in the life of the neighbourhood or attend family festivities.

Professional procuresses, *maquerelles*, who led many innocent girls to damnation (women for whom procuration was only a sideline were, by implication, excluded from this public condemnation) were invited to partake of 'the infernal soup' along with the usurers.[32] These 'courtiers of love' were held responsible for transforming poor *meretrices* into courtesans or kept concubines who wore heavy gold neck chains and held open house in the dwellings of wealthy lovers or worldly ecclesiastics. It was to the procuresses that mothers sold their daughters to earn their *maritagium* with their bodies.

Fornication by a male, even by a married man, is conspicuously absent from this list of public crimes. Although Michel Menot specifies that the man's transgression is fully as serious as the woman's when he breaks his marriage vows (a proposition that he contradicts immediately), he sees only public adultery as deserving of excommunication. This condemnation seems not to be aimed at the husband whose fornication remains discreet – the client of the bordellos or the bathhouses; it is unequivocal only when a man keeps a concubine or abandons his hearth.

Obviously, the denunciation of the concubinage was aimed at ecclesiastics as well. When they kept a prostitute *à pain et à pot* they were guilty of sacrilege as well as public adultery. If they fornicated in the brothel, however, it was up to God to judge them. Olivier Maillard limits himself to pointing out to priests that the women keeping their watch at the foot of the cross were not prostitutes, and that the custom adopted by young priests of dancing with 'prostitutes' following their first celebration of mass made little sense.[33] Priestly concubinage, on the other hand,

---

[30] See Maillard, *Serm. quadr.*, sermon 28, fol. 60; sermon 2, fol. 92; La Borderie, *Oeuvres françaises d'O. Maillard*, p. 129.

[31] As we have seen, Maillard proposed St Louis as a model for the young Charles VIII; Anne of France presented a life of St Louis to the king in 1488 (Labande-Mailfert, *Charles VIII*, p. 163), which was said to have encouraged in the young monarch an enthusiasm for crusades and a sense of justice. This does not mean that he gave up the ladies of easy virtue, however.

[32] The expression comes from Maillard, *Serm. quadr.*, sermon 25, fol. 54v; sermon 24, fol. 130. Similar attacks can be found in sermons in Florence (see Trexler, 'La prostitution florentine').

[33] Maillard is probably addressing his remarks to the clergy when he exlaims, 'vos domini qui vaditis ad lupanar multi sunt sapientes et sunt opera eorum ante Deum et nescit aliqui

was abominable. It led to the discomfiture of the Church and the depletion of its wealth. It was dangerous. Was not the antichrist to be born of such a sacrilegious and accursed union? Their counsel concerning all these 'ecclesiastical whores' was clear: 'You must not tolerate them, but expel them from your houses, and today is even better than tomorrow.' Was this a call to action to the crowd? At the very least it was an appeal to the Lords of Justice of the city and the city fathers, whom the preachers upbraided for their laxity and on whom they called to take rigorous action.[34]

A few cities in fact did impose the wearing of the old distinctive signs (as in Amiens in 1485) as soon as the first calamities struck. Others (Metz, for example) attempted to contain prostitutes within the red-light district. When a city had given up all control of prostitution and no longer kept a *prostibulum publicum*, the city fathers took care to rent or buy appropriate space, this time in order to oblige the women to live there.[35]

---

utrum erit salvatus vel damnatus' (*Serm. quadr.*, sermon 17, fol. 118). See also ibid., sermon 17, fol. 118; sermon 2, fol. 92; sermon 30, fol. 63; sermon 8, fol. 102; *Sermones de adventu*, sermon 15, fol. 33v; sermon 16, fol. 35v, and so on.

[34] Menot in Tours, *Sermones quadragesimales*, sermon 2, fol. 75v; Maillard. *Serm. quadr.*, sermon 30, fol. 64.

[35] After a long period of silence (the ephemeral episode of 1458 excluded), municipalities and other juridical bodies once more took up arms in the battle against private prostitution. The first measures in the Rhône valley date from the highly calamitous years 1473–7 (on which, see below), but such measures proliferated only after the grave crisis of 1481–3. In Paris in 1481 the provost forbade burghers from lodging public prostitutes on the 'good streets' and ordered the women to take themselves to the brothels (see Du Cange *Glossarium*, s.v. 'gyneceum'). In Geneva during the same year, pimps were systematically pursued, as they were in 1486 and 1493 (H. Naef, *Les origines de la Réforme à Genève*, Geneva, 1936, pp. 219ff.). Amiens in 1485 passed laws forbidding inviting 'public women' to banquets and imposing the wearing of the red *aiguillette* (ibid., p. 101, n. 26). In Metz during the same year a decree ordered 'all abandoned women and girls to go to the brothels' *Chronique de Philippe de Vigneulles*, ed. C. Bruneau, 4 vols, Metz, 1927–33, vol. 3. p. 117). In Lyons in 1496 prostitutes were chased out of the district of Notre Dame de rue Neuve (AM Lyon BB 24, fol. 23), and so forth.

There is documentation on the creation of brothels in order to gather in prostitutes in Malaucène in 1473; in Cavaillon in 1477 (see Pansier, *Les courtisanes*, p. 67); in Pernes in 1484 (AM Pernes BB 62, fol. 43); in Valence in 1507 (AM Valence BB 3 fol. 231); in Grenoble in 1545 (J. A. U. Chevalier, *Oeuvres Historiques*, fol. 1, *Annales de la ville de Romans* (Valence, 1897), p. 69). Prostitution was limited to the red-light district in Arles in 1493 and again in 1497 (AM Arles BB 6 fols 106 and 171) and in Tarascon (AM Tarascon BB 12 fol. 226v).

All these regulations insist on vestimentary prohibitions, since too rich an attire on the part of prostitutes 'is apt to lead into error and is susceptible of setting married women and young girls a pernicious example' (Amiens).

False trades as a cover for 'dishonest' activities were actively pursued: in Bruges in 1503, women under twenty-five years of age were prohibited from selling fruit or flowers in the streets (R. Toussaert, *Le sentiment religieux en Flandre à la fin du Moyen-Age* (Paris, 1963), p. 374).

There was increased concern over the brawls and beatings that occurred in the bathhouses, which the city then decided to close or to move. Above all, there was a concerted effort to get rid of courtesans who were priests' concubines.[36]

This repression was slow, spasmodic, tied to the chronology of both calamities and preaching missions, and – in a mirror image of the period of liberalization – interrupted by lulls. As years went by, however, rigour increased, and when religious troubles were added to natural disasters, the municipalities came to the point of officially proscribing prostitution and expelling prostitutes from city territory.[37]

Municipal legislation was often initiated at the demand of the inhabitants of one *quartier* or one street, whether those who lived there were acting in response to the preachers' admonitions, sincerely wanted to protect family honour, or had more complex motives. We can begin to discern a change of attitude toward prostitution within the ranks of the middle class, who came to judge it as more of a corruption than a protection. For the first time, a Dijon craftsman admits soon after 1500 that no one goes to the municipal brothel with no sense of shame. The first even relatively substantial criticism of prostitution appears in Florence in 1511, according to Richard Trexler, when Giovanni Cambi

---

Vagabond prostitutes were now expelled from cities and were considered criminals simply on the grounds that they were vagabonds.

[36] One lay response to the friars' admonitions can be seen in the reasons (stressing clerical responsibility) put forth by municipal councils for the repressive measures they enacted. As early as 1508 the 'honest' women of the rue St Pierre in Dijon put primary blame on priests and monks for attracting prostitutes; the municipal ordinance of 1541 (repeating others of 1518 and 1523) declared the city's intention to combat 'what leads to pestilences, famines and other punishments that the blessed Creator sends on the people'. It was aimed at blasphemers and concubinary clerics in particular (see AM Dijon I p. 142).

In 1563 the procureur of Dijon states that despite several arrests, concubinary clergy and 'scandalous women' had failed to obey the edicts. 'Evil events' had occurred, to the scandal of the 'good' clergy, 'with no regard to the troubles that reign in the kingdom, and which proceed principally from the corruption of the mores of the said ecclesiastics and from the connivance of their superiors' (ibid.).

In 1529 in Tarascon there is a complaint that the houses bequeathed to the chapter were inhabited by 'young, suspect, dishonest' women, for which the rectors and chaplains are held responsible (AM Tarascon BB 14 fol. 114).

[37] For example in Dijon in 1563, where covert prostitutes were threatened with strangling or hanging if they failed to leave the city within twenty-four hours (AM Dijon k. 85). Two years later the people of Dijon were forbidden to frequent brothels, bathhouses and similar establishments (ibid., I 105).

The republic of Geneva abolished prostitution in 1524. In France, the Estates of Orléans forbade all brothels in 1560 (article 101). Municipalities did not resolve to eliminate the public brothel before the mid-century. However, some bathhouses were closed before then.

deplores the presence of courtesans (thanks to their lovers) throughout the city.[38]

Such sentiments were far from widespread in the early sixteenth century, but hostility slowly gained ground, among women in particular. It was at the urgent request of the 'decent women of the rue St Pierre' that the *échevins* of Dijon voted measures against 'priests' housekeepers and dishonest women living lasciviously' in that neighbourhood.[39] They were accused of setting a 'bad example' and of introducing 'confusion'. Perhaps these good wives simply wanted to protect their daughters' virtue. Other women, however, had understood that the liberty accorded to courtesans limited their own freedom. They demanded the right to 'natural' love at the same time that they denounced the prostitutes who corrupted it: 'It is only the most foolish of maidens who rigorously resist these venerable mysteries. They fail to consider – oh vast misfortune! – that they insult heaven and offend benign Nature most grievously.'[40] In Florence, the preachers explained the corruption of women by the influence of the prostitutes; in France, they continually drew parallels between female mores in general and prostitution.

The women who sang of love, or who wanted to keep what little liberty they had recently acquired, obviously did not subscribe to what the friars were preaching. They took the initiative in the conflict, since they knew well that the misogynists were deliberately exploiting prostitution to erode their condition.

The reforming preachers were capable of abandoning all restraint when they spoke of women. Not content with constant reiteration of platitudes of moralizing literature and the vast repertory of sexist bawdy anecdotes, these men also put their fertile imaginations to work. In spite of his exaggerations, Bernardino still maintained some sense of humour when he lashed out at the finery of the women of Siena, but Michel Menot and Olivier Maillard write with a poisoned pen. Beauty is dangerous, and

---

[38] Trexler, 'La prostitution florentine'. The same comment can be found in Venice in 1543: 'in our city the number of prostitutes has increased in such excessive proportions, and neglecting all modesty they show themselves in the streets, the churches and elsewhere so well adorned . . . that the inhabitants cannot distinguish the good [women] from the bad . . . Not without murmurs and scandal from everyone' (see Larivaille, *La vie quotidienne*, p. 39).

[39] AM Dijon I p. 142. There were other recriminations on the part of the citizenry: the inhabitants of the rue des Grands Champs in Dijon protested in 1517 (ibid.); in Lyons in 1478 (but the aims of the 'neighbours' are equivocal in this case); in Tarascon in 1487 (see AM Tarascon BB 11 fol. 162); in Arles in 1493 (AM Arles BB fol. 106). In Florence the inhabitants of the parish of San Remigio take action in 1498 (see Trexler, 'La prostitution florentine', p. 1008).

[40] Hélisenne de Crenne, *Les angoysses douloureuses qui procèdent d'amour*, 1538, cited in E. Sullerot, *Women on Love*, p. 83.

pretty young women are proud, inclined to lust, and 'dishonest' in act or intention. 'It is better to see the Devil than view a finely-dressed woman', 'Golden Tongue' tells the good people of Tours. If a woman has an elegant bearing, she must be a procuress. If she wears the latest fashions, they are the unspeakably filthy signs of wantonness. As for women who 'paint their faces' or beautify their daughters (who are compared to painted idols), they are criminals who are fabricating whores.[41]

How, the preachers continue, can such women be invited to the banquets and dances that have now become so scandalous? In the *carolles* and the *moresques* that they dance (inventions of the Devil), women use lascivious and provocative gestures to tempt, not only the other dancers, but onlookers as well to the sin of lust. Their arms raised, they deride Christ's passion as they whirl about. Even worse, now burghers' wives, their daughters, and their servant women can be seen going to the bathhouse, walking through the streets with head held high and conversing with their gallants. Other women – a thing most extraordinary and abominable – go about in men's clothing, their faces masked, and they attend sporting contests and mummers' plays. Do not ancient prophecies foretell that the antichrist will be born of the Devil when lust and pride have prompted all the young, men and women, to dress in disguises?[42]

---

[41] Examples of such statements can be found in Maillard, *Serm. quadr.*, sermon 5, fol. 97; sermon 24, fol. 52v; *Sermones de adventu*, sermon 30, fol. 64; sermon 41, fol. 53 ('Young ladies who wear split tunics, your husbands are cuckolds'); Menot, *Sermones quadragesimales*, fifth sermon after Easter, fols 136ff. (on clothing and beauty).

On mothers, see Maillard, *Sermones de adventu*, sermon 32, fol. 66v: 'Burgenses facitis filias vestras meretrices ornando et pingendo eas ac si essent ydolass'. See also ibid., sermon 16, fol. 37. A mother who turns her daughter into an 'idol' or a 'temple' is compared to the adulterers, the sacrilegious, and the concubinary in sermon 30, fol. 63. See also ibid., sermon 28, fol. 60; sermon 22, fol. 49, and so forth. 'Young ladies, do you take as much pains to praise God as to paint your faces? Surely I think not, and if it is as I say, may you be damned' (*Sermones de adventu*, sermon 17, fol. 38).

Comparing elegant women to public prostitutes was a time-tested formula among the sermoners: Bernardino of Siena used it, and without compunction held up women's rouged cheeks to comparison with the face of Christ at the Passion: 'Brother club, brother stick,' he exclaims, 'come purify the sin of women who want to be taken for prostitutes.' On the other hand, Bernardino's criticisms are often interspersed with amusing or indulgent remarks. No trace of hatred can be found in Gerson, who well understands women's need for elegance and playfulness.

[42] Our preachers miss no opportunity to criticize all forms of female gatherings, including childbirths (see Maillard, *Sermones de adventu*, sermon 22, fol. 49). Such hostile statements are quite clearly addressed to the men, who were excluded from gatherings of this sort, which occurred frequently and in which women had total sway.

Any gathering among females was suspect. 'Casus est patens de scandalo ponatis, quod sint quatuor mulieres uxorate in una mensa qui loquuntur in presentia virginum de fatuitatibus et lenitatibus suis et tunc est peccatum mortale' (Maillard, *Sermones de adventu*,

The penitence preachers found that confraternity and youth abbey festivities which both boys and girls joined in, an unbearable spectacle. Stinging accusations recur in almost every sermon as the preachers attempted to rally support from those excluded from those new forms of urban recreation: the poor and newcomers unable to afford to take part in the festivities and competitions, but also husbands who thought that their wives were spending altogether too much on frivolous ornaments and their daughters were taking undue liberties – all those nostalgic for an age of order and tradition, in other words.

This situation is reflected in Michel Menot, who speaks of 'proud ladies dressed in gold, silks and velvet, while the poor die of hunger and cold in the squares'.

A comparable moral lesson filters through the poems collected by Montaiglon:

> Girls, when you are doing the *carolle*,
> Dance nicely with the beat,
> For when a girl acts out of measure
> Anyone seeing her thinks her wild.

---

sermon 15, fol. 25). Maillard lashes out at banquets with particular venom, comparing the women in attendance to priests' concubines (*Serm. quadr.*, sermon 8, fol. 102). See also Maillard, *Sermones de adventu*, sermon 25, fol. 55v; sermon 41, fol. 83).

Dancing was equally unacceptable: Michel Menot holds dances as appropriate on only very rare occasions, such as a military victory, a liberation from captivity, or the return of a friend from distant lands. Even on these rare occasions, dances must be performed by 'honest' persons with good intentions, and without excessive gesticulation or lascivious song, or else they constitute a veritable public crime. They are 'rethe diaboli in quo multe filie capiuntur'; 'una chorea confecta pluribus mulieribus vane ornatis proprie loquendo est venatio diaboli. Domina sic ornata in chorea est ut pulchra et frondosa arbor in medio campo onerata fructibus; quilibet ruit super ea oculum'. He continues further on: 'Sed dicimus quod prout hodie dances are conducted cum mala intentione cum pompis et superbye gragues superfluities, concupiscentiis and treacherous glances' (*Sermones quadragesimales*, fol. 34).

On the bathhouses, Menot says, 'At Tours, there are bathhouses that are plain and simple brothels nec est distinctio viri et mulieres, domina burgense vadit ad stuphas et ancilla sequitur step by step et scit quis ibi se debet invenire. O mulier . . . non maior honorem inde habet quod si esset in pleno lupanari' (Menot, *Sermones quadragesimales*, fol. 75v). In Dijon, women did indeed go to the baths with their husbands and their neighbours (AD Côte-d'Or, B 11 360/8).

Against women's participation in mummeries, 'res mirabilis et abominabilis quod una mulier hodie in habitu viri vadat ad ludum taxillorum to mummeries, masked, una larva super faciam suam' (*Sermones quadragesimales*, second Sunday of Lent, fol. 25).

To repeat, critics had long treated these questions, but their attacks had never before corresponded so well to what was actually occurring.

François Garin says much the same:

> On banquets I can scarce keep still,
> Which one sees clergymen hold
> And laymen more usually . . .
> A number of women are conveyed there
> To feast and carry on joyously,
> Start with one and you soon have thirty.
>
> In handsome rooms or gardens
> Instruments and minstrels
> Make [all] dance and sing. One can speak
> Of anything one desires.[43]

This clearly refers to the meetings of confraternities and to the rituals of the bourgeois abbeys in particular.

We now see why the preaching friars deliberately terrorized their hearers. When they called elegantly dressed young women trollops and their mothers criminals, Menot and Maillard were carefully gauging their effect. Non-repentant 'whores' would be damned; until that day, disobedient women should leave the city or be shut up at home, just as the *meretrices* should be confined to the brothels. It is in the course of a sermon on finery that Maillard cites what he considers an excellent custom: in southern Germany, a girl's *ribaud* (her lover) is hanged on the gallows and his mistress buried alive.[44] Is this merely an example that he is citing? When the friar then urges the crowd before him to take up the hunt for concubinary priests, he knows full well what will take place one fine night. The priest has little to fear, for priest-beating was a hanging crime, but raping his concubine was one of the favourite sports of the rowdies of Dijon.

As for Menot, he states calmly that any woman found in dissolute attire or with a dissolute bearing has no right to make a judicial complaint if she is the victim of violence. The good friar was fully aware how often poor young women were subject to gang rape and falsely accused of loose

---

[43] Menot, *Sermones quadragesimales*, second Sunday of Lent, fol. 33; A. Montaiglon (ed.), *Recueil de poésies françoises des 15e et 16e siècles* (13 vols, Paris, 1855–78), vol. 2, p. 19; François Garin, *La complainte de François Garin, marchand de Lyon, 1460* (Lyons, 1978), vv. 1645–50.

[44] Maillard exlaims: 'You burghers' wives, young ladies or virgins, who wear beautiful gloves, it would be better if you left the city like Abraham's cousin to go to distant lands' (*Sermones de adventu*, sermon 18, fol. 42). The German custom can be found in *Serm. quadr.*, sermon 24, fol. 52v, 'Rapacious [widows], who bed like bitches', are compared to the Devil's handmaids (ibid., sermon 16, fol. 38v).

morals.[45] Taken literally, his statements are an invitation to rape, and in my opinion, they are even a conscious incitement to rape for moralizing purposes. From Menot's point of view, it was better to dishonour a woman publicly than to tolerate a beautiful woman, elegantly attired. These learned monks were not trying to persuade women – what would be the use? – but rather to terrorize them.[46] Somewhat later there were solemn professors of jurisprudence who did their utmost to prove that the rape of a debauched woman had never been considered a crime, founding their arguments in archaic custom.[47]

I have no idea to what extent this sort of preaching encouraged the brutality of young men. Laymen, for the most part, still had totally different ideas concerning morality. We can say, however, that municipal authorities more and more frequently prohibited dancing, in particular by females[48] and that the teachings of the friars contributed greatly to the restoration of a momentarily shaky family authority. That was what was really at stake.

'The four sentinels who help women to live decently are the fear of God, fear of the laws that punish adulterers, marriage, and reserve in the world,' Olivier Maillard stated in 1470. These four sentinels stood permanent guard on moralizing preachers' platforms from that moment on.[49]

Although a few Catholic theologians and future Protestant reformers held different ideas on conjugal relations, this was the prevailing ethos

[45] Sermon given in Tours Septuagesima Sunday, fol. 6. For him, as we have seen, 'dissolute' attire is merely elegant dress; 'dissolute' behaviour, failure to observe the rules of modesty (eyes lowered, discretion in speech, and so forth). Menot knew that rape was a frequent occurrence and often refers to the fact (tavern wenches kidnapped and forced into prostitution, for example).

[46] These discourses were addressed only indirectly to women. It was male honour – that of the father, or of the brothers – that was at stake. The reasoning behind this was simple: if a woman within the nuclear family ran the risk of being called a prostitute and 'profaned', it was the men of the family who were dishonoured. Jacob's sons (Genesis 34) avenged their sister (see J. Pitt-Rivers, *The Fate of Sechem: or, the Politics of Sex: Essays in the Anthropology of the Mediterranean*, Cambridge Studies in Anthropology 19, (Cambridge, 1977)).

[47] Joost Damhouder, for example, in his *La practicque et enchiridion des causes criminelles* (Brussels, 1571), p. 98, n. 20.

[48] In Dijon in 1540 there were: an ordinance forbidding *baillyes* (dances performed by young girls before a house in which they then asked for a contribution) (AM Dijon I 105, 1565); the prohibition of assemblies, disguises, masquerades and 'dishonest' songs (ibid.). In Romans in 1543 the consuls forbade the *Enfants de la ville* (the city's youth abbey) from dancing, even in a room, 'given the hate-filled times' (AM Romans BB 6 Fol. 621v).

[49] This phrase is taken from Maillard's Nantes sermon on Mary Magdalene. It is, of course, taken from St Augustine, but there are other ways to interpret the four sentinels. Gerson, too, was thoroughly familiar with Augustine, but he never permitted himself a liberty of this sort (see appendix 1 on the 'quarrel' of the *Roman de la Rose*).

around the year 1500. Marriage was a remedy for the man, thus it had to be a discipline for the woman. The demand for obedience was the key element in a system of incarceration. 'Disorder' could be foiled if daughters obeyed their male kin, and wives their husbands. This is why it was felt necessary to abolish the dangerous custom of engagements, to keep daughters at home, and to disinherit them should they rebel.[50] The man sinned when he broke the marriage vows, but transgression exposed the wife to perpetual infamy. Adultery – female adultery, that is – must once more be classed as a public crime, publicly punished.

François Garin and Guillaume Coquillart had already expressed regret that sentences had been lightened. What had become of the day when the guilty were flogged before the assembled crowd? Evil was gaining ground, they grumbled.[51] Although it is impossible to corroborate their

---

[50] Maillard calls on fathers to be firm and to deprive wayward daughters of their entire dowry if they were disobedient (*Serm. quadr.*, sermon 42, fols 52vff.). Menot recommends thoroughly checking the doors and windows of bedrooms (*Sermones quadragesimales*, sermons 2 and 3 after the third Sunday in Lent). Both insist on the necessity for moderation in conjugal lovemaking. A married man as holy as St Louis, Maillard says, did not commit mortal sin in carnal knowledge of his wife, but any man who makes love daily commits a transgression most unpleasing to God (*Serm. quadr.*, sermon 18, fol. 40) Wickedness in family mores helps to turn the city into a new Babylon. It was in this spirit that learned ecclesiastics rediscovered the times of abstinence and described the dreadful consequences of failing to respect them. Thus Boaistuau (1560) claims that the horrible sin of parents who do not practise abstinence at the required times produces monstrous offspring (see J. Delumeau, *La peur en Occident XIVe–XVIIIe siècles*, Paris, 1978).

[51] See François Garin, *La complainte*, vv. 1429ff.: 'In the days of rigorous law, / Women were stoned.'

Maillard cites the same law, and Coquillart is nostalgic for the days when unfaithful wives were beaten and adultery led to legal separation (see Coquillart, *Oeuvres*, vol. 1, p. 52). Once again, we need to compare these attitudes to Gerson's: he cites this ancient law but says only that adulterers (without distinction of sex) were stoned.

In Tarascon in the mid-fifteenth century, public adultery was punishable by a fine as great as the one levied for carrying forbidden weapons (see AD Bouches du Rhône B 2 041–B 2 043 for the years 1448–73).

Pierre Pansier presents a case in Avignon that throws light on the question. Constance, the daughter of a Tarascon weaver, had married Didier Allemand from Avignon, a baker. In 1472 she left him. Mutual friends intervened. The notarized reconciliation agreement stipulates that whatever happened, the husband would retain the dowry. The implications of such an arrangement are not difficult to imagine: once again, the woman's liberty bore a price (see Pansier, *Les courtisanes*, p. 104, citing the briefs of B. Mollières, 1472, fol. 32). Pansier found that, more generally speaking, the sentences for adultery noted in the incomplete records of the temporal court for the years 1460–70 fall short of the theoretical penalties established by that court. Concubinage was far from unknown among solid bourgeois circles in Lyons where one will out of every 23 or so in the period 1420–48 mentions an illegitimate child (see Lorcin, *Vivre et mourir*, p. 96). Let me also recall that in Metz Philippe de Vigneulles speaks of 'women married over and above their husbands' and that in Dijon a certain number of artisans' wives practised procuration and occasionally 'got their feet wet' themselves.

impression – and adultery figures among the oldest obsessions of social morality – we can be sure that men of that period sincerely believed that adultery was more widespread than it had been, for the simple reason that now justice hardly ever intervened *ex officio* in this domain, and in the larger cities the rites of social control had lost a good deal of their former brutality.

One remedy suggested was inculcating fear in unfaithful wives, following the tried and true methods used against recalcitrant prostitutes. In all the tales of adultery repeated by Olivier Maillard and Michel Menot, the wives who consent to such an adventure end up in infamy, as was right and proper, in the public brothel.[52] More precisely, since it is 'fear of the laws' that keeps women from breaking their marriage vows, Olivier Maillard regrets that France does not follow the Spanish custom concerning adulterous wives: in that country the husband takes his fallen spouse to the city gates, where he tears off her headdress, which he then drops at her family's doorstep. He thus condemns his guilty wife to a life of vagabondage and prostitution and he displays the sign of her dishonour before her paternal dwelling.[53]

Prostitution still had an important place in this moral programme, no longer as an institution that protected decent women and their daughters, but as a means for penitence in this world. The brothel was part of the system of 'fear of the law' that must be imposed on women. No longer an institution for social harmony but of repression, once again its supervision was entrusted to the hangman and his henchmen.

The reforming friars were not persuaded that the 'corrupt' Church was strong enough to enforce discipline, and when ecclesiastical laws proved incapable of restoring order, they encouraged civil authorities to intervene. As we have seen, municipalities were irresolute and slow to act. None the less, the higher court in Orange in 1509 demanded heavy fines for those found guilty of concubinage. Somewhat later, in spite of the tolerance that reigned at the neighbourhood level, the city council of Dijon set public and severe punishments for cohabiting engaged couples. In 1546 the city council of Avignon attempted to oppose 'disorderly'

---

[52] The exempla of Michel Menot include: (1) a woman who had been mistreated by her husband and fell into adultery. Victim of blackmail, she was forced into prostitution when her lover threatened to put her into the public brothel (*Sermones quadragesimales*, 3rd sermon after the 3rd Sunday of Lent); (2) a merchant from Tours seduces a beautiful married woman, has sexual intercourse with her, and orders her to the public brothel, where she is found later (ibid., Sexagesima Sunday, fol. 16). These two examples illustrate the principal causes of adultery: in the first case, the woman is poor, and perhaps even beaten. (In Dijon, procuresses who wanted to enrol a married woman used the argument of flight from poverty and mistreatment.) The second case is simply a case of infatuation.

[53] Maillard, *Serm. quadr.*, sermon 27, fol. 134.

cohabitation, and soon after the King of France intervened in the matter as well.[54]

In the meantime, the jurists had set to work to provide a logical foundation to marital rights. There is a vast literature on the subject in which, as Jean Delumeau has noted, André Tiraqueau's work on *Les lois matrimoniales*, published in 1513, occupies a prominent place. The bourgeois of the legal professions read such works and they discovered, transposed into the wooden prose of the faculty of jurisprudence, just what they had heard in sermons.[55]

Husbands too had an exemplary tale to offer their wives: the story of the patient Griselda. *Grisélidis* had been published in 1495 with the title, 'Singular and profitable example for all married women who wish to do their duty in marriage toward God and husband and have praise in this world: Story of Lady Griselidis.' The 1546 edition was resolutely pedagogical in aim: 'Here begins the story of Griselda and her marvellous constancy and is called the mirror for married ladies.' Formerly, as Evelyne Sullerot has pointed out, the husband had been presented as guilty of many errors; in the mid-sixteenth century, he became a paradigm.[56]

After the religious troubles, certain of the 'abbeys of misrule' that had not been obliged to become penitential confraternities went so far as to serve the purposes of the Counter-Reformation. A ditty entitled *Chanson nouvelle* composed in Lyons to celebrate the cavalcades that took place there in 1566 was dedicated to 'those innocents whom the hen commands'; to men 'who have taken on the sex of hens'. In the city that was presented as the Babylon of the early sixteenth century, the homeland of Bontemps, Louise Labé and Pernette du Guillet, it was imperative to show (in a distant echo of Maillard's admonitions and the Calvinists' accusations) that order was solidly re-established. On St John's Day the archbishop's guard contributed to the festivities by parading with the effigy of 'the night watch's hag' and four women

---

[54] The court forbade *manants* (wealthy burghers) from conversing with their former mistresses, under pain of a fine of 25 *marcs* (Pansier, *Les courtisanes*, citing AD Vaucluse B 1081, fol. 79).

The sentence of Jean Chalopin and Madeleine Viste, discussed above, speaks of 'their wanton, scandalous and dishonest life and the crime of adultery'. They were both flogged publicly; he was banished permanently, and his goods were confiscated. Madeleine was obliged to live in Dijon 'in perpetuity'.

The decision of the council of Avignon is cited above. In 1555 the consuls, in an attempt to reform family life, begged the papal legate to prohibit the frequentation of taverns, by night or by day, on the part of married men and women (AM Avignon BB vol 10, fol. 173).

[55] Bernard Chevalier (*Les bonnes villes*, p. 297), has also discussed Tiraqueau. I might also cite the treatise of Ripa de Sannazar, who wrote in 1522, among other things, that the plague spread through immoderate sexual intercourse (see Pansier, *Les courtisanes*, p. 166).

[56] Sullerot, *Women on Love*.

'ornamented and attired as daughters of joy' marched with the court officers, police personnel, and representatives from the trades. This was, as Natalie Zemon Davis has pointed out, the only allusion to female labour on this occasion. The meaning of the anecdote is clear: in the city, women's place was in the home – or in the bordello.[57]

Before agreement could be reached on this point, however, many men and women who believed that the last judgement took place daily needed to be converted. When women responded to their critics by echoing Mary Magdalene's answer that the danger was hers alone, they had to be persuaded to change their views. Thus the preachers stated repeatedly that the sin of a few individuals could bring punishment on all; that Christ's mercy was not infinite; that He was not alone in arriving at Heaven's decisions, and that the Apocalypse would be no lark.

The advancing Turkish forces and corruption in the ecclesiastical hierarchy were not the only reasons for a resurgence of obsessive eschatalogical concerns, thrust to one side for nearly fifty years: there was also the need to overcome the breakdown of social order. The only way to persuade the indifferent or the complacent seemed to be reiteration of a long litany of examples of divine vengeance: the Flood and the destruction of Sodom and Gomorrah, Jericho, Troy and Rome. 'What was the origin of the calamities that befell the world eighteen or nineteen years ago?' Michel Menot asked in 1508. Where did the 'Neapolitan pox' (syphilis) come from? What was the reason for the sloth, the avarice, and the floodtide of concupiscence that had unleashed the wrath of God? in 1502 Botticelli represented the city of Florence repentant after chastisement in the guise of the Magdalene at the foot of the Cross in the 'Mystic Crucifixion' (now in the Fogg Art Museum, Cambridge, Massachusetts).

After about 1480, the partisans of sweeping social change (out of conviction or for political reasons) called on Christians to recognize the portents announcing the coming of the Four Horsemen – who soon reappeared not only in public platforms but in engravings, stained glass windows, and on tombstones.[58] This is why municipalities punished

---

[57] *Recueil des chevauchées de l'asne faites à Lyon en 1566 et 1578 augmenté d'une complainte inédite sur les maris battus par leurs femmes précédé d'un avant propos sur les fêtes populaires en Franc*, (Lyons, 1862).

See N. Z. Davis, 'Women in the arts mécaniques in XVIth century Lyon', in *Mélanges offerts à R. Gascon* (Lyon, 1978). The event is noted in Nicolas de Nicolay, *Description de l'antique et célèbre cité de Lion*, 1573 (Lyons, 1881), pp. 126–7.

[58] Jean Delumeau (*La peur en Occident*) quite rightly states that 'the last reckoning of accounts proved an effective pedagogical technique for bringing Christians back to the straight and narrow path'. Pierre Chaunu (*Les temps des Réformes*, Paris, 1975, p. 195) notes that Purgatory 'had been welcomed with enthusiasm by popular piety, which explains the violence of the reaction at the summit in the reformers' camp, aimed at uprooting a belief of recent diffusion.' I would agree, but only if the term 'popular' is taken in a very broad sense

blasphemers, concubinary couples and the lustful with a renewed vigour. The good folk of Vienne marched barefoot in procession, their city fathers at their head, to the shrine of Notre-Dame de l'Ile in 1534, chanting, 'Death, famine, and drought are come to punish the sinful city.'[59] Eschatological preaching sowed fear in people's minds for the purpose of better disciplining their passions and their bodies.

* * *

Neither the patricians nor the middling strata had the slightest intention of giving up their time-honoured social practices without a struggle, however. From Lyons to Avignon, 'good society' invited the 'learned Observants' to come to preach, but afterwards they returned to their rituals of *courtoisie*. In Avignon, Lyons and Valence, years of calamity aside, the social scene was as brilliant as ever. Antoine d'Arena, Garganello (from Bologna), all travellers, in fact, remarked on the convivial atmosphere that reigned at the court of the papal legate and in the higher social circles in Avignon: 'In this amiable society, women, married and unmarried, enjoy an incredible liberty, and it is they who rule in all things.' These foreigners were exaggerating, no doubt, but they were not making it up, and what they had to say could just as easily be applied to the ladies of Lyons, whose 'amiability' was famous throughout Western Europe.[60]

Up to 1550, the 'joyous brotherhoods' continued to flourish in large

and if we keep in mind that Purgatory permitted the sorts of social behaviour that I have described.

The preachers described chastisement in vivid terms. They return repeatedly to the notion of collective punishment, taking the recent calamities as proof (as in Menot, *Sermones quadragesimales*, 2nd sermon after the 3rd Sunday of Lent, fol. 73v). Eschatological preaching, which was still moderate around 1480, became more virulent with the passage of time, as did the attacks on immorality.

[59] 'Mortalité, famine, sécheresse/Sont pour punir la cité pécheresse' (AM Vienne BB 15, fol. 93).

[60] This statement was written by an Italian bureaucrat in 1561. Garganello, cardinal Farnese's buffoon, had previously sung of the easy-going nature of the ladies of Avignon. The papal legate had his official mistress, and adultery flourished at his court (see M. Venard, *Histoire d'Avignon*, Aix-en-Provence, 1979, p. 311; see also 'Correspondance de Garganello ou la vie galante à Avignon en XVIe siècle', *Mercure de France*, 1909, pp. 383–404). Judgements concerning Avignon should not be taken too literally. The city remained faithful to the memory of Petrarch and it envisioned itself as the capital of Love. The myth of Avignon – where in 1533 the fabrication of Petrarchian relics counted for more than a penitential sermon – had an overwhelming influence on travellers' sensitivities. Neither did the voyagers invent women's seeming freedom: to recall once again, the appearances of women's liberty were so numerous that they undoubtedly had an influence on the real situation. The same was true of Lyons.

numbers. Although some were intent on diffusing the models of 'urban courtesy' and others specialized in sentimental or bawdy theatricals, all nevertheless agreed on defending man's inalienable right to extramarital sex – as proclaimed from one end of Europe to the other in burlesque *facéties* and riotous farces. This is why, around 1540, the consuls of Alès kept the city brothel open on Sundays so that the young men of the city could encounter 'lovely and agreeable young whores', why the first consul of Nîmes publicly embraced the *abbesse* of the municipal brothel; why the *fillettes* in Arles took part in the young people's foot races; and why the *dame* of the daughters of joy in the court of France offered the king a bouquet of flowers on St Valentine's Day.[61]

Their joy was most probably no longer totally free from apprehension, however. Lucien Febvre discovered, behind the show of sensuality and nonchalance in the great, the anxiety that sometimes gnawed at them, as when the poetesses of love refer to themselves as shameless. At twilight, strange shadows could be seen creeping through the garden of delights.[62] More important, as calamities increased and pauperization spread, the joyous life led by a wealthy minority scandalized others besides the penitence preachers, notably the poor, whose chief concern was their

---

[61] See R. Zapperi, *L'homme enceint* (Paris, 1983), pp. 209ff. Zapperi gives an admirable interpretation of the *facéties* of Hans Sachs, master Nicolas of Troyes, and the Brotherhood of the Cornards of Rouen. The *Contes amoureux* of Jeanne Flore (which were probably written by a man) teach noble ladies that physical love is pure joy and that one cannot declare one's independence from it without offending the gods. The historian Benedetto Varchi considered the banishment from Florence of thirty over-age prostitutes an act of singular barbarity (see Trexler, 'La prostitution florentine' p. 985).

The ceremony in Nîmes was still in practice in 1529 (see AM Nîmes, inventory, RR 5). Léon Ménard (*Histoire civile ecclésiastique et littéraire de la ville de Nismes, Paris, 1754*) dates the closing of the public house in Nîmes during the years 1530–40, but his information is not totally reliable. The Alais house remained open at least until 1537 (see Bardon, MS *Alais*, vol. 2, pp. 460 and 553); it was only after 1555 that the city rented out 'the house in which the public prostitutes formerly were' (ibid., p. 683). In Orange, the city brothel was still functioning in 1552 (AM Orange, CC 433, fol. 20; CC 444, fol. 30v).

The foot races in Arles are documented in 1558 and 1559 (AM Arles CC 564 item 584; CC 318, vol. 111v).

In the court of the king of France the office of *dame des filles de joye suivant la cour* was still in force in 1558, but the moral tone connected with her responsibilities had changed. An Act dated 13 July 1558 states: 'It is expressly ordered that all daughters of joy and others not appearing on the roll of the said lady of the said girls leave the court instantly after the publication [of this decree], with prohibition to those being on the roll to go about in the villages, and to carters, mule drivers and others, to take them in or give them lodgings, or to swear or to blaspheme the name of God, under pain of branding and flogging; and injunction [is given] by the same means to the said daughters of joy to obey and follow the said lady as has been the custom, with prohibition to insult her, under pain of flogging' (Du Cange, *Glossarium*, s.v. 'meretricalis vestis').

[62] See L. Febvre, *Amour sacré, amour profane: Autour de l'Heptaméron* (Paris, 1944).

daily bread, and whose interest in warding off major threats to the community led them to believe in penitence and mortification of the flesh. Such values gradually spread to broad segments of urban society. The Wars of Religion gave the *coup de grâce* to the old life-style, and it was an easy matter to interpret the ensuing generalized poverty as a punishment for past pleasures. Islands of calm continued to exist here and there, to be sure, but society – and men's minds – was left open to invasion by witch-hunters and to a pursuit of the lustful and the sacrilegious. They were one and the same in the preachers' eyes.[63] This was the moment for the friar to come down out of the pulpit and take command of armed bands, and for the hangman to take up permanent residence in what had been the *maison des filles*.

---

[63] For John Calvin, the lecher (*paillard*) was a sinner and loose morals were a sacrilege: 'It is true that a man who has *paillardé* can say, "No one can complain of me, for the two parties came to an agreement together". . . . Is that not tearing asunder the body of the Son of God?' For Calvin, women must hold their honour as more important that their life: 'They should rather let their throat be cut than let their body be visited' (Sermon 129 on Deut. 22:25–1 0, *Oeuvre*, vol. 28, p. 57).

10

A Summing Up: Prostitution as a Mirror Image of the City

(1) The theological justifications for the triumph of prostitution had been laid down as early as the thirteenth century. Once the Church's victory over heretics and concubinaries seemed assured, the more enlightened theologians understood perfectly well that the common good of the *ordo conjugatorum* was inconceivable without an equally well 'ordered' prostitution. This is why they debated the alms, the earnings, the labour and the characteristics of the 'ideal' prostitute. Neither Thomas of Chobham, Thomas Aquinas, Ptolemy of Lucca nor Durand de Saint-Pourçain were troubled by 'matters of conscience' when they discussed fornication with public prostitutes. The debate was taken up unremittingly from one man to the next, and the arguments for tolerance gradually gained ground until they carried the day. These thinkers make a distinction between the lustful woman searching for pleasure (who is the servant of evil) and the impoverished foreigner selling her body in order to survive, the victim of lust or a pitiful receptacle for the unavoidable ardours of unmarried males. Similarly, they take care to distinguish between the fault of simple fornication and the act committed with a public prostitute, which, far from threatening social or spiritual order, reinforces it. It is probably thanks to the influence of these master theologians that the prostitutes' distinguishing mark (the 'sign of Rahab') appears ambivalent: it set prostitutes apart, but just as its prototype was a symbol of alliance, it signified that relations were admissible, since it enabled men to recognize unattached women, with whom there was no risk of the sin of the consummation of lust.

By these arguments the Church, soon after 1300, began to tolerate prostitution as a lesser evil. Prostitution clearly designated, for the benefit of unmarried men, the only concubines with whom relations were licit, and it let it be understood that a brief union with such a woman was only a venial sin, though out of prudence it took care not to say so unequivocally.

None the less, this doctrinal and moral evolution came to an end with more widespread poverty. At that point the urban laity, who when times were good had hardly raised a scruple concerning prostitution, instituted repressive measures to contain this 'gangrene' – reserving the right to ignore their own decrees when the good times returned. Thus the 'sign of Rahab' imposed in the days of St Louis was long held as an emblem of infamy that served to prevent young women from falling into prostitution.

(2) Waves of pestilence at first had little effect on such attitudes: the rupture took place only around 1400. Paradoxically, and despite bitter conflicts, laymen's ideas and the teaching of the clergy converged. Multiple and recurrent epidemics brought society to the brink of disaster, working men delayed marriage, the Turks were pressing hard on a Christendom overwhelmed by the Schism and by internecine wars. Men in Italy, Provence and Languedoc were the first to attribute a total breakdown of the sort to the increased moral laxity and to draw attention to the falling population. Unnatural acts also were not only denounced with renewed vigour, but were also cruelly repressed. At the same time, ecclesiastics obsessed by the problems of social morality shifted to the concrete level of penitential sentences condemnations that had formerly been proffered only theoretically.

The champions of Nature won over new converts. They invoked Jean de Meun and Genius in an effort to ward off vices and to come to the aid of Nature. Extremists among them sang of the pleasures of the flesh and free but fecund love; the moderates thought prostitution a serious problem that needed to be taken in hand. They opened 'workshops of Nature' as a way to turn people away from love's folly (*fol amour*) and crimes against mankind. In this light, brothels seemed not only a means to protect honest wives and virgins, but a preparation for conjugal life. Notables saw public prostitution as an instrument for public health and safety, and one of the central values of the urban ethic.

At the same time, certain folk customs, from the lowest levels of society, could be found even at the French royal court celebrating the life forces at the very moment that the *danse macabre* began to appear on burial vaults. The 'savages' of 1393 and the royal sheepcote of 1398 are milestones along the road leading to the St Valentine's Day bouquet offered ceremoniously to the King of France by the first among his ladies of joy.

It was at this point that the dominant Catholic orthodoxy[1] was forced to shift its position. In the interests of a more effective resistance to extremist currents, clerics attached to the University of Paris adopted ideas that not long before had been held subversive. Jean Gerson, recognizing the extraordinary power of the senses, conceded to married couples the right to sexual pleasure over and above the end of procreation, on condition that they did not jeopardize the fruit of their union. In short, Gerson gave conjugality the charms of naturalism. At the same time, he recognized (albeit implicitly) that the same rights w allowed the unmarried man bedded down with a prostitute.

This was one aspect – but one of capital importance – c 'popularization' of Christianity evoked by Georges Duby.[2] Around i orthodoxy had been forced to open its doors somewhat wider, and the clergy, whatever their personal feelings, were obliged to adapt their catechetics to the new morality. The 'Quarrel of the *Roman de la Rose*', the first literary *querelle* in France, from this point of view was a pale shadow of a major episode in French cultural history. There were a few great preachers who stood their ground, but when calamities and spasms of penitential fever disappeared, somewhat before 1440, signs of the new spirit could be seen everywhere.

(3) For some thirty to forty years, economic, social and spiritual conditions all contributed to the full flourishing of a social moral code strongly affected by naturalism. Business was good, the charitable institutions and other sources of social assistance were functioning efficiently, and the Church, busy tending to other matters, was unable and had no desire to reconsider the concessions it had made. Purgatory had triumphed, which permitted even those shortest on cash to satisfy Nature without fear of damnation. Fear of sudden and brutal death – *la male mort* – subsided; those who had announced the coming of the antichrist seemed to have been wrong. The Christ of Calvary forged a new alliance that allowed men to enjoy earthly pleasures. Thus prostitutes' identifying marks were abandoned, the 'kings' of infamy were dethroned, and the times of high prosperity for the public bathhouse and brothel were also a period of a lusty, bawdy literature and of outrageous farces, a time for the *fillettes joyeuses* to join in the dance when the musicians struck up the *carolle*.

---

[1] We can speak of the dominant orthodoxy since there is no reason that orthodoxy, in the singular, need always be opposed to heresies in the plural. This is all the more true as the sort of orthodoxy that is defined only by its social relation to authority was just as shaken as that authority.

[2] G. Duby, *The Age of the Cathedrals: Art and Society, 980–1420*, trans. E. Levieux and B. Thompson (Chicago, 1981), p. 221.

But the golden age for waged workers was also a high point for male liberty and for young rowdies – true 'savages' this time – to prowl through the Dijon night, insulting their victims before they dishonoured them. They even boasted of their morality! Does this demonstrate the frustration of young men excluded from conjugal opportunities? No doubt, but we can also conjecture that in the back of their minds lay the excesses of depraved sinners cited in popular preaching and that the unbridled exaltation of Nature preached by the youth associations could lead unthinking people down dangerous paths. This is why municipalities practised the dual policy of supporting public prostitution while at the same time encouraging the youth abbeys to adopt the ritualizations practised in bourgeois circles and to propagate 'courtly manners'. By 1401, princely courts of love had responded to the insistence of Genius. By the same token, this change of emphasis in confraternal rites permitted the expression of sentiments and acts praised in the heat of battle by Gerson and the humanists.

The adoption of standards from the world of courtly love, an increased emphasis on consent in contracting marriage, and the exaltation of natural love constituted redoubtable principles of 'disorder', but only a few perspicacious and particularly dour burghers could see the dangers. It was perhaps between 1460 and 1470 (François Garin was then putting the finishing touches on his *Complainte*) that the first signs of opposition to this moral system appeared. The calamities of 1480 helped them spread.

(4) If the apologists for collective penitence succeeded, slowly but inexorably, in imposing their views, it is because even before 1500 they understood that a part of society was ready to accept their words and incited them to greater rigour. One might maintain that what made lay communities fragment was an increasing distance in people's ways of living. The moral code that until 1480 or so had been accepted by all and which the clergy had been obliged to come to terms with, was no longer tolerable to those who were excluded from it: lacking the means to belong to the confraternities and the youth abbeys, they looked on as their daughters became the whores of the wealthy, and they watched the sons of the *mediocres*, the true heirs of the mad and merry times, dance while they toiled to put food into their children's mouths. The 'honest wives' of the artisan class, who enjoyed none of the freedom of young burghers' daughters or girls of humble estate, were all too content to see them subjected to clerical and male discipline. Finally, there were worried souls who dreaded the mortal threat to the community of 'scandals' and bad examples.

Social communities offered sizeable breaches, then, into which the message of the Catholic reformers poured. I ought to add, however, that the reformers' preaching rose in tone gradually and only became vehement as calamities struck and religious polemics grew. At first, the preachers presented themselves as spokesmen for all right-minded people and they bolstered order as defined by men. Later they were able to use the full apocalyptic arsenal to repress the flesh and rebuke their listeners for depravities for which they held women primarily responsible. To bring headstrong young women to their knees, they used pedagogical techniques of three sorts:

1 They systematically and deliberately confused women in general and whores, applying the same term – *meretrix* – to elegant upper-class women, to lusty women of the people, to courtesans, and to prostitutes in the municipal brothel.
2 They drew a comparison, in thinly-veiled terms, between easy conduct and the diabolic rituals described in precise detail in the treatises of the Inquisition. Among the earliest victims of the Vauderie of Arras were 'the abbot of little sense' and a figure that appears to be a former prostitute. This was hardly a coincidence. Maillard and Menot state clearly that the spirit of the Devil presides over banquets and dances, that he had invented the new dances, and that rebellious women must be his devotees. In a prelude to the satanization of women that Jean Delumeau has described, the sermonizers used the model of the witches' Sabbath as perhaps the most efficacious propaganda technique clerics had invented to combat the 'disorder' introduced into society by the mingling of the sexes. The Devil opened the doors to divine chastisement.
3 They wielded a formidable threat: until the supreme expiation came to pass, rebellious women should be punished and shut up in brothels, which were necessary on a temporary basis until the purging of society could be achieved.

This impressive misogyny drew on old treatises by monks, inquisitors, jurists and physicians. It provoked a lively reaction (the *querelle des femmes* in which Rabelais was involved was not a simple repetition of the 1400 dispute) that gradually subsided but never completely disappeared.[3] Reform and Counter-Reform without doubt carried the day, but although it is fitting and necessary to compile the misogynistic statements of the sixteenth century, it is foolhardy to believe that all contemporaries

[3] The triumph of 'masculinism' provoked a reaction from courtly society and the clergy; a hundred years later the reverse occurred. It was the place of women in social intercourse that explains the 'quarrel' prompted by the reformers. In 1400 only a few patrician women were concerned; around 1500 women of all social strata were.

stood behind them. After 1530, the defence of women dared not appear barefaced: our task is to recognize it behind its masks.[4]

* * *

Some final remarks:

1 The Bourgeois of Paris tells us that in 1418, when 'the people', between two massacres, founded the confraternity of St André, the new members wore flowered wreaths on their heads, and the church of St Eustache smelled so sweetly that one might have thought it washed down with rosewater. When Johan Huizinga read this passage, he invented a charming image emblematic of the entire fifteenth century: 'So violent and motley was life that it bore the mixed smell of blood and roses.'[5] This oft-cited phrase weighs like a curse on the history of mores. The history of sensitivities too must be subjected to strict chronology: recent events have taught us that in this domain the short run had a certain importance.

2 There was no conflict between clerical and secular cultures between 1440 and 1470 for the excellent reason that the laity, triumphant, confined priests and friars within what they themselves claimed was their exclusive domain: intercession and preparation for death. A good many men of the cloth had accepted this division of labour, and the dominant orthodoxy had rallied to the support of the idea of happiness. The strictest observants considered this support infamous and soon pictured the culture of the 1560s in all the trappings of scandal.

3. Zealous reformers succeeded in having public prostitution prohibited, putting an end to the era in which the *prostibulum*

---

[4] Thus Yvonne Knibielher and Catherine Fouquet (*La femme et les médecins: Analyse historique*, Paris, 1983, pp. 72ff.), write that Rondibilis 'expresses well the opinion of his contemporaries toward 1530', and somewhat later (ibid., p. 139) attribute to recent progress in medicine the opinion of Ambroise Paré that 'fathers who marry their daughters without consulting them sin against science and natural laws and are responsible for the hindrances that disturb procreation'. This is obviously a moral discourse justified by medical arguments. Where did this idea come from? How long had it been widely held? This resembles the thought of the 'moderate naturalists' whom we have already encountered. This notion was perhaps freely expressed at the beginning of the sixteenth century; soon after it was advanced only under a less vulnerable 'scientific' disguise.

Similarly (ibid., p. 77), it was not in the sixteenth century (the example given is Thomas Sanchez) that theologians attached a price to conjugal love.

[5] J. Huizinga, *The Waning of the Middle Ages* (London, 1937), p. 18.

publicum held a central place in civic imagination, standing at the core of the city between the cathedral and the City Hall. A certain form of slavery disappeared when this happened, but for most people, the 'liberation', was accompanied by an increase in constraints. Not only did male liberty slowly fade away; women, too, saw slip out of reach their momentary hope of being admitted to its pleasures.

4. Medieval painters often portrayed the female sinner in her chamber, mirror in hand. I hope to have shown that this mirror reflects and magnifies images of the city, and that the history of prostitution is in vain without a history of mores.

Appendix 1

The Evolution of Mores and Literary Translations: The Quarrel of the *Roman de la Rose*

The debate concerning the *Roman de la Rose* has been the object of scholarly attention for some time. In addition to the excellent studies by André Combes, Alfred Coville, E. Ornato, G. Guy and Franco Simone, two recent works help complete the necessary documentation. They are: *Le débat sur le Roman de la Rose*, edited by Eric Hicks (Paris, 1977), and Pierre-Yves Badel's thesis, *Le Roman de la Rose au XIVe siècle, étude de la réception de l'oeuvre* (Geneva, 1980).

I make no claim to resolving in these brief remarks the many problems raised by a major episode in cultural history. All I intend to do here is to put a number of questions to historians of literature, since to this date the medievalists have reproduced their terminology, their analyses and their conclusions unchanged.

Johan Huizinga (*The Waning of the Middle Ages*, Anchor Books, Garden City, New York, 1954, p. 117) hinted that what was at stake in the debate concerned something other than 'merely a society amusement', but he presents it as, above all, a literary quarrel between serious love and frivolous love, and involving only the aristocratic circles of the French court and concerning a work that, he claims, evoked a voluptuous mysticism in people's minds.

'Social entertainment or studious retreat, the quarrel of the *Roman de la Rose* was born of chance encounters before a double and doubly obscure background of literary *otium*', Eric Hicks writes; for Pierre-Yves Badel, 'as much as an event in history, the quarrel of the Roman de la Rose is a text. . . . [It is] first of all a group of texts' (Badel, *Le Roman*, pp. 411, 413). Thus it was a quarrel which did not touch on mores or social practices.

Nevertheless, Hicks and Badel have admitted that it was not merely a *disputatio* among a handful of learned men; they speak of 'public opinion, an entire climate of controversy', and Hicks quite rightly quotes Gerson's treatise against the *Roman*: 'Then I saw a great crowd and a flood of people beyond number, young and old of both sexes and all ages, who – with no respect for order and all betwixt and between – tried, one to excuse, another to defend, still another to praise it.' Hicks adds that the arguments Gerson denounces 'do not entirely correspond to those of the declared rhodophiles. In her first treatise, Christine de Pisan refers to her many enemies' (Hicks, *Le débat*, p. xviii).

'The literary existence [of the question] invites us to suppose humbler, or at least more obscure existences, which, although they did not succeed in appearing in written form, must none the less have had some slight existence,' Hicks continues (ibid.). Badel, to end this exchange, notes that Christine de Pisan acts to decide the question early in February 1402 when she invites the Queen of France to judge the debate. As Badel says, 'this gesture, by the same token, called on the court as witnesses. What had until that moment remained to a large extent a discussion among private persons became a public affair' (Badel, *Le Roman*, p. 411). 'From the outset in 1401', Badel continues, 'the *Roman* was the object of oral debates . . . [and] conversations at the court' (ibid., pp. 434–5).

We can agree, then, that there were more participants in the debate than the few authors of epistles and treatises known to us, but the idea persists that the affair was an intellectual quarrel among people privileged by wealth or culture.

For a larger public, the *Roman* served an an encyclopedia, a 'reservoir of ideas' and of images (ibid., p. 431). It 'bore the debate within itself'. This may well be, but in that case why did the debate arise only in 1401? Was it simply a reaction to the *Apparicion Maistre Jean de Meun* written in 1398 by Honoré Bonet? Or was it intended to follow the *Epître au dieu d'amours*, written the following year? Or could it have been an echo of a deep sense of unease arising from social events and the new social behaviour? If Christine de Pisan invited Queen Isabeau to judge the debate in February 1402, thus moving it into the public realm, was it not because in her eyes the 'debate' was already public and concerned political order and the proper government of the kingdom?

If this were not so, why would Gerson have taken the great risk (as early as 1401, but in particular in the autumn of 1402, after he had written his *Traité*) of devoting five sermons to lust, referring explicitly to the *Roman de la Rose* before a large and socially mixed audience in the parish of St Jean-en-Grève in Paris? Because word of the discussions at court and of the epistolary exchanges had in the intervening months reached the ears of Paris merchants and artisans, suddenly attuned to the subtleties of curial and courtly argumentation? Or perhaps because for several years the fire had already been smouldering in the city as it had in the palaces of the princes?

Caution is needed, however: the vestiges of the 'literary quarrel' that have been conserved seem to reflect only extremely imperfectly the true import of the conflict. In this exchange of letters and treatises what was really being said was masked, and heavily masked. Rhodophiles and rhodophobes could not express their thoughts freely *in writing*, or else they did not care to do so. Christine de Pisan refuses, as a matter of principle, to name the facts, objects or places that she finds *inconvenants* (unseemly). Even Gerson – who was perhaps the freest of them all, since by profession he could speak of sins of the flesh and of the soul in order to condemn them – forgets neither the social conventions, nor literary friendships, nor caution. We are among people who were honourable in all respects. Christine de Pisan had, to be sure, committed a serious act by breaking a tacit convention, but in their writings both sides respect the rules of discretion. Even the rhodophobes refused to carry their attack too far, and they avoid personal challenges to their adversaries and abstain from quoting them verbatim. They knew well that direct accusations could have cruelly serious consequences.

Both Hicks and Badel have noted (without satisfactory explanation, however) the embarrassment of the advocates of the *Roman*: 'The defence does not succeed in adopting a coherent tactic' (Badel, *Le Roman*, p. 431). Even worse, the rhodophiles give the impression that everything happens by chance: Jean de Montreuil claims that he read the *Roman* almost fortuitously, at the suggestion of Gontier Col. Here is a work that had served for a century as a 'reservoir of ideas, an Encyclopedia for a broad public' (Badel, *Le Roman*, p. 431), and this scholar discovers it for the first time! Let us imagine for a moment that he had not read the work in 1400: could he really have been unaware of its principal themes? If Montreuil and Col are cautious, occasionally maladroit, and often hypocritical in their argumentation, it is because they have good reason to be so. They are not safe from serious accusations. Does not Gerson speak of *turlupins* and *beghards* and of 'errors of the faith' (Hicks, *Le débat*, p. 81)? At the time these two terms were synonymous with 'heretic' (see J. C. Schmitt, *La mort d'une hérésie*, Paris and The Hague, 1978, pp. 85ff.).

Theologians and moralists of the time took the turlupins quite seriously: 'This current seems to have been underestimated in subsequent tradition. In university teaching the problem of the turlupins was treated as an *exemplum*. . . . Gerson was extremely concerned about it. . . . We do not know whether Gerson's polemic flame also found fuel in the Parisian reality of the time,' Bronislaw Geremek wrote (*Les marginaux parisiens aux XIVe et XVe siècles*, trans. D. Beauvois, Paris, 1976, p. 345).

I totally agree with this judgement. The heretic current of the turlupins was deliberately exaggerated; they were accused of obscenity, and only their more spectacular conduct was taken into account. The few turlupins in the Île-de-France (who were perhaps close in ideology to the Free Spirit movement) were wiped out by the Inquisition between 1370 and 1376. Gerson's reasons for referring to them are clear: they permitted him to caution all who might stray too far or too openly in the direction of a defence of sexual freedom. Such persons were not impervious to accusations of debauchery and heresy. Gerson certainly was not an informer, but there were many other preachers who would make use of the technique of guilt by association with less moderation.

Thus the real arguments of the 'naturalists' can be found more readily in the writings of the rhodophobes. To summarize, they were:

(1) It was imperative to fight for the preservation of the species, which was threatened: 'You say it is in order to continue the human species and to leave off wicked sin . . .' (Christine de Pisan to Pierre Col, in Hicks, *Le débat*, p. 143); 'Marriage is necessary, but that is no reason to reprove chastity. . . . If everyone were a virgin? This is nothing to be dreaded. If the case were to happen, it would be God's will, and then would truly be the end of the world, for some time it must come.' Furthermore, Gerson states that today (under the law of grace) marriage is less necessary than it was at the beginning of the world or under the ancient law, which extended only to the Jews (cited in ibid., p. 85 and Gerson, *Oeuvres complètes*, ed. B. Glorieux, 10 vols, Paris and New York, 1960–73, vol. 7, p. 853).

I shall comment on these statements in due time, limiting myself here to what is most obvious: the rhodophiles were warning of the risks run by humanity threatened with extinction; they stigmatized those who passed judgement on Nature, first among them, anyone who claimed to be chaste.

(2) A corollary of this is the denunciation of unnatural vices. Christine de Pisan says of this aspect of rhodophile propaganda, 'Nature has no need to have her limping foot reset in order to walk straighter' (Hicks, *Le débat*, p. 57); 'You say that it is . . . in order to leave off the wicked sin that should not be named. Response: there is no reason for so much debate on this, for, the gods be thanked, Nature is equal to the task. It is a waste of time and a folly to admonish water for flowing uphill: so with the other sin that he claims is not well-known in France. Gods be praised!' (Christine de Pisan to Pierre Col, cited in ibid., p. 143). The target here is clearly the possible threat of sodomy – or of homosexuality, to be more precise.

(3) If the rhodophiles denounced unnatural vices with so much

vehemence, it was in order to exalt Nature, with the implications that have already been discussed: 'You say that no matter how daring you are, you do not want to say that exercising the aforementioned operation outside of marriage is no sin. Response, without going further: that may well be true, but God knows what you – and other disciples of your sort who dared to say so – think about it. But one must keep silent about this, and for good reason' (Christine de Pisan to Pierre Col, in ibid., p. 143); 'God prohibits lust, in particular simple fornication . . . [The young claim that] it is not in their power to live chastely. . . . Youth must have its fling, and this is the least of sins' (Gerson, *poenitemini*, in ibid., p. 182).

Quite precise acts and ways of thinking are referred to here: young people's convictions and practices in sexual matters and adults' claims to free sexuality outside of marriage. Christine de Pisan had already protested against male behaviour and the frequenting of disreputable establishments in her *Epître au dieu d'amours*.

(4) Pleasures of the flesh were seen as less harmful than love's folly. Jean de Montreuil and Pierre Col return to this theme on several occasions. Peccadillos were a less serious matter than passionate love, both for unmarried men, who thus ran no risk of madness, and for married men, who could then get on with their business without distraction (see Hicks, *Le débat*, p. 99).

Such are the few, muffled echoes of a vast conflict and the emergence in cultivated circles and in a much attenuated form of traumas that had been affecting the whole of society for decades. What we need to do now is to trace the rise of the new social values in the privileged circles of the princely aristocracy.

It has often been said that there was a renewal of the courtly spirit within the princely courts of the latter fourteenth century. It is true that ostentatious display had never been greater than in Paris at the time of Charles VI. But we also need to note that certain of the great courtly displays (the courts of love in 1401, in particular) were organized in reaction to other trends. We need to acknowledge infiltrations into the festive rituals of the court of France from a culture hitherto ignored, at least in the forms that appeared between 1380 and 1400.

In 1393 the courtiers and the king conducted a torchlight charivari on the occasion of a remarriage. Disguised as 'savages', they gesticulated and howled their way through the rooms of the palace, doing their best to frighten the ladies. The charivari, usually carried out by joyous bands in village and town, had a dual function: it sanctioned and protected the new couple, but it was also a fundamental part of a series of collective rites to reinforce the rights of the male community and promote the renewal of the group (see J. Le Goff and J. C. Schmitt, *Le charivari: Actes de la table ronde organisée à Paris (25–27 avril 1977)*, Paris and New York, 1981, 1982). How long had charivaris been organized at the court of France? Had any married king of France before Charles VI ever disguised himself as a savage to lead a thundering saraband through the halls of the palace? The 1393 ball was perhaps not the first of its kind at the royal court, but it counted among the dangerous innovations which preachers had been denouncing since 1389, taking place in the entourage of a monarch who had that year so amiably received the petition of the young prostitutes from the 'great abbey' in Toulouse. Imputing such actions to the influence of the young Duke of Orleans alone is, in my opinion, ridiculous.

Other practices, which seemed less harmful, arose from the same spirit. In 1379 Jean de Brie, the 'Good Shepherd', wrote his treatise, and it found an immediate place in the royal library. In 1398 Queen Isabeau bought a large sheep farm in Saint Ouen, where she and her ladies liked to go; in the same period the court danced to the sound of the bagpipe. The ageing Eustache Deschamps deplored the habit: 'that instrument of bestial men', he called it (Huizinga, *The Waning of the Middle Ages*). Had any previous queen of France played at keeping sheep? It was in the same period around 1400 that the adoration of the shepherds made its first appearance in France in increasingly complex depictions of the Nativity. The shepherds, kneeling before the infant Jesus, offer the King of Heaven a little bell, a wooden calendar, or a pennywhistle. (In Italy, Taddeo Gaddi had already depicted the adoration of the shepherds as early as 1340, but in France only the angel's announcement to the shepherds in the fields had been protrayed. See E. Mâle, *L'art religieux de la fin du Moyen Age*, Paris, 1969, pp. 51–3.)

I agree that at the heart of the aristocracy's values lay a vision of the natural life: hunting in the copses, galloping across ploughed fields, dancing in the meadows, relaxing in an orchard had long counted among the pleasures of the life of chivalry. Nascent humanism and the example of Virgil came to reinforce further a penchant for bucolic living. The 1400s witnessed the triumph of both the pastoral and the literary genre of the *pastourelle*. Although the enthusiasm for the natural life may easily have been merely an elaborate variation on courtly manners, and although 'the bucolic idyll . . . becomes another mask' (Huizinga, *The Waning of the Middle Ages*, p. 135), eulogy of the simple life was also praise for a lusty life. Franc Gonthier and dame Helayne, who were taken as models, contemplate the meadows, admire the flock's amorous frolicking, and lunch on fromage frais, raw onions and brown bread before taking to their couch under the hawthorn tree for more robust sports.

The idealization of the peasant or the 'bestial man' was not found exclusively in this courtly counter-trend and literary tradition. When Honoré Bonet, the prior of Salon, composed his *Arbre des batailles* in 1387, he pleaded on behalf of farmers, their cowherds, their farmhands and their oxen, because it was they who assured everyone's subsistence. 'Today', he declares, 'all wars are against the poor ploughmen' (see A. Coville, *La vie intellectuelle dans les domaines d'Anjou-Provence de 1380 à 1435*, Paris, 1941, p. 271). Bonet was well acquainted with Provence and Languedoc, which had been ravaged by the plague, the Tuchinat uprising and the reaction to it, and the wars of Raymond de Turenne. (The situation in Provence and the surrounding lands shortly before 1400 was comparable to that of Normandy and the Île-de-France some fifteen years later.)

Bonet's *Apparicion Maistre Jean de Meun* was written in 1398. The title is proof that the second part of the *Roman de la Rose* had found an audience, and that certain problems were already attracting attention. After all, the *Apparicion* was written shortly after the terrible news of the disaster of Nicopolis and at a time when the chances of resolving the Schism seemed seriously compromised. If Christians do not regain possession of themselves, Bonet warns, the Saracens will overwhelm them. The Saracens are united; they live ascetically on bread and pure water and they raise their children in these simple ways; they are from lands (as Guillaume Saignet was to say several years later) in which no law obstructs the infinite multiplication of the species; they are (as Gerson was to repeat in 1402) more prone to 'carnality' than other human beings. The Saracen priest ('as black as coal') of the *Apparacion* finds it easy to gibe at the spinelessness of the western knights and the effeminacy of their sons. Bonet concludes, 'to make war on the Saracens, simple farm boys who live on cheese, not capons, would be better'. He calls for robust men, quick to respond to the call of love, and prolific. When Queen Isabeau played shepherdess at Saint Ouen, the image of the rough and ready ploughman echoes that of the victorious Saracen. The *homme sauvage* of whom Jacques Le Goff is so fond completes the image of the lusty peasant, while the figure of the shepherd, who belongs to both the rural community and the forest, borrows something from both of these two images.

In other words, the rapid development, between 1380 and 1400, of a movement that brought courtiers and certain men of letters to sing *pastourelles*, to dance to the strident strains of the *cornemuse*, to weave through the palace in a charivari, and to disguise themselves as shepherds was not without its serious side. Master Jean de Meun quite 'naturally' joined in the *al fresco* chorus, and Genius (so long neglected; see Badel, *Le Roman*, p. 133) urged men and women to watch 'cows and bulls, sheep and rams' sporting in the fields. Gerson responds, in his 1402 sermons on lust, by asking 'Is it a sin to look at things outside among beasts or in paintings or elsewhere?' He adds, 'I answer as before' (Gerson, *Oeuvres françaises*, vol. 7, p. 829). The obsessions that had haunted Italians or the notables of the lower Rhône valley were shared by Parisians when between 1399 and 1401 a new outbreak of the plague struck the entire kingdom.

These new moral trends were not restricted to courtly or curial milieux, as can be seen in the efforts of the Florentines and the Venetians or of the city fathers of Tarascon and Saint Flour to turn the young away from condemned practices, to organize brothels, and to encourage marriage and procreation. It can also be seen in the scandalized reactions to the new mores: the apocalyptical and penitential current is another way of interpreting history; it was an antagonistic reaction that was complementary, but not contradictory. Vincent Ferrier is a necessary counterbalance to Genius.

There is nothing surprising in Christine de Pisan and Jean Gerson joining the debate in 1401. They had their own reasons for attacking the bards or the followers of Genius. They themselves accepted certain of the values of naturalism, and they did not always comprehend just what was at stake. Christine de Pisan, the heroine of a well-mannered feminism and a chaste widowhood, had first wanted, in her *Epître au dieu d'amours*, to combat the excesses of misogyny and the liberty of males who undervalued female honour – a necessary and praiseworthy task. Later, a prisoner of the role she had chosen (in 1401 she was thirty-six years of age, which meant that she was no longer counted among remarriageable widows and was entering old age), her attacks on Jean de Montreuil and the Col brothers were occasionally maladroit and not always without self-interest. Her works resemble the miniatures of the *Très riches heures du duc de Berry* in that they only present one facet of courtly life. Let us leave her, then, to her pastoral ditties and her stylistic niceties.

Gerson is quite another affair. The *poenitemini* sermons that he gave after writing his treatise, *Contre le Roman de la Rose*, give us an opportunity to know the judgements of the most influential doctors of the Church in matters involving mores and sexuality. As we proceed, two essential facts must be kept in mind:

> 1 These sermons denouncing lust and praising chastity were drafted at the height of the battle, in a crisis when the 'naturalism' that drew justification from the *Roman de la Rose* was all the rage. As Gerson says, 'Master Jehan de Meung published his book for young people who went too far with it. . . . Take this book away from your daughters and your children, good people, for they will draw evil from it and leave the good. . . . If I had the only

remaining copy of *Rommant de la Rose* and it was worth a thousand *livres*, I would burn it rather than sell it for publication as it is' (see Gerson, *Oeuvres complètes*, vol. 7, pp. 829, 831, 839, 852, etc.). Thus Chancellor Gerson was brought by logic to harden his position and to insist on severity.

2 This teaching was given at the exact time that the preachers of the Apocalyse were stirring up fear of infernal torments.

Jean Gerson was no terrorizer. There will be troubles at the end of the world, he says, but since we have revelations only through Scripture (ibid., p. 815), we should refrain from such inquisitive questions and speak primarily about the Advent 'that takes place at the death of each person, for that is when Jesus the judge appears' (ibid., p. 810). Is he speaking sincerely, in a desire for moderation? Perhaps, but this also shows a preoccupation with tactics, at a moment when – at least in Parisian society – a great many people were mocking the censors: 'lust prevents believing sermons' (ibid., p. 825); 'a person occasionally lustfully inclined takes no thought for the universal judgement because it seems to him still remote, as the thief said to the goodwife when she told him he would account for his thieving on the day of judgement. "That is a long way off," he told her. I will speak to you of your particular judgement.' Is this another *exemplum*? Some years later, was there not a doctor who took immense pleasure in revealing that he had had to treat a student from Montpellier stricken with madness by listening to Vincent Ferrier preach?

Thus Gerson took on the task of putting in its rightful place 'the whore Lust', born of Gluttony, whose six hideous daughters, like their repulsive mother, make men forget God, shorten men's lives, bruise soul and body alike, and bring on evil and chastisements. The *exordium* absorbed, more concrete lessons followed: lust is powerful; it has no equal in turning men away from studies and from wise conduct, outside marriage even more than within. 'From this it follows that so few people are contemplative and see God intensely' (ibid., p. 825), for if a life of chastity is not impossible – we have the example of the saints – it is 'strong and arduous, serious effort, and strong temptation' (ibid., p. 836). Here we have a significant concession to the all-powerful Nature that many preached: the praise of chastity was to re-establish an equilibrium. 'Carnality' was natural: 'Shall I deny that Nature and God grant company to man and woman? Surely, I will never deny it' (ibid., p. 853). However, if 'the young, to whom foolish youth and silly hope promise a long life, have some excuse and consolation', men of mature years have no such excuses. It was thus to them above all that Gerson addressed his appeals for repentance and penitence. They should waste no time in renouncing lust.

Gerson assured young and old alike that, contrary to accepted ideas, simple fornication was indeed a mortal sin. However, he follows this with two further statements which modify these premises a good deal:

1 Loose women (and when he speaks of *folles femmes* he has the official prostitutes, the *meretrices*, particularly in mind) are not capable of salvation, but it is good to suffer them, and the Church ought to receive their offerings as long as they are not the fruit of theft or fraud. Gerson states explicitly that simple fornication with such women is not normally a reserved case for special judgement, but that should there be any doubt concerning the woman's estate or her ties, one should confess the act.

2 The simple fornication that he denounces is of a quite different sort: 'Consider the evils that would follow if God abandoned all unmarried women to any man on your mad demand: marriage would disappear ... procreation would be greatly hindered, wives and progeny would be abandoned. I ask you, if you have unmarried young daughters, sisters, or cousins, would you like them abandoned to all men? Or your sons to all women? Or your own mother if she were a widow?'

This is where true 'disorder' lay; this was the insidious erosion concealed in the lessons of the *Roman de la Rose* and the comforts of city life. It encouraged *le fol amour* – love's madness – as distinguished from 'vulgar pleasure' and far more pernicious. This was why *fol amour* was condemned time after time (ibid., pp. 811, 812, 824, 825, 830, 831, 835, and so forth). Gerson equated forbidden 'simple fornication' to concubinage and free union, those insults to the sacrament of marriage and to social order.

'Carnality' must thus be subsumed in the 'honesty of marriage'. As a counterpart to his relative severity towards fornicators, Gerson offers an interpretation of marital practices that is generous in at least three aspects:

1 The choice of a partner. The corollaries of consensualism are far-reaching: a maiden may make a vow of perpetual virginity against her parents' wishes if she is of marriageable age (ibid., p. 849). One can infer from this that if a vow of virginity is licit, so too would be a sworn engagement. Is it kidnapping if a girl leaves her parents' house 'she being willing' but against their wishes? Yes, says Gerson, 'if the girl is under age'. Therefore it is not considered kidnapping if she is of marriageable age (ibid., p. 821). 'Are the oaths sworn by mad lovers to be respected? I say some, yes, and some, no, according to the good or evil to be seen in them. If the oath is honest and possible (i.e. made in good faith

and capable of being kept), it should be kept' (ibid., p. 831). There is no possible doubt that Gerson is talking of the engagement promises exchanged by young people. His conclusion is thus an energetic way of reminding families of the rights of young people that the Church had long recognized.

2 'Carnal union', under the condition that the decencies of marriage be respected, permitted a good measure of enjoyment. The husband pursuing carnal pleasure for its own sake was not sinning mortally; he could have intercourse with his pregnant wife as long as the child's life was not endangered; he could approach his wife on many other occasions, and if he demanded that she fulfil her conjugal duty when she 'has received the body of our Lord or if it is a major feast day, I still say that she should obey.' If a husband demands marital relations with his wife and she is unwilling, she must obey, and only the husband will be committing a sin (ibid., pp. 819, 863). Thus Gerson makes broad concessions in his discourse on sex within marriage: 'The bride must take pains to please her husband and the husband his wife to their common profit for the marriage' (ibid., p. 855). Where are the obligatory times of abstinence? What had become of the rejection of pleasure?

3 In spite of his hierarchical conception of the couple, Gerson seems to recognize a condition for the woman that approaches that of the husband's. He proclaims that adultery is just as serious a matter for the husband as for the wife; he invites the couple to concord and discretion when one of them strays. He also shows extreme prudence concerning priestly control over conjugal life: 'As far as going to church is concerned, I say that on Sundays and days of obligation, the husband cannot reasonably forbid his wife to go to church and hear the entire mass; the other days he can forbid her to do so, according to the needs of the household.' As for the secrets of marriage, one should confess them, but to a priest unacquainted with one's spouse.

In this way, Gerson does everything he can to augment the attractions of marital bliss and refurbish the lustre of the conjugal state. His words on the excellent qualities of marriage rival the lyrical flights of the champions of 'civic humanism' ('Virginity comes and is born of marriage; by it friendship is engendered and conserved through an entire lineage or in a town', and so forth; ibid., p. 859). Conjugal union establishes social harmony, reinforces peace between families, generates alliances and concord. So necessary is it that certain persons 'can on occasion better be saved through marriage than through chastity'. Much is permitted in connection with marriage and in its support: writing love letters, singing secular songs, dancing, dressing in fine apparel, and more. After this, Gerson devotes several fine pages to chastity, for 'it must not happen, just because marriage is necessary, that virginity be diminished or criticized' (ibid., p. 853) – even though nowadays 'there are too many priests'.

To conclude: whether out of personal conviction or for tactical reasons, Gerson abandons a good deal of ground to the 'naturalists'. Certain of his positions – on consensualism, for example – merely restate long-standing doctrine with force and precision. Others, however, show proof of an impressive *aggiornamento* taking place among the most prestigious circles of the secular Church. In short, Gerson permits unmarried men fornication with the *meretrices*, on the condition that they mend their ways with maturity and marriage. Sensitive to naturalist propaganda for 'natural pleasures' and procreation, and above all attentive to shifts in social practices, Gerson embraces the new ideas, but as applied to the institution of marriage. In the thick of battle he appears lucid and moderate, quite probably strongly impressed by changes in morality, and intent on conserving what he considered essential. That a dignitary of his stature should be rallied to the cause of the innovations or the ideological adventures of the end of the thirteenth century says a good deal about the discomfiture of the secular Church, the strength of the lay moral code, and the true significance of the 'quarrel' of the *Roman de la Rose*. It also permits us an insight into a good many characteristics of social morality in fifteenth-century cities.

The censors of mores lost a decisive battle between 1390 and 1410, at least in France. For another twenty years a few privateer captains (the 'popular' preachers) continued to win a short-lived victory here and there, but the ground lost around 1400 was not to be reconquered before the end of the century.

Appendix 2

Documents

Acts of Violence

The Road to Ruin

(AD Côte-d'Or, B 11 360/16, 1492)
Jeanne's road was unfortunately a common one. Poverty forced her father to place her in service in a *rôtisserie* when she was fifteen years old. It would have taken her fifteen years of work to save the minuscule dowry that might perhaps have offered a way out of domestic service – if, of course, she did not fall sick, her employers respected the contract, and she spent nothing. She gave up her place after she was raped one night, and she then did day work, supplementing her earnings with occasional prostitution. She soon landed in a sinister private bordello, and doubtless ended her youth in a municipal brothel.

For a moment she thought she might break loose. She lived with other young women like herself who also did day labour. They rented a room together from an old lady named Jambe de Fer (Iron Leg) in a house near the Porte Guillaume gate in Dijon, and the neighbours, many of them recent arrivals from the country, accepted the little community. Occasional prostitution, a furtive embrace in the workplace, at times submission to the insistence of the journeymen or the master were all part of this life. A certain discipline reigned in the hovel she lived in, however, and when Jambe de Fer learned that Jeanne was now prostituting herself regularly, she had to leave: the house at Porte Guillaume was not to be a brothel. There is also the enigmatic silhouette of Claude, who worried about her companions' destiny and tried to preserve her liberty.

* * *

Jehanne, daughter of Claude Joly of Charentenay, near Roy in the county

of Burgundy, aged about fifteen years, as she says. Witness sworn on the
Holy Gospels of God our Lord, says and deposes by her oath that it is
true that about one year ago the said Claude her father, because the
mother of the deposant went from life to death and because he had charge
of other children, brought the deposant in this city of Dijon to serve a
master. And put her in the *rôtisserie* in this city of Dijon in the service of
one named La Pucelle, where she lived during about ten months and even
on a certain evening of this past winter [when], as she was going by
candlelight up to the town to get wine on the order of her mistress, a
companion whom she did not know and knows not who he might be
came to her and extinguished her candle and dragged her and lay her
down under a sign for selling meat in the said butcher shop and because
she attempted to start to scream covered her mouth with his apron,
tumbled her on her back and knew her carnally. And from that day [she]
has done no evil with her body. When the fields were being weeded the
deposant went [to work] by the day in a certain field outside the new gate
with other girls and women, among whom there was one who was named
Claude, whom she did not know otherwise, who interrogated her on her
lodging and the earnings she made from her service, the deposant
answering that she earned two francs, and the said Claude said to her that
this was not much, and that it would be better to go weeding at the
harvests and the grape harvests by the day than to serve a year for two
francs, and if she wanted to leave her said service she could be well lodged
with others in the house of an old woman named Jambe de Fer living near
the Guillaume gate of the said Dijon. And by this means she was so
induced that she left her service and went to the lodging of the said Jambe
de Fer, where she requested to be lodged to go work her day like the
others, paying for her lodging for every night one *niquet*, and on which
she was received. And from that time went on some days to hoe the fields,
and on other days stayed home and went down from the city and over the
moat, and since it was known that she came and went and was idle, she
was immediately hunted by the young men of the city, who pursued her
so that she began to give them pleasure of her body, and she could not
name them except for a carpenter who she said to be the son of Mongin
the Carpenter, who brought with him other companions by night before
the house of the said Jambe de Fer. The which some fifteen days later
remarked the behaviour of the deposant, who had known the said Pierre
Bouju when he was plastering the house of Philibert Truchot in the said
butcher shop near the house of the said Pucelle, and whom she had served
by carrying the mortar, and from then had known that he lived in the said
faubourg of St Nicholas. She met on a certain day the said Pierre and
asked him if he could lodge her in his house, who answered her. And in

fact the said deposant went into that house where she was in the daytime, and until this present day has only slept two nights.

Jeannette Pingeon

(AD Côte-d'Or, B 11 360/14, 1483)
The way this drama unfolds could easily serve as a model for many others:

1 Seven or eight men pose as the night watch, break into a house, beat an elderly couple, and carry off their servant girl, Jeannette. She is raped by Lord d'Anvillers, and, when he has had enough of her, passed on to one of his men.
2. A good half-dozen adult, able-bodied neighbours have observed the scene and heard the screams of the girl as she was dragged off by force and beaten. 'Let us close the window, or we will have stones thrown at it,' is all the bailiff can find to say to the priest.
3 The next day, about noon, Jeannette is finally set free: her masters lodged a complaint. She is interrogated by the prosecuteur: did her kidnappers give her anything? The question is crucial and cruel, for woe to the girl who accepted a few pennies, as she would thus have shown consent and complicity. How many victims, after a night of brutalities, had the courage to refuse what was put in their hand?
4 This aggression could be qualified as 'semi-legitimate', at least in the eyes of young men. Two years earlier, when Jeannette was fifteen years old and perhaps already an orphan, she had had to serve as the concubine of one or several men. This was in 1481, when times were bad, so she had sold herself to survive. Two years of irreproachable conduct were not enough to win back her honour.

* * *

To your very honourable lordship, My Lord the Mayor of this city of Dijon, or your lieutenant:

Beg most humbly and in pity Aubert Aubriot, locksmith, a poor man aged about eighty years, and Jehannette his wife, living in the rue St Philibert, and also Jehannette, their servant, an orphan aged about eighteen years. Being that for long years the said supplicants have been people of the town and always lived quietly and decently with their neighbours and all others without causing disturbances or discussions or bringing harm to others and with no reproach to their estate. And the said

Jehannette their servant and co-supplicant, for the two years that she has been living and staying with these said master and mistress co-supplicants has also so well and decently conducted herself in her service without complaints or pursuits from anyone and without sinning with her body that she was until recently on the way, by her good and quiet conduct to be well placed for marriage in the said [city]. . . . And that they and their said goods as inhabitants of the said city are totally, they and their goods, in the safekeeping both of the law of the said city and in that of the king, our lord. Nevertheless, Wednesday evening of the seventeenth day of the present month of September and about the hour of nine hours before midnight of the said day and by night at an undue hour and the said supplicants being in their dwelling peacefully without making noise or saying or doing displeasure to anyone at all, there arrived in the dwelling of the said supplicants Oudinet Boudier, Jehan Courtot, the young Odinet Godrant, my lord the forest warden, Jehan de Courcelles, Lord Danvillers, one named Channeaul, cellarer to my lord the bailiff, their consort, accompanied by several others whom the said supplicants did not know. The which, their being at the said dwelling and under colour of saying it was the watch of the city, furiously and evilly moved to courage, with great violence took the said Jehannette servant co-supplicant by force and against her desires and will, while saying to her many insults and doing her many outrages and beatings about her person and dragging her by the hair and pulling her by her arms and the sleeves of her overdress by force because she did not want to go with them to accomplish their damnable will, and because she defended herself they also beat the said Aubert and his said wife with a stick and with torches and . . . as has been said, they took away by force the said Jehanette to the dwelling of Sir Danvillers, where they or some of them held her all the night and the next day and had their will of her against her wishes, as has been said, and until about one hour after noon of the said day of Thursday following, when they or some of them opened the door of the said dwelling for her and gave her permission to leave. The poor girl left, desolate, and took thought to come to the house of the said master and mistress, begging them to receive her back in their house and service as before, about which they were as they still are hesitant, fearing to have in their said house again such and similar outrages as above done to them by the abovesaid or some of them, about which they bragged and the said Courtot is still bragging about it. By means of the said outrages and violences the said poor servant is rejected and has lost her good and her honour and to such an extent that she finds almost no one who will receive her or take her in, for fear of the abovesaid malefactors and is on the way to being completely abandoned and talked about, when she wanted only to do good. These things are to the great dishonour, prejudice and damage to the said Jehannette servant and rejection of her good [actions] and those of the other co-supplicants, of which they and each one severally present to you complaint and grievance and also [declare] that it would be more to them if by you, most honoured lord, were the source of remedy by justice . . . as it please your grace and in aid of law and of justice . . .

* * *

Information taken on the content of the request hereto sewn and attached Wednesday, 23rd day of the month of December of this year 1483 by myself, Jaques Bourestel, sworn clerk of the court of the chancellery of the Duchy of Burgundy and substitute procureur for the honourable man, Giuillaume Billocart, procureur of the city and commune of Dijon.

Jehannecte, daughter of the late Gabriel Pingeon and of Ysabeaul aforesaid, his wife, of Fahy, near Langres, servant of Aubert Aubriot, locksmith, and of Jehannette his wife, her master and mistress, aged of about eighteen years, summoned, interrogated, and examined on the contents of the said petition she has read word for word says by her oath given on the Holy Gospels of God to know all the said contents to be true. And she says to know it because the evening and about the hour declared for the said case she was taken, beaten, dragged by the hair, and taken away by force against her desire and will . . . And was taken screaming through the streets by those named in the said petition to the house of my Lord Danvillers and there had carnal company of her the said Lord Danvillers, the forest warden, and also one named Loys Regnart of Auxonne at the said house and knew her several times and [she] lay with the said Danvillers of whom she complains and of whom also demands justice. And says that they started by beating her and her said master and mistress. And the next day the said Sir Danvillers ordered his lackey to open the door of the said house and to put her out. Which he did, and she went back to the house of her said master and mistress, who did not want to receive her, fearing to be beaten, and asked whether the said lords and Loys Regnart gave her anything, says that they gave her only blows with their fists in spite of all that has been said above, and more she does not depose.

* * *

The venerable person, messire Jaques Jarry, priest, aged about 46 years . . . says on his word as a priest, his hand to his breast, that of the taking of the said servant he knows only what follows. To wit, that the evening she was taken, he was not in his house, which is fairly close to the house of the said Aubert. But it is quite true that the said evening that she was taken and about the hour declared . . . the deposant was in the dwelling of Monsignor de Langres, where he sleeps every night, as he says, in a lower room facing the street with Estienne Julien, first bailiff of the parliament and servant of the said Monsignor de Langres, where they were talking together. And while talking together, the deposant heard in the street a voice which was crying out as if coerced, on which, to know what it was, he went to the window, and to the iron grille before the said chamber. And heard and understood from the said voice that it was the servant of the said Aubert, whom people he did not know were leading away. And who went screaming words such as, 'take me to my lord the mayor, who knows me well, I am not as you think I am.' Some of those following after were saying to her, 'Go to, go to, wanton whore.' To which she responded that she was not, and that she was not what they thought, still crying out to them to take her to my lord the mayor. And then, the one who speaks to you now cried out. 'Hola! Hola! Gentlemen, do not use force! You are in a good city; you might regret it.' And at that those who were leading her pushed her and went off by the rue de la Poullaillerie. And then the said Estienne Julien, bailiff as above, told he who now speaks to you to close the said window so that no one would throw stones through it, the which he did. And regarding the fame and reputation of the said girl, says on the damnation of his soul that since the said girl has been living in the house of the said Aubert (and it will soon be two years), no matter how surly and obstinate the said Aubert may be, this Aubert and his wife have just as carefully and gently kept and governed the said girl than as if she were their own daughter, whom he who speaks has always seen to be a sweet and humble girl of handsome and good countenance, and does not see her gossiping or anything nor wandering about the city, nor of bad behaviour. And he is their closest neighbour. And says that if he had seen or known her to be of bad behaviour he would not have suffered it so close to him, for when he knows that there is some bad behaviour on the said street, he goes to complain to my lord the mayor. And also the neighbours of the said Aubert also know well that the said girl behaves herself well and simply. And he knows no more than he says.

Marguerite Guillaume

(AD Côte-d'Or, B 11 360/4, item 369, 1449)
Little trace has come down to us of acts of violence leading to a girl's ruin that took place within the household. Marguerite's father by adoption was an 'honourable' and the circumstances of the crime seemed

worrisome to the people of the neighbourhood. Although no plaintiff came forward, Jean Rabustel opened an inquiry. Indeed:

1 The servant complained once before to two female neighbours, who, oddly enough, did nothing but warn her mistress. The second time they intervene, and to good effect. This is a somewhat paradoxical response, as the defloration (which was what constituted a crime) had taken place two months earlier.

2 Humbert le Ravet's wife had undoubtedly begged her neighbours to keep silent on this matter, as a formal complaint would have involved dramatic consequences for the couple. The rape had taken place 'fairly close to Easter, and more than that I cannot remember', the victim says, having been well lectured. Thus it was certainly during Holy Week, perhaps even on Good Friday, a day of strict interdict respected by all. (Good Friday would also explain the wife's absence from the house.)

We do not know what happened after.

* * *

Thursday, Day of the Ascension of Our Lord
22nd day of May 1449

Marguerite, daughter of messire Jehan Guillaume, aged fifteen years, as she says, summoned by myself, J. Rabustel, concerning a certain act that is said to have been committed on her person by Humbert le Ravet. Item: She says by her oath . . . that one day during Lent last passed, and it was fairly close to Easter, but otherwise she does not remember the day . . . the wife of the said Humbert and gone to St D. . . de Vergey. And when the night of the said day came, she who is speaking went to lie on a pallet in the bedchamber of the said Ravet, where she usually slept, the said Ravet being already lying in his bed in the said chamber, who got up and came to her, took her stark naked and brought her to lie in his bed, and as soon as she was there, lay with her and put his hand over her mouth, and opened her legs with the other hand and stretched himself out on top of her and took his member, which he thrust in her nature with great force and pain, and after moved on her for a very long time, it seemed to her at least a half-hour. And when he had done this for the said time of about a half-hour, and breathing hard and sweating mightily, he got off and left her soaking in and out of her nature, but she did not know with what until the morning, when she made the bed, she saw blood on the sheets. She further says that after the said Ravet had done this, she attempted to get up, but he held her with her arms behind her back and held her there until it was nearly day, when he suddenly mounted her again and did what he had done before. And after arose and went his way into the city, leaving her in the said bed and forbidding her to say a word or he would beat her.

Interrogated as to why she did not cry out the first time or the second, she said that he held his hand over her mouth as she had said and that she could not cry out. Interrogated as to why as soon as she had arisen she did not complain of what has been said, she says that in the morning she did speak of it and complained to Jehanotte, the wife of Jehan Vournant, and to the daughter of Jehan Firaut, barrelmaker, who told the wife of the said Ravet, but she paid no attention to it. And more than that she dared not speak of it. She says further that yesterday around midday, at the which hour her said mistress was out of the house and working with Jehan le Blanc in the butchery, the said Ravet went up to sleep, and told her who is speaking that when it was time she should go wake him. She did so, and suddenly the said Ravet took her by the arm and threw her on his bed and put his hand over her mouth as before and did as he had done the other two times, and was at it almost an hour, and then went away and left her there. And at that, she who is speaking took her distaff and went into the street, where she found the wife of Perenot Viaulot, the wife of Favier, and the Chapelier, Pageot, and the Cordurier girls, whom she told weeping of what had happened to her, and showed them her nature and the state she was in, and when they had seen and visited her, the said Pageot girl went to tell her said father, and more than that dared not tell him.

The Baths: Sociability, Prostitution, Eroticism

Who Went to the Baths?

(AD Côte-d'Or, B 11 360/8, 1478)
Marie Dami's statement gives us a vivid portrait of burghers' habits. Women – neighbours, merchants' or artisans' wives – go to the bathhouse together. Even better, it does not seem extraordinary to damsel Marie to bathe in the company of her husband and two other couples. Such details, reported in court calmly and incidentally, show that men and women bathed on the same day, at least when they had chosen their own company. The same customs can be found in Geneva and in many another city. Miniatures that present nude couples coversing with no sign of shame in the baths are neither invented nor distorted. The artists were simply reproducing ordinary habits held to be perfectly decent. This may give more credence to the violent denunciations of such practices of the preachers of the end of the fifteenth century.

The episode related here had just occurred. It shows that the burghers and the artisans of the parish of St Philibert continued to frequent the bathhouse of Jeanne Saignant in spite of a reputation of which no one could have been unaware. It took threats to a respected family (the immediate cause of the inquiry) to interrupt bath-going for a time.

* * *

Damsel Marie, wife of Pierre Dami, burgher of Dijon, aged approximately twenty years . . . Says that the eve of the feast of St Philibert last, which was a Tuesday, the women were going on their usual day to the bathhouse, and she who is speaking and two of her neighbours, to wit, Jehannote, wife of Guillemain Petot, mason, and Jehannote, wife of Jehan Butain, vintner, decided together that they would go to the baths of Jehannote, wife of Jehan Saignant, so that she who is speaking went around the hour of five hours after noon of the said day to the said bathhouse to know who was in it. To the one who is speaking the said Jehannote answered that there was no one but a man who was getting dressed and getting ready to leave, as the said Jehannote said, saying also to she who is speaking that she should go back to her house to undress and get ready and that she would clean the said baths, which would be ready before she who is speaking returned. For which reason she who is speaking returned home with the intention of getting ready. And when she was in her said house, the said Pierre Dami her husband said to her that he wanted to go bathe with her, but she answered him that he should not do so unless one of the husbands of her said neighbours went with him, for otherwise the said neighbour women would not go. And then she who is speaking went on ahead to the said baths with her said two neighbours, but when they were about to enter into the baths, she heard some people talking inside the said baths. She asked the said Jehannote who were those people in the said baths, who answered her that they were two priests of the chapel, and when she who is speaking complained to the said Jehannote that she was a bad woman and was not showing her great respect by thinking that she could put her in with the said two priests, the same Jehannote answered that if she did not wish to wait until they had finished bathing, she could go in with them with no fear, for they were two proper men and good companions, at which she who is speaking left the house of the said Jehannote and went back home with her said two neighbours.

Bathhouses in Lyons

(AM Lyon, FF, unnumbered, 1478)
The baths of La Pêcherie were among the oldest and the most richly

appointed of Lyons. Illustrious citizens had been its proprietors, and they had never given a thought to limiting its facilities: baths and steam rooms, gaming tables and prostitutes, all furnished handsome revenue to their ecclesiastical and burgher owners.

The wholesale fishmongers who in 1478 claimed they were 'scandalized' and demanded the closing of the establishment were not persuaded of their own 'moral' arguments. One of their allies, Janin Courtois, a sergeant of the guard, had built his own prostitutional bathhouse in 1471 in the neighbourhood of the Augustinian monastery and some of them had frequented the establishment that they attack here. Furthermore, they were unable to prove their accusations. In reality, they were counting on arguments of another nature: the immense house was managed by foreigners and could take in several hundred clients (conceivably, foreigners) at a time: this constituted a permanent danger for the city, hence for the kingdom.

The decent folk of the rue de la Pêcherie lost their case. In 1483, Casotte Cristal still headed her little band of chambermaids, and the bathhouse was closed only forty years later, along with all the other bathhouses.

What were the neighbours trying to accomplish in 1478? Were they attempting to protect their children's innocence? To proclaim their own respectability? Or perhaps to protect their own business interests?

The petition is contemporary to a period of commercial expansion and the reconstruction of Lyons' river ports, and these *marchands-poissonniers*, all of whom made their living from navigation, fish wholesaling and wheat transport, had no wharf convenient to their places of business. The destruction of the baths would have enabled them to create a large port; it would also have raised the property value of houses in the neighbourhood. In 1493 they petititoned the city council for support to do this, but in vain. The monumental baths of La Pêcherie continued to welcome 'great multitudes of people' two steps from the city's principal church (St Nizier) and from the city hall (St Jacques).

* * *

Accusation

And first Jehan Colin, fisherman, living in Lyons, aged forty years or thereabouts . . .

Says that the baths of the Casotte mentioned above and in the said affidavit are situated on the rue de la Poissonnerie of the said place of Lyons, near one of the gates of the said place of Lyons named the Porte Chenevier, in the which bathhouse live and remain continually seven or eight public women, if not more.

Interrogated on the second article, [he] says that on the street on which the said baths are situated live and reside several notable persons, merchants and others, who are of good life and honest conversation.

On the third and fourth articles [he] says that both because the said bathhouse is close to the said Chenevier gate and for other reasons these baths are a most suspect and dangerous place for the said city of Lyons. And also for the king our sire, for the said baths are next to the river Saône and quite close to the said fishmarket, where there is a great quantity of boats. By means of these one could easily put people at night in and out of the said city or take them out and move them into the house of the said baths under cover of going to bathe, who could seize and open the said gate and by this put enemies in the said city. [He] further says that because of the proximity of the said baths and the said river Saône, one could easily throw and drown from the house of the said baths into the said river Saône divers persons frequenting the said baths and the street in which they are situated. [He] says also that under cover of going to bathe in the said baths one could in time of war and eminent peril conspire and machinate in the house of the said baths against the king and the wealthy burghers and inhabitants of the said city and other particular persons of this city without anyone noticing them for the great multitude of people frequenting the said baths. [He] also says that those who frequent the said baths can descend from the said bathhouse into boats being on the river Saône behind and adjoining the said baths by means of the cord with which water is drawn from the said river into the said bathhouse, and from there by means of the said boats leave out of the said city without passing through the street and without being seen.

On the fifth article interrogated, [he] says that the said bathhouse is next to a small alley called Charbonnier leading from the big street of the said baths to the said river Saône, by which one can enter into the said baths by means of one of the doors of the said baths which is on the side and next to the river Saône, and one can also easily go out of the said city by means of the boats that are there and also put enemies into the said city.

On the sixth and seventh articles . . . [he] says that the said Casote and Massin, her husband, are natives of the lands of Flanders, and because of this many foreigners and unknown persons from the said lands of Flanders repair to and frequent often the said baths, indeed, more often than the other places of the said city, as he who is speaking has several times seen and known, and also because of the public women of the said bathhouse, who are for the most part of the nation and language of the said Massin and Casote.

On the ninth and tenth articles, [he] says that for the last six years he who is speaking has several times seen and known of several foreigners and unknown persons, coming out of the said bathhouse by night and by day, beaten with murderous and prohibited clubs and who were wounded and hurt and made great insults in the street in which is the said bathhouse. And several times has seen and known that they fought each other both in the said street and inside the said bathhouse. By means of which beatings and insults the neighbours and inhabitants of the said street several times have come out of their houses to pacify the said fights and insults. And many times have been scandalized by them.

On the thirteenth article . . . [he] says that several times passing and repassing before the said baths he has seen from the street that the women of the said baths and the protectors and several others frequenting the said baths cling to one another and kiss, and has also seen several times that the public women being in the said bathhouse call out to the journeymen passing by and made signs to them to come and speak with them publicly, both in the said street and at the doors and the windows of the said bathhouse, at which many women of good life and honest conversation feared to pass in front of the said baths next to the said street, and often were and still are constrained to remain in their houses to avoid seeing these said things.

Defence

The said city of Lyons is one of the notable and ancient cities of this kingdom in which there are usually three or four fairs held each year and several market days during the week which many persons regularly attend, both to sell and otherwise; and for the great abundance of the people who live in the said city and who pass and repass, there are many markets, lodgings, hostelries and public places which are set up to welcome the said merchants coming and going. And among the other places there are certain hostels set up and established from all time and antiquity, and even some for such a long time that there is no memory of the contrary, to keep baths and bathing places common to all people capable of this, and in these places have been accustomed to conversing with women willing to apply themselves to serve the men in the said baths.

And with this presupposed, it would be true that some twenty-four years ago and during the lifetime of the recently late King Charles, may God absolve him, the said Thomassin, who was native of the free city known as Arras and living then in that city, left the said city and the said land and came to live in the said city of Lyons, in which he has always lived since, and has so well and honestly governed himself that he has been, as he still is, prevost of the workers of the said mint, and some time after he came to live in the said city of Lyons he was [word missing: united?] in marriage with the said Casocte Cristalle who is native of the bailiwick of Tournesis, and since, the said Thomassin and his wife, to find a means to live, about the year 1469 took on a contract of rent and perpetual lease a house situated and standing in the said city of Lyons in the street named La Pescherie, for the price of 70 gold francs, for the value of one hundred *livres tournois* or thereabouts, that they took on and put themselves under obligation to return and pay back for each year at the accustomed terms to those who leased them the said house, of which sum the better part was to be used for the payment of several ground rents and debts of which the said house is perpetually charged to several churches and burghers of the said city of Lyons.

And in which house and from all time and antiquity of which there is no contrary in memory there have been established baths common to all manner of persons, as with the other bathhouses of the said city. The which baths the said Thomassin and his wife have kept and exercised in the said house from the said time to the present in such a way that from the said time there has never occurred anything untoward or any scandal. They say that although the abovesaid [person], according to reason and all equity, should not be bothered or molested in the enjoyment of the said house nor in the use of the said baths for which this house is established and of long date, as has been said, and that because the said house has from all time been destined to the said baths, they had taken it at great expense and on an extremely onerous contract, as of a hundred *livres* per year, for if it were not for the use of the said baths, the said house would not be worth one quarter of the said charge, and by this means the holders of the quit-rent and the long-standing investors who have heavy holdings in the said house would be frustrated of their rights and could not be paid.

Courtesans

(AD Côte-d'Or, B 11 360/8, fol. 20, 1461)
Claire Berbisey, the wife of the 'honourable man', Jean de Molesmes, secretary to the Duke of Burgundy, a young woman of twenty-four in 1461, had frequented the bathhouse of Jeanne Saignant for several years. She and Jeanne had become friends, and she brought woman friends to Jeanne's baths and on days reserved for men she met there 'the grandest people around'. To anyone reproaching her for such conduct, she answered 'that she was a tender woman, and would go to the baths when she wanted'. Who would have dared attack the wife of a ducal counsellor?

There came a time, however, when everyone in Dijon knew that Claire's moments of abandon were many and that Jeanne was using blackmail to keep her chambermaids. A quarrel between the two women led to defamatory statements in public and menaces made before witnesses. The city intervened against the mistress of the baths. The testimonies gathered for the preliminary inquiry leave no doubt of Claire's misconduct. Four years later, when she had lost her protectors, Jeanne was sentenced to be put to death; Claire, however, managed to escape the punishments that usually resulted from such deviant conduct.

The anecdote aside, the fact remains that several 'women of estate' had for some years met or picked out their lovers in Jeanne Saignant's baths. They ate well there, they conversed, they shone; were they not prototypes of the courtesan?

* * *

Testimony concerning Claire de Molesmes:
Philippe, wife of Jehan Cuer of Roy, aged approximately forty-six years:
And knows [her] well and saw her many times, several times, drawing water at the well, as she says, [she saw] coming to the said baths a woman of fine bearing and gentle estate whom she named etc., always alone, on the days that men are there and should be there. And when she was there saw fine jugs of wine and meat being brought by a nurse to make good cheer there. But she knows no more and will refer only to what happened. For concerning her, saw no harm done by the said woman of estate, but she deposing knows well that the neighbour women have reproved the said woman of estate for not having great honour in coming all alone to the said baths on men's days, and that the men had their days to go, and the women also had their days to go. The which answered them that she was a tender woman, and would bathe when she wanted, and anyone who wished could talk, for she was doing nothing bad, as she said. And more does not know.

* * *

Jean Felix, burgher of Dijon, aged about twenty-six years:
. . . and it displeases him to say that a good woman of the parish of St Jehan goes to and frequents so often the said Jehannote. He who is speaking remonstrated with the good woman and said that she was taking on a great responsibility for her honour to be with the said Jehannote, advising her strongly not to go there any more, for her honour's sake . . .

* * *

Jehannote, wife of Jehannin Malarbe, master cloth-shearer . . . aged about thirty-six years:
Many proper men and women and some of the greatest of these parts repair to the said baths and have good cheer there . . .

Says also that there have been many times women of estate who have come there and taken good cheer. And because she who is speaking was a chambermaid, they sent her several times to get wine or other things in the city and to do in the hostel what was to be done. This was no reason for her seeing everything going on in the chambers.

* * *

Katherine, wife of Henry de Maroilles, formerly wife of Michiel Chaulvirey, aged about forty years (she lives facing the house of the baths, and the window grille of her room gives directly onto the alley and the upper rooms of the said baths):

And knows well and has seen more than a hundred times a woman of estate whom she named and who will not be named here, for good reason, coming always alone to the baths of the said Jehannote in broad daylight on the days that men come and should be, and never on the days when women should be there. And when the baths and everything was ready, the said Jehannote went to call the gentry and nobles who live in St Benigne, who soon after would send wine, pasties, meats, spiced wine (hippocras) and other things. And they came after and were closed in the chamber in which the said woman of estate was bathing and where they all made good cheer. And when some other men came to bathe, they were told in the presence of she who is speaking and who was spinning before the said house that the furnaces were not hot, so that they would go away. Which they did. And the woman of estate has a nurse who sometimes came after, but she who is speaking has heard from men who were leaving the premises and from the manservant of the said house named Jacot, who was leaving, and from the chambermaids that the mistress was 'riding' downstairs and the servant-nurse was 'riding' upstairs, and so were all the maids. And she knows well and has seen a hundred and a hundred times and even again this week the domestics and a page from the house of the said woman of estate coming to a barn and wine press being in the said street to steal hay, wine, and other things belonging to the husband and to the said woman of estate that were being carried to the house of the said Jehannote to drink and for her horses.

Bordellos and Public Prostitution

Founding a Municipal Brothel

The King of France Authorizes the Consuls of Castelnaudary to Open a Public Brothel, 1445
(Published in Leah L. Otis, *Prostitution in Medieval Society*, Chicago: University of Chicago Press, 1985, p. 116)

The founders of a public brothel always operated under the mask of social decency. It is true that the containment of prostitutes and municipal protection of prostitution permitted the cities to satisfy the demands of rigoristic clerics and some 'honourable men', to clamp down on pimps, and perhaps to limit scenes of public depravity (but what were the conditions of life in Castelnaudary around 1440?). The consuls' petition is also a public and solemn proclamation of the sexual needs of bachelors. Purification of the city? Officially, yes, but the outcome of the consuls' project would be to spread prostitution by creating a city *prostibulum* to answer the needs of journeymen and apprentices not native to the city to supplement the bordellos that the city's own young men would continue to frequent. The city thus eliminated the 'noisy disturbances and unfortunate incidents' from which the city suffered, imputable not only to the *ruffians*, but also to confrontations between the city's own young and outsiders.

According to Leah L. Otis (*Prostitution in Medieval Society*, pp. 34 and 171, n. 60), financial difficulties prevented realization of the municipal project. The construction of the house was left to private initiative in 1452, and it remained in private hands until 1482. The project would not have been very costly, however, since the city could simply have rented a house. Thus it seems to me probable that the city fathers' attempt to take command of the situation was a passing fancy, abandoned when new establishments opened to respond to the same demands. On the other hand, in the latter years of the fifteenth century, the city did indeed take over responsibility for public prostitution, following the wishes of the reformers and the example of other cities. At that time private bordellos most probably disappeared.

* * *

Charles, by the grace of God King of France, to the judge of Lauragais or his lieutenant, salutations. The consuls of the city of Castelneuf d'Arry have exposed to us that the said city is fairly large and populous and many young men and unmarried menservants come there or live there; also [that it is] lacking in public women or girls, at least those public women who are there have no hostel and house for that express purpose, in which they must be found and live separated from honest folk, as it is the custom in other cities of good governance, from which there sometimes arise noisy disturbances and unfortunate incidents in the said locality. For this reason the said exposants have deliberated among themselves to sponsor the construction and edification, at their expense, of a hostel outside the city and separated from honest folk, which will be called the *bordel* [and] where these girls will live and be found. The said petitioners

[ask] that we give leave or permission and licence to do so, as they humbly beg. For this reason, having considered the abovesaid things and in order to avoid the said disturbances and incidents, we instruct you and command you, because you are our judge nearest to that place, when you have called our procureur or his substitute in your jurisdiction and others who are to be called, to choose and consign an appropriate place or location and to permit and give our licence to the said exposants to have built and edified, at their costs and expenses, outside the said city in an appropriate place, the said hostel called *bourdel* for the reason given above, and to have public girls or women retire there and live there, emptying the said city of them as regards continued residence and throwing them out of it. For thus it pleases us that it be done, and to the said exposants we have granted and we grant it, as a special grace by these presents, *non obstant* any letters on this matter obtained or to be obtained to the contrary. Given in Toulouse the nineteenth day of November of the year one thousand four hundred forty and five, and of our reign the fourteenth. By the Council.

Procuration: The Customs of the 'Trade'

(AD Côte-d'Or, B 11 360/)

In 1476, Damsel Marie, daughter of a lord of the region of Abbeville and widow of a knight, wanted to get out of a remarriage undoubtedly imposed by her family (with an 'old man fat in body' but who was a bailiff). She decided to make her suitor forget her and she left with her retinue (five persons, valets and serving girls) on a pilgrimage, then stayed at the house of a female friend in Valenciennes. In an inn outside that city, separated from her servants, she fell into the hands of a band led by one Drouhet, who was attached to a noble household. She yielded to him under duress, but when she was freed, she pardoned him and his companions and even went off with Drouhet, who began to sell off her jewels and soon announced that in Burgundy he had a 'good master and good acquaintance who will do many good things for them'. So off they went, on foot, from city to city, using Marie's remaining jewels to pay the innkeepers. When they arrived in Dijon, they lodged for a few days in an inn in the parish of St Nicolas, after which Drouhet led Marie to the rue des Grands Champs.

The *bonne rue* in Dijon is described in a few precise strokes (the prostitutes, seated in front of the house, chat among themselves), and we witness the rituals for entry into the Grande Maison. Drouhet had come twice before to arrange matters with the prostitutes, their mistress, and probably the police. The ritual took place not far from their workplace, in the house of the 'mistress', Jeanne Robelote, who had managed the house for some time. Marie is presented to the group by her 'fiancé', and the assembled women then accept wine and coins, the equivalents of the 'wine of the trade' and the 'right of welcome' demanded by all professional brotherhoods.

Was it Marie's despair that made Drouhet give up his project? This was not the first experience of the sort for this cruel man. He must have had to renounce his plans because the prostitutes and their abbess, who at first thought this a simpler affair, were unwilling to become accomplices to forced prostitution: the kidnapping of a noblewoman was punishable by hanging.

Marie took refuge with the procureur of the city and lodged a formal complaint. Drouhet was imprisoned, but she withdrew the accusation of murder and pardoned him his crimes a second time. We have no information on what happened to him later.

* * *

Item: When the said three days had passed, the said Drouhet let her know that he wanted to take her to his master, where there were good people, about which she was happy and believed him, but he took her behind certain walls into a certain nasty street where there were sitting before a house several women who were doing nothing, whom she greeted, and she asked them how they lived because they were doing nothing, thinking that they were working silk, and they began to laugh at her and answered her that they earned money from the men who came to them. And they also told her that the said Drouhet who was leading her knew very well what they lived by, and that he had been in their hostel twice only two days earlier, by which he knew well what they lived on. The which Drouhet then said to the said damsel that this was the place to which he wanted to bring her and leave her and in which she must live and earn money with the other women for the two of them, at which she was so astonished, so saddened, and so displeased and so shameful that she knew not what to do or say. One of the women said to the damsel that a worthless wretch had played such a trick on her, and then she began to weep and to embrace the said Drouhet, and she begged him for the love of God to take her out of the said street and not make her enter into that house, but he led her to another house near there where there was the mistress of the said women. To whom he said that he needed to have a room there to sleep with the said damsel, who would earn money with the others, and the said Drouhet sent for all the other women, [and he] sent for wine, and he gave them to drink and gave them money and said to them that the said damsel would stay with them to earn money, about which she was even sadder and more astonished than before and she so embraced the said Drouhet and wept so on his face that it was drenched with tears, and she reproached him, saying that he was not a gentleman but was a nothing, a robber, a cheat, and a lecher for having taken her to that place, and said to him that he could no longer stay with her if he did her this dishonour, and that she would rather see him hanged than stay there, and carried on so much that he took her back to their lodgings. Soon after [they] dined, and after found lodgings in the hostel of Estienne Sambenet, where they lived about fifteen days, and where the said Drouhet spent for her and had others spend what she had and made her sell her coifs, her wimples, and several other rings, and made her dress like one of little estate, saying that if he were not better turned out he would mistreat her, and threatened to cut her throat if she did not earn money and if she did not provide well for him. In fact, he beat her cruelly many times, which saddened her and distressed her for the dishonour that he had done to her and because he had thrust her out of her place, out of the hands of her relatives, out of honour, and made her lose her goods (which he could never restore) and brought her into a foreign land where she had nothing and where he treated her badly and dishonestly and was, as she said, in danger of dying by his hands. And knowing that he was cruel and that she could not furnish him and also that she did not want to do evil and that he did not keep his word about what he had taken from her, she decided one day and thought how she could find a way to escape from the hands of the said Drouhet to save her life and her honour, and she begged a certain notable woman to take her in until justice could be notified about her case, which she did. And she let her case be known to his lordship the procureur of the city of Dijon, who sent for her and kept her in security in his house and of whom she begged and requested that he save her life and her honour and take her out of the hands of the said Drouhet who wanted to dishonour her and wanted to cut her throat if he found her, as he said. To the which procureur the said damsel said her poor story, which is just as it has been told.

Legal Exploitation

The brothel, even when it was municipally sponsored and when prostitutes operated under the protection of their *ruffians*, remained a business venture like any other, and the manager of the brothel was intent on earning maximum profits. We can suppose – but it is only a supposition – that the girls were less harassed when a woman, an 'abbess' who had often come out out of prostitution herself, took up the farm contract for the house. This was often the case in the fifteenth century. But 'abbot' or 'abbess', such brothel managers had many other legal and less than legal means than procuration and protection for extracting money out of the prostitutes. Both the formal complaint lodged with the court of Toulouse by the city prostitutes, demanding liberation from the oppressive tutelage of an 'abbot', and the statutes of the Joyous Castle of Pamiers reveal the importance of the table in this system. Even the worthy Jeanne Robelote, who ran the city brothel in Dijon for eighteen years and whose girls did not complain of her, requested reimbursement from the mayor's office in 1476 because when an epidemic threatened in the course of her last contract period and her girls had remained in the rue des Grands Champs she had paid their living expenses.

* * *

1. Suit brought before the Parlement by the public prostitutes of Toulouse against the terms of the farm contract for the *prostibulum* and the rights of the 'abbot'

(AM Toulouse, FF 177, 1462)
Published in Leah L. Otis, *Prostitution in Medieval Society*, Chicago, 1985, p. 117–20)

. . . And the said defence [the 'capitouls' and the Toulouse city council] further said that the said prostitutes are usually women of great dissoluteness and greater extravagance in their drinking and eating than other people, for it was [the manager's] custom to give them four meals a day – that is, in the morning, fried foods or pasties to break their fast, for dinner boiled and roast [meat], and for the afternoon pause some other dainties, then for supper more good meats and always good wines, white, red, and claret, so that their expenses are higher than for other people. By the statements of the defence, always taken in a prejudicial sense, it appears clearly that the said procurer, called 'abbot', is responsible for leading the said women into even greater dissolution by means of good wines and various meats and *datus est ad multiplicanda vicia, et inconveniancia.* Which is denied *tamquam absurdum et detestabile quia vicium et mulieres apostatare faciunt etiam sapientes.* It is true, however, that *quot parcitas cibi potusque therit et renprimit luxuriam*, as our masters have complained on several occasions.

* * *

. . . And it is thus that without noise or uproar, day and night, they could go where they wanted, as they are accustomed to do in Paris, throughout the kingdom of France, and elsewhere. . . . And in order that the said court, and your lordships of the commission can clearly perceive that the said supplicants and petitioners do not intend to pursue any suit in this direction that is not reasonable, they and each one severally offer to the said court that they will be happy to pay five *sous tournois* apiece *qualibet septimana*, to be used in the repair of the said hostel, the chambers, the beds, and other things necessary by the hands of the Master of Hours chosen by the king in Toulouse or by another whom the court will prefer. And these five *sous* will be recorded in a book, along with the names of the women who are there or to be added in future times, by a merchant of Toulouse chosen by the court, who will pay each his due and the viguier of Toulouse or his lieutenant will give satisfaction to the said receiver [of funds] with a reasonable salary for his trouble. Further, [the prostitutes] will pay the table charges if they want to eat or drink. And the eldest among them, who in Toulouse is usually called the abbess of the bordello, under whose discipline the others are accustomed to live, *circa familiaria dicte domus*, along with the said Master of Hours, now and for the future, will consult and provide each month, by visiting the said hostel, all things necessary for the report that the Master of Hours and the said abbess, together with the said receiver, will be expected to furnish, and which he will furnish by taking receipt from the said Master of Hours containing in detail the reason [for each expenditure] and what it has been made for, and he will be repaid. By this means the worst will be avoided – that there be *ruffiens* found among the sheep, and should they be found there, it is clear how they should be punished. They offer [this] as above.

* * *

Extracts from the statutes of the 'Castel Joyos' of Pamiers, *c*.1500

(AM Pamiers, BB 11, 123r–v, undated
Published in Leah L. Otis, *Prostitution in Medieval Society*, p. 127–9)

Item: it was decreed and ordained that any woman desirous of living in the said house of the Castle of Joy, if she wants to eat at the table of the abbot, will pay for each meal, that is, for dinner and for supper, four *ardits*. And the said abbot will be obliged to furnish them with good bread, wine and reasonable accompaniments according to the season.

Item: it was decreed and ordained that if certain women do not want to eat at the abbot's table but at their own expense, the said abbot will be obliged to sell them foodstuffs, bread, wine and meat at city prices.

Item: it was decreed and ordained that aside from what is stipulated above, the said women will be obliged to give and to pay to the said abbot for their lodging, bed, fire, service, and light two *ardits* per day.

Item: it was decreed and ordained that if some foreigner or citizen sleeps the night with a woman in the said house, he will pay the abbot one *double* for the bed.

Item: it was decreed and ordained that the women of the said house of the Castle of Joy will be obliged to eat and drink inside the said house and not in the city; they must sleep at night in the said house, exception made for a legitimate excuse.

Public and 'Secret' Prostitutes

(AD Côte d'Or, B 11 360/9, 1464)

Five public prostitutes (of a relatively advanced age) entered a complaint to object to unfair competition from a private bordello. They relate the failure of an expedition that, according to them, was instigated by several 'decent women'. Their declared objective was to have a drink with the clandestine prostitutes and get to know them; to share the ritual 'wine of the trade' and the 'welcome' with them. Their probable true objective was to force their competition out of their lodgings or to carry them off forcibly to the city brothel.

I see no reason to suspect their version of the facts. 'Honest women', in these circumstances, put more store in the efficacy of the prostitutes than in that of the law courts.

The incident at least reveals that in spite of a number of unfavourable elements, a confraternal solidarity existed among prostitutes. They did not hesitate to take joint action to defend their earnings and their theoretical monopoly in the city. This monopoly had of course never been total, but in the 1460s it was fast disappearing. The communal house in Dijon continued to operate, to be sure (although some cities were abandoning theirs), but it stood witness only to strong city government.

* * *

Thursday last, 21st of this month of March 1464

Mariete, called la Bauldemonte, aged about thirty years,

Olive la Boyote, aged about thirty years,

Jeanne Quarreliere, aged about thirty-four years,

Jehanne Sandre, aged about twenty-eight years,

Margot des Prés, also aged about twenty-eight years, all common women, declared on their oath given on the Holy Gospels of God interrogated on this Sunday the 24th day of the month of March 1464 by myself, Jaques Borestel, sworn clerk of the court of my lord, the duke of Burgundy and substitute procureur for the honourable Jehan Rabustel, procureur of the city and commune of Dijon, that Thursday last they and several other public women of the house of this city of Dijon were before the door of the prison house of Dijon, where a number of women of the neighbourhood of the hostel of St Eloy near porte Guillaume came to look for them and to speak with them to ask them to go and remove certain common women living in a room near the hostel of the said St Eloy. Considering, as [the plaintiffs] said, that there are so many secret common women in this city who do them so much harm that only with great difficulty can they earn [enough] to pay the mistress of the said city house, they went to see what [the situation] was, and as they say, in the street near the hostel of St Eloy, my lord the keeper of the Seal of [the bishop of] Langres commanded and ordered them to go take and carry away certain common women being in a room near the said hostel where they operated and kept a bordello, according to the said keeper of the Seal and the neighbours there. So they who are speaking entered the said room with the intention of drinking with the said women and getting to know them, saying that they wanted to do them no harm. In the room they met and found three women, whom they did not know, and found with them three companions, to wit, Loyson, who is unmarried, one named Girard the Red, a seamster, and a leather-worker named Christofle, whom they knew fairly well because they have often seen them in the city house. But as soon as they were in the said room, the said Olive and Margot des Prés, who are speaking, returned to the entrance of the said room to guard the door so that no one could leave or enter and the said Mariete, Jehanne Quarreliere and Jehane Sandre began to remonstrate with the said three women and the three companions, and according to the same Mariete, Jehanne, and Jehanne, at that point the said Girard the Red suddenly took up a stick and chased out the said Jehanne Sandre and denied God our Lord two or three times and swore that if anyone laid a hand on the said women he would beat them. At that they who are speaking returned, and they declare that they know no more.

The said Olive and Margot des Prés say that they did not hear the said Red deny Our Lord because they were at the outside door with their backs turned.

Municipal Aid

Repentance and Retirement

Extracts from the Statutes of the House for Repentant Prostitutes of Sainte Marie Madeleine or Notre Dame des Miracles in Avignon, c. 1480 (Published in P. Pansier, *L'Oeuvre des Repenties à Avignon*, Avignon, 1910, pp. 125–45)

The house for reformed prostitutes in Avignon, probably founded around 1280, did not reach full development until a century later. Between 1362 and 1370 additions were made to the buildings, and in 1376 a rule was drawn up for the establishment. The extracts presented here are taken from the translation into French made soon after 1450.

In the preamble we see the double aim of the foundation: to admit sinful young women to penitence, and to protect respectable men from such seductive creatures. The novices had to be young and beautiful; they must enter the institution to leave the world, not because the world has passed them by. They seemed all the more dangerous because, moved by love of lucre and above all by lust, they were held fully responsible for their heinous past life. Living cloistered and subjected to abstinences and prayers, the repentent sisters of St Mary Magdalene not only atoned for their own sins but for those of their accomplices and their benefactors.

The consuls of Avignon had been closely involved with the foundation of this community and they administered its holdings until 1370. After that date, although their rights became theoretical, the Conservators and Protectors from the city council never missed their annual visit to the convent (followed by a dinner at city expense), thus demonstrating to the citizenry at large the symbolic value that they attached to the convent.

* * *

I. What women should be received into the said monastery and how they should be received:

Item: We decree and ordain that from this moment on, there will be received in the said monastery only young women of the age of twenty-five years who in their youth were lustful, and who by their beauty and formliness could still be prompted by worldly fragility and inclined to worldly voluptuous pleasures and to attract men to the same totally. Other women as well can be received as sisters in the said house, as seems advisable, according to capacities and size of the said convent. And one of these sisters or others sufficient [shall be] placed and instituted as governess of the said house with the fifteen nuns of the said convent named below. Such reception cannot be made without the consent and goodwill of the governess and of the prioress and of the greater part of the said fifteen sisters, after having first proven and tested the person they may want to receive for eight or ten days in order to know and understand if in doing this she is moved by a good spirit and if she will be entirely humble and obedient in bearing the burdens and the discipline of the other sisters; and that during the time of eight or ten days, information about her will be duly had by having her instructed and admonished by the confessor of the said sisters and by the said governess and prioress to do penitence and to learn about good morals and conditions.

IV. Of the quality of the clothing and conversation of the said sisters:

Item: we decree and ordain that the robes and vestments of the said sisters be uniform and decent, to wit, not tight, nor difficult to put on, of white wool cloth neither delicate nor precious. The mantel or cape of black wool, with no lining of fine wool cloth or wild beasts, and this for the robes as well as the mantels. They are to be veiled in the manner of decent widow women. The veils are to be of mediocre quality and honest, with nothing curious or precious. So that by exterior honesty their intrinsic purity can shine through to be an example of good life. . . .

The conversation and life of the said sisters is to be humble and honest, laudable and of good example, peaceable, full of charity and modesty, not voluptuous, proud, wandering, or idle. To the contrary, they are to exert one another to do true penitence in divine praise, in vigils, prayers, abstinences, and licit and honest manual labours to provide for their necessities and the needs of the commonality, and [they should] bear them without, however, ignoring for them the hours designated to the divine office. Nevertheless, those who are disposed to learning will occupy themselves with lessons of the Holy Scripture from matins after mass until the hour of tierce and from the hour of nones to the hour of vespers.

V. What masses will be said during the week and in observance of the requirements of the book of anniversaries:

Item: Each week on the day of Monday, if this day is not a solemn feast, a mass will be said from beginning to end; and on another appropriate day a mass of Mary Magdelene will be said; and on a later day, [a mass] of Our Lady, according to the dictates of the confessor of the said sisters, except in Lent, when the said masses will be said or left off at the discretion of the confessor or the procureur. And in all things shall be observed the ordinances of those who have left their persons and their goods in this monastery, as contained in the book of anniversaries.

VI. On fasting, abstinence, common life, and manner of sleeping:

All the sisters will fast and observe the fasts ordained by the Church, . . . The other days, the same will eat only two times a day, to wit, at dinner and at supper, in the refectory, in total silence without any word. During dinner and supper some lesson from the Holy Scriptures will be read to them continually. And after dinner they will go two by two to the church to give thanks by singing humbly and devoutly.

VII. On keeping silence, and in what time and how, and with what persons the sisters will speak, and of the persons who can enter to them:

The said sisters will abstain from all illicit and dishonest words, from blasphemies, from shameful statements, from murmurs, detractions, lies, foreswearing, oaths, insults, shouting, and any sort of noise whatsoever; indeed, they will always keep silence from the hour of compline when the sacristan has rung the bell until the first hour that the bell sounds again the following day, at the discretion of the governess and the prioress. They will likewise keep silence in their hearts when divine service is being said, in the refectory while dining and supping, and from Easter to the exaltation of the cross from the said bell after dinner until nones.

At the wheel, however, and at the large grate they may speak with honest women, likewise with their confessor, their attorney, the porter, also with a man of their kin and affinity, and with messengers who might be sent to them, the governess or the prioress being present and within earshot, and not otherwise.

IX. On the punishments for the sisters who do not observe the things described below:

Item: Those who shout out and who say illicit words at the abovementioned times and places, will eat bread and drink water on the floor before all the sisters of the convent. Those who refuse to enter the dormitory in the evening or who go to bed nude, the sisters assigned to tasks if by their failing the community cannot gather for dinner and for supper, and the sacristan, the porter, and the *quistante*, if they are negligent in their office, will incur similar punishments. Those also who proffer insults and say shameful things to the other sisters, or who eat and drink in the chambers of the dormitory, or who do not sit in the refectory according to the order and place given to them, and those who will not learn to say their lessons will incur similar punishment, or greater if the case requires.

Index